"*Instead* is a beautiful meditation on th[ ] concerns of women without kids: nonc[ ] and the children who are not 'ours' but w[ ]... ..o our lives. A generous and honest portrait of a trail-blazing child-free life."

—RUBY WARRINGTON, author of *Women Without Kids: The Revolutionary Rise of an Unsung Sisterhood*

"*Instead* is a deft, utterly readable memoir about one of the most profound decisions a human being can make: the decision not to have children. It's a huge subject and requires a writer of great courage who can tell a story beautifully, but never turns away from the gravity of the decision and its life-altering consequences. Thankfully, Maria Coffey is exactly that kind of writer."

—IAN BROWN, award-winning author of *The Boy in the Moon*

"To embark on the journey of parenthood (or not) stands among the most poignant decisions we must face, yet the doubts, worries, hopes and second-guessing tend to live in the shadows. Never have I seen such profound questions explored as deeply and humanly as in this compelling memoir."

—BRUCE KIRKBY, author of *Blue Sky Kingdom*

"Maria Coffey's evocative memoir about making tough choices takes us on a wild, round-the-world adventure, culminating in a tender and intimate finale. Masterful writing."

—BERNADETTE MCDONALD, author of *Keeper of the Mountains: The Elizabeth Hawley Story*

"I absolutely love this book and its encouragement to find your own best life and seize it with enthusiasm. In prose as immersive and engaging as my favourite novels, Maria Coffey encourages women everywhere to do the hard work of unburdening themselves from society's expectations so they can freely and truly follow their own hearts."

—ANGIE ABDOU, author of *This One Wild Life: A Mother–Daughter Wilderness Memoir*

Books by Maria Coffey

NONFICTION
Fragile Edge
A Boat in Our Baggage
Three Moons in Vietnam
Sailing Back in Time
A Lambing Season in Ireland
Visions of the Wild (co-authored with Dag Goering)
Where the Mountain Casts Its Shadow
Explorers of the Infinite

FOR CHILDREN
A Cat in a Kayak
A Seal in the Family
A Cat Adrift
Jungle Islands

Instead

Navigating the Adventures of a Childfree Life

A Memoir

Maria Coffey

RMB

For information on purchasing bulk quantities of this book, or to obtain media
excerpts or invite the author to speak at an event, please visit rmbooks.com and select
the "Contact" tab.

RMB | Rocky Mountain Books Ltd.
rmbooks.com
@rmbooks
facebook.com/rmbooks

Cataloguing data available from Library and Archives Canada
ISBN 9781771606400 (softcover)
ISBN 9781771606417 (electronic)

Design: Lara Minja, Lime Design
Cover image: Vik_Y/istock

Printed and bound in Canada

We would like to also take this opportunity to acknowledge the traditional territories
upon which we live and work. In Calgary, Alberta, we acknowledge the Niitsítapi
(Blackfoot) and the people of the Treaty 7 region in Southern Alberta, which includes
the Siksika, the Piikuni, the Kainai, the Tsuut'ina, and the Stoney Nakoda First
Nations, including Chiniki, Bearpaw, and Wesley First Nations. The City of Calgary
is also home to Métis Nation of Alberta, Region III. In Victoria, British Columbia,
we acknowledge the traditional territories of the Lkwungen (Esquimalt and Songhees),
Malahat, Pacheedaht, Scia'new, T'Sou-ke, and W̱SÁNEĆ (Pauquachin, Tsartlip,
Tsawout, Tseycum) peoples.

We acknowledge the financial support of the Government of Canada through the Canada
Book Fund and the Canada Council for the Arts, and of the province of British Columbia
through the British Columbia Arts Council and the Book Publishing Tax Credit.

For Agnes and Hannah
And for Bac, wherever you are

Contents

Part One   1

Part Two   17

Part Three   39

Part Four   61

Part Five   87

Part Six   131

Part Seven   177

Part Eight   223

There is something threatening about a woman who is not occupied with children. There is something at-loose-ends feeling about such a woman. What is she going to do instead? What sort of trouble will she make?

—SHEILA HETI

Author's Note

A few years ago, just before pandemic times, the approach of old age suddenly took me by surprise. My husband Dag was bemused – I was in my sixties, surely I had known it was coming? We were both healthy, and still roaming the world. But suddenly I had started wondering where we would go, what we would do, when we got really old, and frail. Dag suggested sticking to our usual modus operandi – no grand plan, just always keenly aware of what we *don't* want to do, open to what may unfold.

Meanwhile, I turned to another familiar tactic: looking back to help me go forward, exploring my past through personal narrative. I hadn't been writing for a while, but now the stories poured out. I wrote about earlier experiences, when I was in crisis and afraid, how I survived them and what I had learned. About the chance and circumstance that led me to Dag. About the decisions that allowed us to carve out an unconventional, exciting path. How those decisions had shaped my relationships, my work, my identity – and my amnesia about ageing.

As the stories began to morph into a book, tumultuous events happened in the world at large, then in our personal lives, and the thread holding the book together became clear. A key decision, made decades ago, was to be "childfree" (not a word I like, but a widely recognized term for someone who has chosen not to have children). All else had hinged on that. Despite being the right choice, it was complex in the making, wrapped up in the expectations of others. It stretched back into my childhood and ahead into the future.

Today, an unprecedented number of people in our society are making the same choice, yet it is still often questioned and harshly judged. I hope my story can help to challenge and change those attitudes. And that, whether nonparents or parents, we can understand and support each other as we navigate our lives, and the nuanced outcomes of our personal "insteads."

To maintain privacy, I have changed the names of certain people and locations. While some dialogue has been reconstructed, I have striven to capture the essence of those conversations.

One

I love the physical world and the experiences
I get to have in it so deeply and completely
that it threatens to break my heart every
minute, and I have made countless life
decisions – in addition to childlessness –
to ensure that I can be out and in the world
on my own terms almost all the time.

—PAM HOUSTON

1

I was engrossed in writing when I heard him calling from downstairs.

"I'm heading out, honey."

Leaning out of the top floor window, I saw him pushing his bike through our front door and into the narrow, steep lane. He was wearing a light shirt, shorts, sandals, and a helmet. It was four o'clock, in early October. The sun would set in just over three hours.

"Where are you going?" I asked. He looked up.

"Just for a quick ride around. Love you."

"Love you too." It was my unspoken rule to share such endearments whenever we parted, even for a short time. A way to assuage the separation anxiety that, decades after my previous partner died in a mountaineering accident, I had never been able to completely shake.

Presuming he would follow one of our regular routes, past orchards where fruit-laden tree branches hung over the county roads, I added, "Bring back some pomegranates." As he wheeled away on the bike, I remembered that his phone was broken. A few days earlier, we'd been hiking up a river canyon, and he'd dropped it into the water. All efforts to revive it had failed.

"Dag, take my phone!"

"I won't be long," he called over his shoulder, just before he disappeared around the corner. Later, he admitted he nearly turned back to get it. But then he thought, *Just this once.*

~

For the past 11 months, we'd been living in Catalonia, a northeastern province of Spain, in a village situated on the banks of a river that flows through a wide valley of fruit orchards and olive groves. Behind the village stretches a series of rugged hills dotted with a few remote farms but otherwise frequented only by wild boars and the occasional walkers or intrepid mountain bikers. The original plan was to base ourselves there for the winter, take some trips to India and Africa for our adventure travel company, Hidden Places, and return to Canada in early summer. Then along came COVID. The first case in Spain was reported at the end of January. By late March, the country went into one of the world's strictest lockdowns. Canada's prime minister implored all citizens overseas to return home. But it wasn't so easy. Most flights from Barcelona-El Prat Airport were grounded. We would have to take trains for 500 kilometres to Madrid-Barajas Airport, and that, plus several flights with long layovers, seemed more dangerous than simply staying put.

In May, things appeared to ease up travel-wise. We booked our flights to Canada. Days later, they were cancelled. We tried again, multiple times. It was always the same story. Booked, paid for, cancelled. Early one morning, we were up on our terrace drinking coffee. Swifts were zooming around. An eagle floated by. The sun was already warm.

"Let's stop trying to get flights," said Dag. "Let's see what a summer here is like."

I thought about it. In truth, I didn't feel like going anywhere. This was the longest I'd been in one place for...well, I simply couldn't remember. Over the last few years, increasingly people had been asking me when we were going to slow down, retire. It was a fair question – I was now 68, Dag 63. But it always infuriated me. I was never going to retire, I claimed. I loved our big life, constantly bouncing around the world to lead trips, scout for new ones, and have our own adventures. COVID-19 brought that to a shuddering stop. During lockdown, we'd spent weeks mostly inside our house, running up and down the three flights of narrow stairs to keep fit, and hanging out on the terrace. Eventually, restrictions eased so we could go on our daily hike in the hills to a high point with sweeping views. On some afternoons we'd cycle along country roads, or drive to the beach to swim and paddleboard. With our travel business in hibernation, I had lots of time to write, and Dag was learning the violin. The village cafes were still closed, so at night a small group of our neighbours would gather in the lane. We'd set out a long table to allow social distancing, and everyone would bring their own food and wine. I loved the rhythm of the days, the simplicity of life, the beauty of the area, the camaraderie. Though it was a strange state for me, I had to admit I was content.

And so we stayed, throughout the perfection of June, the steamy heat of July and August, and into late September. By then, I was wondering if it was time for us to return to British Columbia. I knew things would be different. We wouldn't be able to throw our usual big "We're Home" party in our apartment and have impromptu get-togethers with friends in local pubs and restaurants. I wouldn't be hopping on a floatplane to Vancouver to see my niece Hannah. Dag wasn't keen to leave, but I felt a pull back to Canada, even though I wasn't sure how being there during a pandemic would feel. Weeks later, I would find out.

∽

My back began to ache. I'd lost track of how long I'd been standing at the high writing desk in our bedroom. I looked up from the computer and through the windows. The house is southeast facing, but I could register from the light on the river, the colours of the clouds, that the sun was low in the sky. Dag had been gone longer than I'd expected. I felt a pang of worry and frustration that I couldn't reach him by phone. Then I told myself he'd be home any minute. I decided to make soup for supper. We had a cauliflower, onions, some good Parmesan. I headed down to the living room and kitchen. I was reaching for the vegetables, a knife, and cutting board, when I heard a loud knocking at the door. *He's forgotten his keys again.*

"Coming!" I called, running down the stairs to the windowless entrance hall. I pulled open the wooden front door. Instead of Dag, there was a swarthy, solidly built man wearing heavy boots, a dark sweater, workman's pants. He started talking to me rapidly. What I understood sent adrenaline spiking through me.

"Your husband is in my van in the square. He is very broken."

I went into autopilot. "Please wait," I told the man. I raced upstairs, grabbing a bottle of water, one of Dag's sweaters, a scarf, a first aid kit, keys to our vehicle, my phone.

Very broken.

The square was deserted, chairs and tables piled up under the trees outside the two cafes, which were still closed because of COVID. The man's van was parked next to ours, its back passenger door slid open. Dag was sitting sideways on the seat, stripped to the waist. His left leg was stretched out; his shirt, blood splattered, was tied below his knee. He was leaning over his calf, holding it. He looked up at me, his face ashen and drawn, his eyes pale.

"I was off-road, way up in the hills. I fell. I've broken my leg. It's really bad."

I eased the sweater over his head, tied the scarf around his neck, got him to drink some water. I wanted to ask, "What were you doing up in the hills?" But it wasn't the right time. He was clearly in shock.

"I had to haul myself for ages before I found this guy. I asked him to take me to the hospital, but he insisted we come here."

The man was staring at the river, smoking. I could only imagine he was concerned about COVID.

"You have to help me move into our van," Dag continued, "and drive me to Emergency."

"No, I'll call an ambulance."

"It will take too long, Maria, it will be quicker if you drive me. I need to get to the hospital. When I tell you, put your hands very gently under my leg to support it, and I'll push myself forward. Ready? Okay, now."

Dag has always had a high pain threshold and a stoicism when it comes to physical suffering. But with that slight movement, he let out an anguished scream, like a wild animal. I jumped back, horrified.

"Dag, we can't –"

"Try again," he said, through gritted teeth.

"No."

"Yes, now!" Again, that unbearable, gut-wrenching sound.

Another car pulled up, our young neighbour Izan stepped out.

"My God, what's happened?" he said.

"Izan, come here, help me move," Dag insisted. The third round of screaming was too much for all of us. Izan called an ambulance.

~

I sat in the small waiting room of the emergency department. There were four rows of plastic bucket seats, half of them with yellow tapes stretched between the arms to maintain social distance. It was a quiet night; only a couple of other people came in for treatment. A suspected broken wrist. Bad stomach pains. Their companions sat across from me, masked, silent, blinking under the harsh fluorescent light. I stared at the vending machines, the colourful soda cans and chocolate bars. The messages taped up explaining COVID procedures. The bottles of sanitizer. My phoned pinged, texts from people in the village who had heard about Dag's accident. I had nothing to tell them. I kept standing up, walking a few steps to the glass window, tapping on it to alert the receptionist sitting at a computer. She had nothing to tell me. I must wait.

Eventually, a young doctor appeared and called me into an office. He wore blue scrubs. He looked rumpled, tired, a bit sweaty.

"Your husband is okay," he said in English. "But his injury is bad. Not the worst possible, but very complicated, and he will need an operation. Tonight he will go to the trauma unit. Tomorrow the surgeons will examine him. Don't worry, they are good."

"Can I see him?" I asked.

He shook his head. "Because of COVID, in Emergency you are not allowed."

He registered my eyes welling up. "Okay, a little while."

Dag was lying on a gurney, propped up against pillows, dressed in a hospital gown. His left leg was in a cast. A tube ran from one arm up to a bag of saline solution. He looked calm. Morphine was working its magic. Next to him was a tray with a dinner, untouched. As we talked, I cut up the chicken and potatoes, fed him bits, eating most of it myself.

He told me he had planned to cycle along the riverbank, then go partway up a trail we sometimes hiked and loop back. But my request had got stuck in his head. He remembered a particular tree we'd cycled past a few days earlier, its branches hanging over the lane, heavy with ripe pomegranates. He decided to go exploring, find his way up and across the backcountry to the tree, and bring home some of my favourite fruit.

"The track got progressively worse. I was heading down a steep rutted section with lots of big rocks and gravel, and I remember thinking, I've got to be careful here. Then I skidded sideways, tried to correct. Suddenly, I was in the air, dirt and stones flying around me. I think I might have blacked out briefly. Next thing I knew I was on the ground with the bike on top of me."

Both our bikes were electric-assist. They were heavy road bikes. We'd bought them because of the hilly terrain, so we could go longer distances together and get over passes, so I would always be able to keep up with Dag. I'd never felt comfortable about him going off-road on his own.

"I lay there for a bit, while the reality of what had happened sank in. I got the bike off me, sat up. I knew my leg was mush. I tied my shirt around it. Then I tried to stand up. The pain was horrific. It was like I'd stood on a land mine."

But he had to move. He knew the general direction he had to go to reach the country road, where hopefully a car would come by and stop. He knew he couldn't wait too long. The sun was getting low in the sky. A cold night ahead. No phone, no extra clothes, no food or water, no first aid kit.

"Typical professional guide, out on his own, right?" he said. I shook my head. When he was guiding our trips, he was fanatical about safety, to an extent that made some clients complain.

He managed to get out from under the bike, to stand on one leg. He managed to lift the bike and tried to mount it, thinking he could push it with his good leg. He fell. He lay again for a while, waiting for the agonizing pain to subside a little, building up courage to face it once more. He threw away his bike pannier so he could sit on the back rack. He covered some ground, then fell yet again.

"This time..." He paused. I was clutching his hand.

"This time, I thought, it's too hard. I can't face the pain. I knew it was likely no one would come by there for maybe days or more. The sun was close to setting. I'd soon get cold; I was in shock. I thought, well, I've had a good life. And then – " He looked up at the ceiling, swallowed.

"I thought, I can't leave Maria behind. I can't do that to her."

He stopped. I couldn't speak. When he carried on, his voice was shaky.

"Somehow I got up. But it was so fucking hard. It was like I was looking up at this huge mountain wall. Life was on its far side. It was impossible, but somehow I had to climb up and over it. I knew if I fell again, I wouldn't be able to get up. It would be over. So I had to plan every little move before I made it."

He had no memory of how long all this took. Later, we estimated he'd covered about two kilometres across steep, rugged terrain for maybe a couple of hours. Eventually, below him, he saw the road. Above it, some olive groves. And a car. A man emerged, walking toward his vehicle.

"I yelled *Ajuda! Ajuda!* I saw the guy stop and look around to see where the sound came from. But he didn't look up. He got into the car and drove away, down a rough track and onto the road."

"That must have been..." I couldn't find the right word.

"Yeah. Desperate."

He kept going, down the slope, his focus extreme. He was worried that, even if he reached the road, someone driving past might not stop – they might think he was crazy, it could be dark by then. Then he glimpsed another parked vehicle, a van. He started yelling again. "*AJUDA!*" A man stepped out from between some trees. He saw Dag.

"*Què va passar?*" he asked.

He'd been tending to his olives that afternoon. He was about to leave for the day. A few more minutes, and Dag would have missed him.

The doctor put his head around the curtain. "Sorry, you must go now. Tomorrow in the main hospital they will let you be with him – just one family member can visit."

I walked out into the cold night air. Still on autopilot, I drove the nine kilometres home, my headlights picking out orchards along the roadside. The village was silent. It was against the restrictions to go inside anyone's house, so I sat in the kitchen, poured a glass of wine, and tapped out quick replies to my neighbours. I went to bed. I knew the following day would be a long one. I needed to get some rest, be able to help Dag. But I was wide awake; I lay staring at the ceiling. It was only then that the autopilot snapped off and the realization hit: I had nearly lost him.

It's not unusual for my mind to go rogue on sleepless nights. Worries and fears surface and swirl, with nothing in those dark hours to distract or push them away. Sometimes I get up, make tea, read a book, check my email – anything to put things into perspective. But on this night I felt pinned to the bed, my mind out of control. I kept imagining Dag on the mountain, alone, howling with pain, the horror of every movement. And then an image lodged in my brain. Of a cold room, a big drawer pulled out from a wall. Identification. Of looking at one of his hands, the long fingers, the nails. That is the only part of him my mind would allow me to see, but it forced me to keep seeing it, again and again.

Finally, I sat up, wrapped my arms around my calves, and buried my head in my knees. *He's alive*, I told myself. He's safe in the hospital; the surgeons will fix him.

But my mind wouldn't let up.

What if they can't fix him? What if he's disabled and can't ever hike, run, swim, cycle, and surf like he used to? He was defined by his physical abilities and strength. How would he cope? How would I cope? For over 30 years, he'd been my rock, the centre of everything.

I lay back, breathed deeply, tried to calm myself. It didn't work. Long ago I'd been swept out to sea by a riptide, and this felt the same. Everything had changed in an instant. Everything was beyond my control. I was afraid and profoundly lonely. Who to turn to at such a moment in the middle of the night? There was my niece in Vancouver, my brothers in England and Ireland, our worldwide tribe of friends. I just had to call, text, email, and I knew they would offer support. But suddenly I longed to reach out to someone who was part of Dag and me. A child, grown up now.

The thought was so unexpected, so visceral, it propelled me from the bed. I opened the window shutters and stood gazing at the river, the moon casting a silvery path that lit up the contours of its currents. Of course, there was no child. I'd decided that long ago.

2

December 2018

The plane overshot the coast, then turned back for the approach to landing. As it banked steeply, I saw the sun begin to slide behind the horizon, where the Atlantic meets the sky.

I was flying into Morocco from Indonesia, where I'd been leading a trip. Dag had driven down from Catalonia; he had been in the country for a couple of weeks and was at the airport to meet me. We headed south from Agadir for over two hours on a highway winding through bare, rolling hills. Night had fallen by the time we stopped in Tiznit to buy fruit, tea, and milk. The vendor sat by a pile of oranges. He wore a long, striped *djellaba*, the hood pulled over his head against the evening chill. He was watching a video on his smartphone. A donkey tethered to a post nearby flicked its tail.

Forty kilometres on, we took a narrow road through the edge of a small town, past shuttered shops and dark houses.

"Does this look familiar?" asked Dag.

I shook my head.

"It was just a one-street village then. There was nothing beyond except dirt paths."

Some months before, Dag had told me about a place in Morocco that was a mecca for paragliding, a sport he loved. He suggested he should go there while I was in Indonesia. Then I'd join him, and we'd explore the country together. I'd always talked about returning to Morocco to see the places I'd missed because of my long-ago accident. So this plan fitted together nicely.

"The town's called Mirleft," he had said, and I'd stared at him in astonishment.

"That's where I drowned."

~

He had rented a small apartment on a beach. "I don't think it's the same beach," he said on the way. "There's a bigger one with a notorious rip current half an hour's walk along the cliffs. We can go there tomorrow."

We zigzagged down, the road becoming a gravel path ending at a small parking area. Stepping out of the car, I heard the pounding waves, inhaled sharp, salty air. A man darted from the darkness, took our bags, let us into the apartment. Framed by the bedroom window, the moon lit the breaking surf. My journey had seemed endless, through many time zones. I was blurred with tiredness. I longed to lie flat, to hold Dag, to sleep. I closed the shutter on the ocean. Tomorrow, I thought. Tomorrow.

~

I woke to a dull roar, the repetitive thump and hiss of waves hitting the beach. Dag brought me a cup of tea. He opened the shutters, and bright sunlight flooded the room. I sat up, blinking. Looked out. The ocean shimmered. Surf foamed over yellow sand.

Our apartment was in one of a few simple stone buildings straggling along the head of the beach where it met the bluff. We walked to a small cafe for breakfast. Two steps up from the sand led to a patio. Earth-hued cushions were scattered over stone benches, low plastic tables set before them. It was grimy yet cheerful. The owner emerged from the dark interior, greeting Dag like an old friend.

"Mohammed, this is my wife, Maria," said Dag.

Skinny and tall, with stained teeth and a long blue scarf wrapped around his head, Mohammed bowed to me, folding his palms together at his chest.

"I have been waiting for you. Your husband has been with me here a lot. He has missed you."

Mohammed served us eggs cooked in a brass pan with olives, tomatoes, onions, and lots of oil. We scooped up the mixture with pieces of flatbread. Then he brought us little glasses of sweet mint tea. When I finished mine, I excused myself. I wanted to walk on the beach alone. I headed to the jumble of black rocks marking its northern end. Scrambling onto the highest rock, I looked around. Dag was right. I had always described a larger beach, with higher bluffs. But this was the right shape, like a horseshoe. I jumped down and followed the tide line, walking barefoot on damp, hard sand to the far bluff, sheer like a cliff.

Just before I reached it, I stopped and stood very still.

The memory was visceral. Sprawled out on my stomach, one cheek pressed against the sand, opening my eyes, seeing the arm lying next to my face, realizing with a shock it was mine. That I was alive. A babble of voices, then hands lifting me, carrying me, the pain of that, the agony of every breath.

It was here. Right at this spot. I was sure, I could sense it with every cell in my body. I sat down. Hugged my knees to my chest. Stared at the waves. A dog trotted up, wagging his tail. Yellow-furred, long-legged, a jaunty red scarf around his neck. He curled up next to me. We stayed that way for some time.

I looked along the beach to the rocks. Squinted. There I was, with my friends Claire, Eileen, and Margaret. Twenty-one, slender as a reed, hair down my back, a long patchwork skirt and T-shirt over my bikini. We had just walked from the village. I threw my bag and clothes on the sand and ran into the shallows to play with some other young travellers. Carefree and laughing, jumping in the foam of the broken waves as they rolled to shore. After each jump, landing back on my feet, never out of my depth. Then the shout, someone was beyond the break, in trouble. People started forming a chain to reach him. I was a weak swimmer. I should have backed away. Instead, I made a split-second decision and reached out my hands. Suddenly, I was in the chain, moving out, standing on my tiptoes in chest-deep water. The people on either side of me held me fast when a wave rolled in and lifted me off my feet. But the next wave was much larger. As it curled up above us, I stared at its belly, smooth like blue glass, at its foaming, teetering head. Then the shocking crash, the tumbling over and over like a rag in a washing machine, no idea of up or down.

Surfacing: at first the relief of air, then the realization I couldn't touch the bottom. I was being pulled away from the beach where my friends stood staring at me in bewilderment. Only later did I learn about the notorious rip current, too strong and fast for anyone to swim against. That I could have swum parallel to the shore to try to escape it, as the man we had been attempting to rescue had already successfully done. That eventually the rip would peter out in much deeper water, or curl back toward the beach, so I should relax and let it take me. Had I known this, I would have kept my head above water and waited for the current to release me, knowing I'd end up somewhere I hadn't expected to be but that I'd be okay. Instead, I panicked. As another wave churned over me, I coughed violently, sucking in water. I saw it rolling toward the shore, rearing up as it reached the surf break. I was beyond that now, and my friends had become tiny figures.

∼

The mind protects us from the unbearable. For most people, it is impossible to imagine the moment of death, the prospect of not existing. But I know what it's like to die, at least by drowning. Waves slapping against my face, water filling my mouth, my nose. The choking, the sense of being suffocated. The desperate struggle, limbs flailing, hands clawing uselessly at the ocean. The mind slowing into lucid waves of sorrow, regret, and anguish. I imagined my body smashed against the rocks at one end of the beach, or drifting down into depths, rolling around on the ocean floor. I thought about my parents, how they would find out, their terrible sorrow. I remembered the spat I'd had with Claire that morning. I would never be able to apologize to her. I'd miss the rest of university, miss meeting my future husband, miss travelling the world. The beach was far away now. I kept fighting, choking, clawing. The loneliness, the desolation was profound. And soon so was the darkness.

A young German man had walked from the village a little while after us. From the top of the bluff, he saw people running around by the rocks. Wanting solitude, he took another path, down to the far end of the beach. As he reached the sand, he spotted a body washing about in the surf. He ran in, grabbed my hair, carried my limp body to this spot. My lips were blue. I wasn't breathing.

~

I stood up and slowly walked back across sand, the yellow dog trotting along beside me. At the cafe, it flopped down at my feet.

"This is the beach, isn't it?" said Dag. He was looking at me with concern.

I nodded.

"I found the spot where I was resuscitated."

Mohammed set down another cup of mint tea. "Your husband told me of your accident, madam. I am sorry. The sea is very dangerous here. It has taken many people. You are lucky. Allah was with you. You were reborn."

I breathed in deeply. Ocean air moving easily through my lungs.

Mohammed was right. I had been returned to life – but differently. The invincibility of youth had been stripped away. Underneath it was a raw understanding of the fragility of existence. It was a knowledge that would impel me to chase my dreams and inform the biggest choices I was to make in the years ahead.

Two

She hadn't chiselled the fact that she didn't want children into stone; she came on to it naturally, gradually. It was something that made sense to her as she lived her life. Sometimes we don't "know" for sure, and maybe we never will, but we just have to live each day in the way that feels most natural for us.

—EMMA GANNON

3

September 1971

I woke early and lay watching the late September light shafting through the curtains. I could hear my parents speaking in the next room. I was 19, and I had just spent the summer hitchhiking through Italy and sleeping on beaches in the Greek islands. It had been my first big adventure, and already I longed for more. The previous night I'd returned to my childhood home in Wolverhampton, a gritty town in the industrial centre of England. In a few days, I would head to Liverpool to start my second year at university.

I slipped down to the kitchen, prepared a tray of tea, and carried it upstairs. Mum and Dad sat up in bed. She wore a cotton nightdress and a net pulled over her permed hair. Dad was in checked pajamas. Above them on the wall was a painting of the Virgin Mary. Across from them, Christ hung from a heavy wooden crucifix. While they drank the tea, I perched at their feet and babbled about Italy and Greece, giving them a heavily edited version of my trip.

"I was so worried about you," said Mum when I took a breath. "But I'm glad you went off and got travelling out of your system."

I stared at her, aghast. My plans for the following summer had already started taking shape. I launched into an impassioned speech about how I loved travelling, that it was what I wanted to do with my life more than anything else. I didn't know how yet, but I was determined to make it happen. I went on and on and finally announced, "And when I'm 70, I'm going to walk across the Sahara!"

During the silence that followed, I must have looked as startled as my parents. I had no clue why I'd said that, where the idea came from. Walking across the Sahara at 70? The words just popped out as if I was channelling someone else. My parents' teacups were frozen between their saucers and mouths.

"So that's what I've decided," I lamely concluded, and fled downstairs.

∼

I was born in the early 1950s to working-class Irish Catholic parents who had lived through the Second World War and wanted nothing more than peace, stability, and the chance to push their three children up the social ladder. My mother's decision to work full-time until we all left home had been out of necessity. She would have much preferred to be a stay-at-home mum, at least while me and my brothers were small. This was the societal norm at the time, and it was what she hoped I would do. In her eyes, my going to university was, in part, about finding a husband with good prospects. She wanted me to have a career, but one that fitted in with family life. Teaching, she kept telling me, would be ideal. I could take a long break when I started a family, return to work once all the children went to school, and then be with them during the holidays. And it wasn't just Mum extolling this. Marriage and a family were the expectations of most of my friends, even those who had career ambitions. I didn't know anyone else who dreamt of wandering around the world unfettered.

The second wave of feminism, which started in the United States after the publication of Betty Friedan's *The Feminine Mystique*, arrived on the shores of England just as I was heading to university. Female factory workers were striking for equal pay. The first Women's Liberation Conference was held in Oxford. The 1970 Miss World beauty contest in London, broadcast live on television to 100 million people worldwide, was disrupted by a group of feminist activists protesting the objectification of women, who pelted the stage with flour bombs and rotting vegetables.

It would be a couple of years before I fully appreciated what the second wave feminists were fighting for – equality for women in the workplace and home – and joined them. At that point, my self-centred self just saw the chance to shake off the expectations I'd grown up with. Away from the eyes of my mother, I went to a "family planning" clinic to ask for the contraceptive pill. Introduced in the UK in 1961, for most of that decade it had only been prescribed to married women, but now it was freely available. Finally, the lurking dread of an accidental pregnancy, which would scupper my dreams, was lifted.

During our first university summer break, most of my friends went home, several of them hoping for a proposal from their boyfriends. One of them, Marie, was in love with a dental student – whom she would marry and start a family with after graduation – but I managed to winkle her away from him for a couple of months to go backpacking with me in Europe.

~

We arrived in Rome at night. I have only vague memories of a taxi, a cobbled street, several narrow flights of stairs to our room, a bathroom with a stained claw-foot tub down the hall. But I vividly recall waking up the next morning. Staring at the high paint-cracked ceiling and a slow-moving fan. Registering that the light had a different quality, the air an unfamiliar smell. Marie was still asleep in the other narrow bed, her red hair spread over the pillow. I padded quietly across the wooden floor, pushed up a window sash, and stuck my head out. Lines of bright laundry stretched across the narrow lane. Below me, a man pushed a cart heaped with green, speckled watermelons. A woman in a black headscarf approached him. He set down the cart, cut a slice from a melon, and offered it to her. And I thought, *I'm here*.

This was long before cell phones, credit cards, the internet, or guidebooks for backpackers. In youth hostels and cheap hotels we got advice from other young tourists. Our plans were loose, and we were never quite sure where we would find ourselves at the end of each day. But we wanted to get to the Greek islands, so we hitchhiked south through Italy to the ferry port in Brindisi. Tollgates were the best place to snag rides, especially for two young women in skimpy shorts and T-shirts.

Hitchhiking was just one of the many firsts for me on that trip: travelling by plane; sleeping on beaches; watching dawn break over the sea; seeing my moon shadow; sunbathing nude; dancing barefoot under the stars on warm sand...taking drugs.

On the island of Ios I met a gorgeous young American. We chatted one night in a cafe, and ran into each other on the beach the following morning.

"Would you like some Windowpane?" he asked.

I had no idea what he was talking about. But, keen to impress him, I simply nodded.

"Put out your tongue," he said. I did, and he placed something very small and light onto it. I swallowed, and it was gone.

"That's like Holy Communion," I giggled. "But easier, it didn't stick to the roof of my mouth."

"LSD *is* a form of communion," he said seriously.

I stared at him.

"You have taken it before, haven't you?"

No, I confessed. He looked horrified.

"Any psychedelics?"

No.

"Marijuana?

No.

"Any drugs at all?"

"Um, lots of alcohol."

The world became intensely beautiful, everything amplified. I could hear the flap of a sail on a distant boat. Sky and sea merged into a great dome of blue, a vast cathedral I walked through, dumbstruck. As I passed people on the beach, their faces dissolved, then reformed. In the evening, I grew paranoid, clinging to the stone wall of a village cafe like a gecko. I was convinced everyone inside hated me for being so high. The American was kind enough to take care of me during those mind-bending 12 hours. Later that night, we sat by a beach fire. I stared into the flames as he massaged my shoulders.

"Who is she?" I heard someone ask.

"Just a lady coming down," he replied.

It was years before I took drugs again. I didn't need them; I was high on new experiences, thrumming with childlike wonder. I had no idea where my life was heading, but I wanted this feeling to last. I knew I couldn't find it in the life my mother wanted for me. And I knew that was going to be a problem.

4

The only joke I can ever remember goes like this:

Question: How many Irish Catholic mothers does it take to change a light bulb?
Answer: None. They'd rather sit in the dark and suffer.

That was Mum. She was nurturing, tender, and supportive. She had a great sense of humour, laughing easily and often. She was also a fierce and controlling matriarch who brandished guilt like a weapon.

My parents' quiet suburban street was flanked by two rows of small semi-detached brick houses, with neat gardens and windows covered by lace curtains. For them, this was a haven of security after the hardship of their early lives in Ireland. Dad came from a family of farmers. He was the youngest of eight children, and there hadn't been enough land to go around. He left for London in the late 1930s, took a job as a bus conductor, and struggled to find a room in boarding houses with signs that warned, "No Children, No Irish."

Mum emigrated for a different reason. Her parents were alcoholics, prone to explosive arguments, emotionally abusive to each other and their three children. When she was 19, she followed her older sister, Madge, to London to train as a nurse. She first saw my father when they were both walking toward a church for Sunday Mass.

"A fine figure of a man," she recalled, "his long legs in wide trousers that flapped in the wind as he strode along."

Soon after that they met at a dance. Within months they were married. The first baby, Michael, arrived within a year. Almost a decade later, they had another boy, John, and finally me, the longed-for girl.

When Madge moved to Wolverhampton, my parents followed. Dad got a job at a paint factory. For years, Mum did night shifts as a nurse so she could be home when we woke up and when we returned from school. She cooked us porridge for breakfast, soups and stews from scratch, delicious apple pies, creamy rice puddings. On Sundays, we had roast lamb; on Mondays, I helped her to mince the leftover meat to make shepherd's pie. As a child, she'd always been dressed in hand-me-downs; now she scraped and saved to buy me new clothes. "Only the best," she would say, admiring how I looked in expensive smocked dresses, fine wool cardigans, and shiny patent leather shoes. She sent me to Irish dancing lessons and elocution classes. She hired private tutors to help with my studies, so I would pass exams for grammar school, the only route back then for a working class teenager to a possible spot at university.

"I want you to have everything I never had," she'd say.

This master plan included a big white wedding. When I was 7, she started saving for it. From then on, she talked about the fabulous dress she'd buy for me, the hat she would wear, the limousine that would take Dad and me to the flower-filled church, the lavish reception in a country club. How the wedding would be the talk of the parish. How I'd settle down close by so my children could run in and out of her house. But despite these dreams for my future, she also dreaded me growing up.

"The happiest times of my life were when my children were little and needed me," she'd often say in later years.

As I headed toward my teens, she railed against me switching from white socks to nylons. When I wanted a bra, she just laughed and pointed out that it wasn't necessary because my breasts were tiny. When I got my first period, she simply said, "Oh no, it's all started," and I felt ashamed.

When I was 13, Mum started menopause. It was never talked about, except when my Aunty Madge took me to one side and explained about "the change." We were both hormonal messes and fought terribly. She forbade me to pluck my eyebrows or wear cosmetics. I did both. I used to sneak out and plaster on foundation and mascara in a department store "powder room" before heading to a coffee bar I wasn't supposed to go to. The eventual arrival of boyfriends, when I was 15, brought suspicion and curfews. None of it worked. The harder she tried to cling, the more I drew away.

"I sacrificed everything for you," she would wail. "I didn't ask to be born!" I'd yell back.

She never explained what those sacrifices were; only with hindsight did I realize how many of her desires had been subsumed by devotion for her children. I didn't want to follow her example.

Despite working so hard, she rarely bought anything for herself. When I was 15, she came home one Saturday with a new purchase, a sheepskin coat. She'd saved hard for it. It was to be her "best coat." The next day, she and Dad went to an early Mass. I stayed in bed; they were aware I'd lost all belief in Catholicism, but they still expected me to attend Mass on Sundays, and I knew they would start reminding me later in the morning to get ready for the eleven o'clock service. At around nine o'clock I heard their car pull into the driveway. The front door opened, and Mum's footsteps came quickly up the stairs.

"He's ruined my coat!" she cried, bursting into my room. She sat on the bed, leaned over to pull open the curtains, and thrust an arm toward my face. "Look, look! Oil!"

I saw the stains close to the furry cuff. As her body started shaking with sobs, she blurted out the story. Dad had decided to put some lubricant on the handbrake. He'd been too liberal with it. He hadn't wiped off the residue and hadn't warned her about it. On the way back from church, one of the sleeves of her new coat made contact with the oily brake handle.

"I never have any luck," she gasped. "I've wanted this coat for years, and now I might as well throw it away."

I tried to reassure her. The oil would come off. We'd take it to the dry cleaner's. She couldn't be consoled. The stains were almost completely removed, but they left a shadow that always reminded her of the incident. Poor Dad felt guilty for months. And, strangely, I felt guilty too. I wanted to make it all better, but I couldn't. I wanted to make her happy. I'd done that as a child, but now it seemed impossible.

Over the years, I came to realize Mum often set herself up for disappointment. Both my brother John and myself were at high school when she and Dad had their 25th wedding anniversary. We'd consulted with our eldest brother Mick, who had moved to London by then, about what we should do. We bought a card, a present, arranged for a lunch out with my parents and Aunty Madge. All went well on the day, until the evening newspaper was delivered. When the *Wolverhampton Express and Star* was pushed through the letter box, usually Dad got to it first. But this time it was Mum who snatched it up. Standing in the hallway, she turned to the announcements, looking for the congratulations message from her children. (Which, of course, we hadn't thought of.) The meltdown was awful. Tears, recriminations, everything ruined.

"Why didn't you tell us to do that?" I asked Mum.

"I shouldn't have to tell you!" she cried in fury. "You should have known!"

I felt awful about that for years. I still do. It was such a small thing, and it would – maybe – have made her happy.

～

Even as a child, I was restless. In primary school, my favourite book was *Alice in Wonderland*. I wanted to *be* Alice, wandering through strange worlds full of wonder, surprise, and danger. As I got older, these early inchoate cravings turned into burning desire. Life in Wolverhampton was claustrophobic. I felt suffocated by my mother's love, hemmed in by suburban life, by Catholicism, by my convent school, by my parents' need for security and safety. I longed for something bigger and exciting; I couldn't wait for my real life to begin. Such longings served me well. I realized that, if I flunked my exams, I could get stuck in Wolverhampton. A period of relative calm came when, at 16, I decided to knuckle down and work really hard at school. I stopped fighting with my mother. We went clothes shopping together, and she bought me lovely dresses that *I* chose, that showed off my body. She seemed excited about my future.

On a hot August day, my A Level results arrived: top marks across the board. With them came the chance to sit exams for admission to

Oxford or Cambridge University – but not until the following year. I couldn't face the prospect of continuing to live at home and staying at convent school to prepare for the exams. To my parents' disappointment, I accepted a place at Liverpool University to read geography. Weeks later, they drove me there – 150 kilometres and as many light years away from my life to date. Mum was distraught at her youngest child's flight from the nest. I was ecstatic, in free fall, the earth spread out beneath me like an endless carpet, the horizon a giant, beckoning curve. I had no ambitions except to take on life in great big bites. In some ways, that has never changed.

Mum fell apart. Whenever I called her, she wept down the phone, saying how much she missed me, asking why I didn't want to come home every weekend. When I went back in the middle of the semester for a few days, there were more tears and recriminations, with my father sitting awkwardly on the sidelines, at a loss for what to do. By then, I was deep into a love affair with a medical student, Keith, whom I'd met shortly after I arrived in Liverpool. A few years older than me, he was handsome and worldly. He drove a vintage sports car with a leather strap across its hood. He played classical guitar. He wore pink, bell-bottom, corduroy pants, army-issue jackets, and high-top sneakers. He was curious and funny and fabulous in bed. Blinded by young love and lust, I thought it was a good idea to invite my Jewish boyfriend to my traditional Irish Catholic home for Christmas.

It was a disaster. When he asked for some rags to wipe up oil from the engine of his beloved car, my mother responded, "Why don't you use some of the ones you're wearing?" My father informed him that the Jews killed Christ. My brothers laughed when he was served with a plate of bacon and sausage at breakfast. And on it went, for two excruciating days, until he decided to cut short the visit. As he was leaving, my parents pinned him in a corner of the hallway and hissed, "Our daughter is very precious to us." They spent the rest of my time at home telling me he'd never marry me because his family wouldn't accept a gentile. And even if they did, they would insist the children were brought up in the Jewish faith. He's only my boyfriend, I told them. Settling down and having a family – I hadn't even considered these things as part of my future.

"Well, it's time you started!" my mother retorted.

I returned to Liverpool an emotional wreck. It took me a while to stop imagining my mother staring down at us when Keith and I were in bed. I never talked to my parents about him again, but I knew they were constantly worried about us being together, and what it would lead to. Almost three years later, when I broke up with him, he said I was letting my family wreck the relationship. But there were other reasons.

Keith had refused to travel with me in the summers; instead, he'd gone off on his own adventures, riding a motorbike across America, hiking along the coast of Crete, cycling through Sweden. He said he didn't want to feel responsible for me, and that he wanted to sleep with other women. There was no need to worry, he assured me, because he never got involved. I was his girlfriend, and he knew he was coming home to me. But at any mention of men I'd met on my journeys, he became suspicious and questioning. At first I put up with it, struggling quietly with my own jealousies. Then, 18 months into our relationship, I joined a women's group. I'd like to say it was attending its meetings, and reading books by Betty Friedan and Simone de Beauvoir, that began opening my eyes to the fact that my boyfriend had controlling tendencies, and that I was being compliant. But what really kicked it off was Keith's insistence that, instead of joining my friends to see the Rolling Stones at the Liverpool Empire and the Who at the Students' Union theatre, I ought to go with him to concertos by Beethoven and Handel. The fact that I missed seeing young Mick Jagger and Roger Daltrey in small venues is something I never quite forgave him, or myself, for.

One of my flat mates, Nigel, was an International Marxist and called himself a feminist. He became a good friend and always offered a sympathetic ear for my woes about Keith. Eventually, he offered an alternative bed.

Those Keith-less university summers were full of my own adventures. As well as Italy and Greece, I went to Morocco, France, Israel, Sweden, and Russia. I worked as a chambermaid, as a grape picker. I returned reluctantly from each of these odysseys, wondering how I could make travelling a lifestyle. Despite not studying much, I scraped through my exams and emerged as a teacher at a Liverpool high school. Exactly what my mother had always wanted. But it wasn't part of a plan to settle down and have a family, nor was it a vocation. At the time, I simply couldn't think of any other career, and the long summer holidays were a huge appeal.

Leaving student life was a terrible shock. The routine of my new job appalled me. I hated knowing exactly how each week from September to July would pan out. I resented the strident bells that divided up each day. Staff room politics baffled me; I regularly sat in the wrong chair, or used someone else's mug, or forgot to bring cake on a Friday when it was my turn. I often turned up for work with a hangover. I was teaching something called "general studies," a mishmash of different subjects with no real academic aim, which gave the headmaster, Mr. Tucker, an excuse to saddle me with the toughest kids in the school. My pupils were 14–16 years old, a lot of them regular truants. Some of them had been in trouble with the police.

"Your chief job is to keep bums in seats," Mr. Tucker instructed me. "And whatever happens, don't let them out of the classroom before the bell rings."

Sometimes I was dealing with near riots. Once, when things were getting really out of hand, I barricaded the door with my body. Two of the boys yanked me aside, while the others spilled out and raced down the hallway. While I stood there shaking, one boy stopped long enough to write "Mr. Tucker is a Fucker" on a wall, in big letters, with an indelible ink pen he'd snatched from my desk. Later, I got reprimanded for allowing him to do that.

Little wonder I was drinking so much, and that at lunch hour I would sometimes go to the nearest pub – where I usually ran into some of my students.

"Don't let on about our age, Miss, and we'll behave better," whispered a tall 16-year-old boy one day as we both stood at the bar. We struck a deal, and school life got a bit easier after that.

To finalize my teaching qualifications, I had to stay in the job for one academic year. Halfway through it, my post-Keith boyfriend, Nigel, left for Peru to do his PhD research on South American trade union politics. As soon as the last bell of the summer term rang, I bought a year's return ticket and joined him. My mother was beside herself, this time on several counts: Because I was giving up my teaching position. Because I accidently let slip to one of her Catholic friends that I would be living in Peru with a man, not realizing it was supposed to be a big secret. Because I would be 10,000 kilometres away. Most of all, because I was leaving her again.

Nigel and I lived in Arequipa, a colonial town of white stone buildings in the foothills of the Andes, beneath the picture-perfect, snow-capped volcano Misti. I taught English part-time to adults in a small private school. Walking to work was a joy. I crossed a bridge with a clear view of Misti, then passed through the main square, where couples strolled arm in arm around the fountain, old men sat chatting on benches shaded by tall palm trees, and women wearing bowler hats and layers of long skirts arranged potatoes, maize, and bunches of herbs on sackcloth spread over the smooth stones, waiting patiently for customers.

For three months we travelled through Peru, across Bolivia and Argentina, and down to Patagonia. I loved the high plains, the thin air, the mountains, the intriguing cultures. I dreamed of staying forever. Then Nigel started talking about his plans for an academic career in England, "when we move back there." This was problematic. By then, I was thinking of breaking up with him. I was trying to find a way to broach the subject when he announced he wanted us to marry and have a family, and that he would agree to a Catholic wedding for the sake of my parents. He also said that, as he was the last male in his family, it was okay if I wanted to keep my own name when we married, but our children would have to have his surname.

"So much for your feminism," I said, which sparked a big row.

Not long afterwards, the recurring nightmares began. I dreamt I was walking down the aisle toward him, wearing a white dress and veil, when I started to panic, scream, and struggle with my father, who was trying to stop me fleeing from the church.

"What were you dreaming about?" Nigel would ask after shaking me awake.

I never told him.

When the date of my return ticket approached, I considered tearing it up and going to Ecuador on my own to find work and a place to live. The knowledge of how this would affect my mother, mixed with fear about leaping into the unknown, caused my courage to·fail. Back in England, I ended the relationship – badly – by having an affair. I got another high school teaching position, this time in Manchester. My brother John sensibly suggested I should buy a house – because of my job, I could get a mortgage and rent out the spare bedrooms to cover the payments. He helped me find a place, and my parents gave me the deposit. They were relieved that I seemed to be settling down. Mum kept asking if there were any nice young single men working at the school. During the year I'd been away, several of my friends from convent school and university had got married. A couple of them were pregnant; another had already given birth to a son. "It's good to have your babies when you're young," Mum said, when I told her. "You can grow up together."

In the staff room at work, I listened to my colleagues talk and plot endlessly about career paths to becoming heads of departments, heads of schools. I had a new recurring nightmare: being at my retirement party after 40-plus years as a teacher.

I longed to be travelling again, for life to feel open-ended and full of surprise once more. I took evening courses to get a diploma in teaching English as a second language, and started applying for jobs overseas. I had interviews for teaching positions in Buenos Aires and in Ulaanbaatar. Neither was successful, but I had a feeling I would be third-time lucky. Then those plans came to an abrupt halt.

Through my brother Mick, who until recently had been an active mountaineer, I got introduced to the climbing scene in North Wales – or at least the social side of it – and started spending weekends there. Back then, climbing and hard partying went hand in hand. After a Friday night pub session, everyone would pack into a small cottage for more booze, marijuana, hash, and magic mushrooms, and hours of dancing. The following day, hangover cures consisted of greasy breakfasts and endless cups of tea before a hike to the nearest crag. Then back to the pub.

Though this group, I was introduced to a rising star in the mountaineering world, Alex MacIntyre, who was moving to Manchester and needed a place to live. He rented a room in my house, and since it was only eight kilometres from the airport it soon became a base for his climbing partners. Sometimes I had a whole Himalayan expedition sprawled on my living room floor. I didn't climb, but I was accepted into this tribe of free-spirited nomads, which at that time was male-dominated. They dazzled me. They were like knights heading off to slay dragons in high, wild places, returning with stories of walking a fine line between life and death. Perhaps this resonated with my drowning experience – I too had glimpsed the void. I was drawn to their aura of risk, their reckless zest, their charged energy. Compared to the predictability of my teaching life, this was heaven.

But I vowed not to get involved with a mountaineer. I'd pitied Mick's girlfriend when he left on long expeditions. I'd met the wife and children of a man who had been killed in an avalanche. I'd decided it was enough to just be mates with these guys, to enjoy the parties and the joie de vivre. I was having a long-distance relationship with a man who, like me, was on the edge of the climbing scene. We met up twice a month; it was casual and eventually we both began seeing other people. From the outside, it seemed like I was having a fine time: lots of men, lots of sex. But the complications and jealousies were making me unhappy, and emotionally I was lonely. By then, Alex had become a close friend, and I confided in him.

"You need to ditch all these blokes and start again," he advised. "There's a big party in Wales on Saturday. I'll give you a lift, and you can get going on the hatchet job then."

At the party, in a corner of the crowded kitchen, a man was holding court, recounting a horrifying descent down a Himalayan mountain in a storm and turning it into a funny story. I recognized him from photos in magazines and newspapers, and through Alex and other friends I'd heard a lot about the famous Joe Tasker and his daring climbs. I watched him across the beer and wine bottles, through a pall of cigarette smoke. He was lean, rangy, broad-shouldered. He wore a fisherman's sweater with the sleeves pushed up. He had strong forearms and beautiful hands. His hair was receding, his blue eyes framed by fine wrinkles. He caught my gaze and smiled.

"You're Mick Coffey's sister, aren't you?" he said. "I met you once at a party, but you were high on something and you wandered past me. You probably thought I was a lizard."

For the rest of the weekend, we circled each other. The man I was attempting to "hatchet" sensed my interest in Joe and became uncharacteristically solicitous. Later, Joe told me he had to resist the urge to walk over and hold me in his arms. When Alex decided to stay on in Wales to do some climbing, Joe offered to give me a lift back to Manchester. I accepted.

I hadn't expected to fall in love, never mind so fast or so deeply. I knew it was folly. He made it clear to me from the beginning that mountaineering was his first priority. He wanted me in his life, but on his terms. He would be away a lot on expeditions; if I couldn't put up with his absences, and his preoccupations with work when he was home, he would understand. And there was another woman in his heart, but far away and unavailable. It was, quite simply, a "my way or the highway" arrangement. But when he did turn his focus on me, he was fully there, and full of tenderness. He was the most interesting and engaging man I'd ever met. He had a sharp, enquiring mind, honed by the classical education he'd received at a Jesuit seminary, where he had trained for the priesthood before making mountains his vocation. He was witty and wry, a raconteur with many compelling stories. He fascinated me, and with him I felt content and calm in a way I never had before.

I stopped applying for jobs overseas. I got a position at a refugee reception centre, one that allowed me to arrange my own holiday time. I suggested to Joe that I accompany him on some of his expeditions, trekking as far as his base camps. He said it was out of the question, that my presence would disturb his focus. This was another hard condition, yet I accepted it. When he was home, I curled my life around his, caring for him, becoming a domestic creature I hardly recognized. When he was gone, I caught up with friends and I travelled. I drove across the United States, I worked as a waitress in California, I wandered around Europe. But it was a way of filling time, of allaying worry, until I knew he was safe and on his way back to England.

We were a couple for 30 months – for half that time he was on long expeditions. Six weeks after the start of our love affair, he left to climb K2, the world's second-highest mountain. He was buried in an avalanche, barely escaped, and promptly went up the mountain again for another try. He returned painfully thin and plagued by nightmares but with his ambitions stronger than ever. Twelve weeks later, he set off to attempt a winter ascent of Everest. After that, Kongur, a Chinese mountain. Then to Everest again, and its unclimbed Northeast Ridge, which he tackled – like the other mountains – in a small team without supplementary oxygen.

Mum had been horrified to discover I was dating a mountaineer. She had always been terrified about my brother Mick's climbing, a fear that was compounded when she learned about his accident during a crossing of the Patagonian icefield. A snow bridge collapsed under him, he tumbled headfirst into a crevasse, and got stuck where it narrowed, staring into the depths, freezing. News of this near-tragedy, and his dramatic rescue by another member of the team, Don Whillans, reached England before Mick got home. Mum found out when a newspaper journalist rang her for a comment just before the story ran. Since then she had been disparaging about anything to do with climbing, so I guessed the announcement about my new boyfriend wouldn't be kindly received. I tried to soften it by telling her about his Catholic background, how he had trained for the priesthood. I thought this might give her some common ground with him.

I was wrong.

"Why would you choose a man who takes such risks?" she asked me.

It was a fair question. I recognized the irony – I'd become one of those women I used to pity. I told her what Joe's peers said about him – that he was a supremely talented mountaineer, that he knew how to manage danger, that he was considered invincible. I didn't tell her I wanted to marry him.

Since the debacle with my Jewish boyfriend, I'd been wary of introducing anyone to my parents. They only met Joe once. We were driving to his house in Derbyshire from London, where he'd given a presentation about the Everest in Winter climb. As we approached the motorway turnoff for Wolverhampton, I suggested we stop for a quick visit. Joe said he needed to get back to work on a book he was writing.

"Just for a few minutes, Joe. It's not far from the motorway."

We were in my car, I was at the wheel, and when we came to the off-ramp, I took it. Joe was furious.

"What are you doing? You know I need to get back."

"I just want to say hello to my parents. We won't stay long."

"You're only doing this to make a point," he said tersely.

"What point?"

"About your independence."

"I thought you appreciated my independence."

"In this case it's selfishness. Hardness. Insisting on what you want."

I was flabbergasted.

"Selfishness? I fit in with your schedule all the time."

"You do that because you want to. I don't ever ask it of you. You can go and see your parents anytime. It's not fair to force me to go with you when I've got pressing things to do."

By now, we were almost at the house. This was long before the days of cell phones, so I couldn't warn Mum and Dad of our arrival. But it was a Sunday afternoon. I knew their patterns – they would be home. I thought my mother would be overjoyed to see me, and to meet Joe. It was a misjudgment.

"Your dad and I are watching a program," she said coldly when she opened the door. "I'll make you some sandwiches when it's over."

I sat awkwardly with Joe, listening to the television in the next room. He wanted to leave. I said we had to stay. We ate sandwiches and drank tea with my tight-lipped mother and my silent father before brusque goodbyes.

"Well, that went really well," he said nastily as we drove away. "I hope you're happy now."

It was my turn to be furious. But I couldn't speak. Tension filled my small car until finally he softened, put a hand on my knee.

"I'm really stressed, Maria. There's so much to get done before the next trip and every minute counts. I wish I could be like normal people and just relax when I feel like it. But this is what I've chosen to do."

The Jesuit discipline. His calling. It always came first.

In bed that night, tenderness returned and tensions melted. But the situation in Wolverhampton was never discussed. Our relationship was fragile. There were no firm commitments, and the times between his expeditions felt so precious I was afraid to speak up about my insecurities, my deepest feelings, my hopes for our future. At 28, I had no idea of what a mistake this was, how it would haunt me for years to come and become one of the biggest lessons of my life.

In a phone call to Mum, I broached the subject of the visit. "I'm sure he's a decent man," she said. "But he'll break your heart into pieces."

~

Mum and Dad were visiting me in Manchester in early June 1982, when I got the news that Joe and his climbing partner Pete Boardman had disappeared without a trace on the Northeast Ridge of Everest. Mum watched helplessly as I fell apart that day, desperately wanting to ease my pain. For the next three years, she watched as I threw myself at one thing after another, trying to make sense of my life. I remortgaged my house to go to Tibet with Hilary Boardman, the widow of the man who had disappeared with Joe, and trek to their advance base camp on Everest – an attempt to find peace with the fact that they were never coming home. I sold the house, moved to the Derbyshire countryside – not far from where Joe had lived – and completely renovated an old cottage. I ran a marathon. I chased men who were bound to reject me, and rejected a man who loved me, and who Mum had hoped I would marry.

Meanwhile, the carnage in the high mountains was unrelenting. Six months after Joe and Pete's deaths, Alex, who had become like an annoying younger brother, was hit by a falling stone on Annapurna, in Nepal, and killed instantly. Another friend, Pete Thexton, who had climbed with Joe, succumbed to pulmonary edema while on Broad Peak, a mountain straddling the border between China and Tibet. Two more – Jean Pierre Hefti and Roger Baxter Jones – died in the French Alps. I was one of a growing band of young widows and devastated parents. Each time bad news broke, it felt like my wounds had been ripped open.

Finally, I fled across the world to Canada, hoping I would find something there to fill the grief-gnawed emptiness inside me.

Three

From the beginning of my life I have been looking for your face, but today I have seen it.

—JALĀL AL-DĪN MUḤAMMAD RŪMI

5

When people ask how we met, Dag claims I stalked him in the produce aisle of a supermarket in Nanaimo. And that a few days later he was sleeping on a ferry from Vancouver and woke up to find me staring at him.

It's partly true. I did spot him for the first time in a supermarket. He was standing in a checkout line. He had an unusual haircut, short at the back, long and flopped to one side at the front. A white scarf was thrown casually around his neck. I watched him pay and stroll through the doors – tall, long-legged, his feet slightly turned out.

Later, I phoned my friend Christine. "I saw the most beautiful man today," I told her. "He's like a Russian dancer."

"What, in Nanaimo?" she said. "You need your eyes tested. Are you coming over this weekend? The snow conditions on Whistler are supposed to be good."

Christine was from Glasgow. Like me, she was on a one-year teacher exchange in British Columbia. I was stuck in a small town on Vancouver Island; she was living and teaching in downtown Vancouver. I was jealous of her placement but grateful she let me stay with her whenever I wanted.

Originally, I had applied for a teacher exchange in Australia. Then one spring afternoon, my friend Robin popped into my Derbyshire cottage to see if I wanted to go to the pub. He had just returned from a climbing trip in British Columbia.

"Forget Australia," he said. "Apply to Vancouver, it's a great city. And there's so much outdoors stuff around. You can ski in the winters and sail in the summers."

I wasn't interested in sailing then. But I had learned to ski and loved it, so the idea of being near winter snow was appealing. Most of all, I desperately needed a change.

The day after Robin's visit, I contacted the exchange agency to enquire about Canada. Within half an hour it called back. We had a perfect match, the woman at the other end of the line told me. The exchange would start in just four months. The only glitch was that my placement school was "a bit of a way" from Vancouver, in a town whose name she struggled to pronounce.

"Na-neeee-moo," she said. "But apparently it's only about 25 miles from Vancouver as the crow flies. That's not too far, is it?"

It was the distance I drove twice each day for my commute to and from Manchester. No, it wasn't too far.

I met Robin again that night in the pub. I bought him a pint, set it on the table in front of him, and told him my news. He stared at me, then put his head in his hands.

"Nanaimo? Are you serious?" he said, looking up. "It's on Vancouver *Island*, Maria. You know – separated from the mainland by a stretch of water? You have a degree in geography – couldn't you have looked at a map? It's an absolute shithole. Don't go."

"It's too late," I said weakly.

He sighed and took a drink of beer.

"Oh well. Maybe you'll meet the man of your dreams there."

He didn't sound convinced.

~

I had flown into Vancouver the previous August on a perfect afternoon. As the plane started its final approach, I pressed my face to the window, gazing landwards at the city and the jagged peaks beyond it, barely noticing the glittering sea dotted with islands below. A few days later, I stood on the stern deck of a ferry taking me across that sea to Vancouver Island, sadly watching the range of mountains grow smaller across the horizon.

Nanaimo appalled me. It was originally a coal mining town, but by the mid-1980s its big employer was a pulp and paper mill. I hated the pervasive, rotten-egg smell from the mill, the lonely suburb where I lived, the soulless malls, the depressing downtown area with its rough pubs and bars. I knew I was being prissy, but after escaping hardscrabble, small-town Wolverhampton in my late teens, I felt like I'd been spiralled back to its Canadian version.

The high school students I taught loved my British accent, but there were subtle language differences that sometimes made it difficult to keep them under control. When I innocently asked if anyone had a rubber I could borrow, or suggested that a chronically late arrival should get someone to knock her up every morning, the class erupted into laughter. My fellow teachers were friendly, but we had little in common. I was invited out for a Friday night pub-crawl by several of the physical education department. The third place we walked into had a small stage, where a woman wearing only a large live cobra was swinging around a pole. I'd never been to a stripper bar before; I was shocked that a bunch of teachers would casually stroll in and sit at a table right in front of the stage. Yet this woman intrigued me. She was built like a gymnast, lithe and leanly muscled. Shortly after finishing her act, she reappeared, fully clothed minus the cobra. I joined her at the bar, bought her a drink, and struck up a conversation. She was happy to answer my questions about her background – she was indeed a gymnast and was now putting herself through university with this job, which she called "exotic dancing." From the corner of my eye, I could see my colleagues staring at me in consternation. One of them came over to tell me they were heading to the next pub. I let them go on alone. They never got over the fact that I'd talked to the exotic dancer, and to my relief never invited me out again.

∼

For the first six months in Nanaimo, almost every weekend I fled to Vancouver. I went clubbing with Christine, and we got friendly with a group of lovely gay men. When the ski season began, on Saturday mornings I would wake up early on Christine's couch, get a bus to the ski resort at

Whistler, slide around the slopes all day, then return for a night out in the city. Once, on the ski lift, I met a nice guy, Jeff, who – astonishingly – lived in Nanaimo. He had twinkly eyes, a big moustache, and a wicked sense of humour. He ran his own business, making fibreglass bathtubs and showers. We went on a couple of dates, realized there was no spark, and decided to just be friends.

After one of these weekends away, I took the bus from downtown Vancouver that drove onto the ferry for Nanaimo. I came up the stairs to the passenger deck. There, in a window seat, leaning his head against the glass, his eyes shut, was the man from the supermarket. The white scarf. Broad shoulders. Nervously, I sat a couple of rows away, facing him. He opened his eyes and looked out at the darkness. He seemed sad. No doubt sensing the full bore of my gaze, he glanced toward me. I was about to say something – I had no idea what – when suddenly Jeff appeared.

"Maria!' he cried, sitting down next to me. "Were you in Whistler this weekend? I was too! I wish I'd known."

By the time I looked back at the man, his eyes were shut again.

~

To help pass the lonely weeknights in Nanaimo, I had turned to evening classes in a local community hall. Aerobics on Tuesday. Tai chi on Thursday. I was new to tai chi. The instructor, Nelson, was an elegant Chinese man, a martial artist, light and agile as a cat. I struggled to emulate his graceful movements and wasn't encouraged by the fact that, while I was the only beginner, my classmates were little better than me. We were an odd bunch. There was a man with a hairline so low it almost met his eyebrows, and dark sideburns that spread right across his cheeks. He reminded me of a werewolf. One woman had lost the lower part of her left arm and had a prosthesis with a metal hand in a fixed position. I admired her bravery, but the sight of the shiny, clawed fingers moving through the air disturbed me. Then there was a guy who breathed hoarsely and heavily. And the man who sweated a lot and didn't smell so good. In the midst of them, there was me, wobbling about in bright yellow sweatpants and T-shirt, trying to put together the moves and remember their names: hold the moon, strum the lute, step back to repulse the monkey. I was hopeless, but I kept trying.

One Thursday evening, our motley group had assembled in the room as usual and was standing in front of Nelson waiting for his cue to begin. There was a line dancing class going on in the room directly above us, and the stamping and hollering was a bit distracting. Even more distracting for me was the prospective student who arrived and asked Nelson if he could watch the class. He stood to one side, leaning against the wall, his arms crossed. That floppy hair. The white scarf. Our eyes met; he looked slightly puzzled.

Awkwardly attempting tai chi in front of a man I'd fallen in lust with but not yet met was excruciating. I only looked over at him once. He was watching me. Feeling a blush spread from my neck to my forehead, I turned the wrong way and bumped into the lady with the metal hand.

When the class finished, the prospective student went to talk to Nelson. I slowly put on my shoes and coat and made sure we headed to the door at the same time. He stopped. I looked up at him. I saw the scarf was silk. Noted the generous lips. Deep brown eyes.

He denies this now, but I swear it's true.

"Haven't I seen you somewhere before?" he asked.

If I'd had my way, the whole thing would have started that night. But he was reticent. We went for a beer at a pub that overlooked the harbour. We sat side by side at a high table, next to a window. He arranged his long limbs with an easy grace and leaned back, smiling, as he answered my questions. His name was Dag, pronounced with a long *a*. He was Canadian, had grown up in the east of the country and in the States, until his family moved to Germany when he was 14. He went through university there, getting a veterinary degree in Berlin and starting his PhD on fish pathology in Munich. The previous summer he had arrived in Nanaimo to do his research at the Pacific Biological Station. I couldn't believe I'd been in the same town for over six months and not stumbled across him earlier.

"You seemed so sad when I saw you on the ferry," I said.

Again, I watched him gaze out into the darkness. He said he'd been returning from a weekend with a woman he'd met last summer through his research work. They had just broken up. I felt a selfish pang of hope.

He decided to take the tai chi class. We arranged to meet there the following Thursday, have a beer again afterwards. Just in case, I gave him my phone number and address.

He turned up on my doorstep the following Monday. It was a cold night. He was wearing the usual silk scarf, an Icelandic wool sweater, tight German army pants that ended just below his knees, thick wool socks, and hiking boots. I had to hang onto the door frame.

"I just popped by on the off chance you might be home," he said.

We still only talked. He admitted he found me rather frightening, defended by a tough shell. It was true. I was terrified of being hurt again. Because Joe had disappeared without a trace on Everest, there hadn't been a body to say goodbye to, no concrete fact of death. Even going to the mountain myself hadn't helped to shake the feeling that one day he might just turn up. But there was a problem with that too – after he died, I'd learned about his infidelity. It was little wonder I was now so defensive.

At the next tai chi class, I stood behind Dag and off to one side. He wore loose cotton pants and a muscle shirt. He had a lizard tattooed on his left shoulder. It was my worst class ever – I couldn't take my eyes off him.

I had just turned 34, and over the weekend I threw a party for myself. Christine came from Vancouver and brought a cake. I'd made a few other friends in Nanaimo by then and invited them all. Everyone was single, and most people didn't know each other, so I thought I should have a strong welcome drink to get the group loosened up. As each guest arrived, I made them a tequila pop. In a narrow glass, add one-third tequila, two-thirds ginger beer, put your hand over the top of the glass, slam the bottom of it on the counter, and, as the contents fizz, drink them down in one gulp.

Within minutes, the room filled with chatter and laughter. Dag was late. Nervous that he might not turn up, I drank one too many tequila pop. By the time he walked in, I was flying high. Christine produced the cake. I blew out the candles. Then, without forethought, I grabbed two oranges and a banana from a nearby fruit bowl, stuck the banana end up into the middle of the cake, and positioned the oranges on either side of it. I picked up the knife and cut right through the middle of the banana and into the cake.

There were groans from some of the men in the room, weak laughter from the women. Dag looked horrified.

Why did I do that? I think when I first saw Dag, a door in my heart that had long been shut suddenly swung open. As much as I wanted to step through it, I was terrified of the consequences, of more loss. I guess I was trying to scare him away. I almost succeeded.

I didn't hear from him for a few days. One afternoon after work I stopped by unannounced at his studio apartment. It was my first time there. His bed was a mattress on the floor, and his clothes lay in a heap beside it. The scant furniture was made from driftwood he had collected from beaches. A gnarled stump for a low table, logs and rough planks for bookshelves. While he brewed some tea, I looked through his books.

I picked up a heavy tome titled *Stress in Fish*. "Is this a joke?" I called to him.

He stuck his head around the corner. "What's funny about that?"

A late snowfall had been forecast, and through the balcony window I could see flakes drifting down. As we drank the tea and starting talking, it began falling fast and thick. He cut up some cheese into slices and arranged them artfully on a driftwood board. He lit candles. Poured wine. He told me about a woman in Germany he had loved since he was 17. They had broken up and restarted many times but could never make it work. It hurt him to think of her.

Since arriving in Canada, I'd only told Christine about Joe. Now, hesitantly, I started to talk about him. His four long Himalayan expeditions while we were a couple. The problems that grew between us when he was home. How I wanted a commitment, which he was unwilling to give. And then, when I was waiting for him to return from Everest, a friend and climbing partner of Joe's turning up at my door to break the news. Six months later, my own journey to Everest, a pilgrimage to follow in Joe's last footsteps, as far as I could go.

I talked and talked; the whole story spilled out. By the time I stopped, there was a drift of snow on the balcony. Dag was silent. I looked at him and in the candlelight I could see tears on his cheeks. He reached for me, wrapped me tightly in his arms, and held me for a long time.

~

We stopped going to the tai chi lessons.

"We've got better things to do right now," said Dag one morning in bed. "We can take it up again when we're old."

Right there, a hint of a future together.

There's a German word – *fernweh* – that describes an ache to explore faraway places. We both had that. We both wanted an unconventional life. We shared some important dreams. We loved being together. So what was in the way? There was the woman back in Munich he still thought about. There was the ghost in my life. And there was the fact that he'd always imagined having a family – a large one.

"Five kids would be perfect," he had said blithely, shortly after we'd met. "That way, they could all look after each other. They'd never be lonely. But I don't want to start until I'm in my 40s, after I've got some big adventures out of the way."

I had fears around motherhood, rooted in trauma. The near-drowning experience in my early 20s had taught me all I needed to know about the fine line between life and death; nine years later, this was compounded when Joe disappeared on Everest. The moment I learned of his death, I understood there was no way to defend oneself against such pain, except not to love so deeply. Since then, love had been shadowed by fear. No matter how I tried to rationalize it, the thought of having a child, of opening myself up to the possibility of the worst kind of bereavement, terrified me.

I decided not to worry about it. I was five years older than Dag. When he was ready to start a family, I would be well past being able to have a baby, even if I wanted one (never mind five). Besides which it wasn't clear if our affair would go anywhere. *Just enjoy this*, I told myself. *Don't project into the future.*

6

I'd been so busy hating Nanaimo that I'd hardly paid attention to its quaint Fisherman's Wharf, a bustle of tugs and seine boats, or the two small islands in the harbour beyond. But now Dag had decided to rent a cabin on one of the islands, called Protection, and he was about to move there. His brother was arriving from Germany for a long visit, and they would share the place.

He'd been raving about how amazing the previous summer had been, his explorations of beaches in the area, all the swimming he'd done. He couldn't wait to be living on Protection, crossing the harbour each day, getting into sailing and kayaking. None of which sounded so great to me. Since my near-drowning accident, I had a fear of deep water.

He rowed me over the harbour in a borrowed boat. It was cold, a bit windy, and waves sloshed against the hull. For the 1.5-kilometre crossing I clung to the gunwales with a white-knuckled grip. He tied the boat to a wobbly wooden dock.

"Careful, the boards are slippery," he warned. I clutched his hand as we walked along the dock and onto the island. The tide was going out, and from the muddy beach there was a sharp smell, part rot, part iodine. Trees with convoluted trunks and branches bent over the shore. Their bark was red and peeling, revealing a bright green layer beneath, smooth as stone.

"Arbutus," Dag told me. "These tall, straight trees are cedars, and those are Douglas firs. The island was logged long ago. This is all second growth."

The island was only 153 acres in size. We wandered through the forest along winding dirt paths, muddy from the recent snowmelt. We passed a few cabins tucked in among the trees, smoke curling from their chimneys. The one Dag would soon be renting was small, built of wood, with a steep roof. Two windows either side of the front door, another smaller one tucked under the eaves. It reminded me of a cuckoo clock.

He led me to a beach where slabs of sandstone had been weathered to patterns like intricate honeycombs. In places there were smooth hollows, large enough for us to sit in. Dag was as excited as a child, peering into tidal pools, watching seabirds skitter along the tide line. He filled his pockets with stones and bits of driftwood. He pointed out barnacles and got me to lean in close to hear their sucking sound. This was a whole new world, and I could hardly take it in.

The wind picked up, making me anxious about our return journey. I endured the crossing and was relieved for once to get back to Nanaimo.

When Dag told me he'd bought a second-hand motorboat, I imagined sitting safely and comfortably in the cockpit behind a glass windscreen as we whizzed over the waves. On the evening he took possession of his new craft, I met him at Fisherman's Wharf. He was tinkering with the outboard engine when I arrived. I stared in horror at the state of the boat: old and battered, its hull a patchwork of fibreglass repairs; completely open, without a cockpit or windscreen; a couple of wooden planks serving as seats; and around Dag's feet, a bailing jug afloat in a few inches of greasy water.

He looked up. "Hey, honey! Come aboard! The engine's a bit temperamental, so give me a few minutes."

Gingerly, I stepped into the boat and sat on a plank. Dag pulled at the starter cord. Nothing. He pulled again. And again and again. Once he pulled so hard he almost fell backwards. Eventually, the engine spluttered into life, and we chugged slowly out of the harbour. Dag looked happy. Halfway to Protection, the engine died.

"Don't worry," he said, yanking the cord. "We've got a couple of oars."

∽

By late spring, Dag was swimming every day. I wanted to get past my fears, and he promised to help me. We started in the calm waters of the channel between Protection and the island across from it, then called

Newcastle, now renamed Saysutshun Marine Provincial Park. I stood on the rocky beach wearing a pink, high-cut swimsuit that hadn't yet been anywhere near the sea and a pair of newly bought water shoes. I waded in and took a few strokes. When I tried to touch down, and felt only water under my feet, a visceral fear gripped me, and panic closed my throat. Gasping for breath, I thrashed back to safety.

"I'm right here," said Dag. "Let's try again."

Eventually, by telling myself land was within easy reach, I could swim in circles just out of my depth. I relaxed enough to watch great blue herons skim by, their long legs trailing behind them, then flexing as they landed on nearby rocks. I laughed when a curious seal popped up its head to regard me, before sliding beneath the water's surface again, nose last. I couldn't follow suit; I swam with my head poking up on an uncomfortably elongated neck. But it was progress.

Dag had a favourite spot on the north side of Protection, where he could jump off the rocks into deep water. One sunny July day, I decided to be brave and join him. Jumping wasn't an option for me, so he found a place where I could step on submerged rocks, then launch into a swimming position. I stepped, squatted, and pushed off. A ferry had steamed by, and when its wake reached us, waves started rebounding from the shoreline. As they tossed me about, I kept my eyes on the mainland mountains, determined to stay calm. Dag swam backwards, watching and encouraging me. Later, he said he would never forget how my face changed when a wave slapped against it, how terror flooded my features. I started choking and flailing my limbs, unravelled by flashes of memory, by the trauma that lived deep in my body rising up to engulf me. I could have drowned right there, but Dag guided me back to shore and calmed me down.

We returned to the gentle waters of the channel. I counted my strokes – 10 away from the beach, then 20, then 30. A woman I befriended on the island became my other coach. Barbara Jane patiently swam alongside me every day, encouraging me to put my head under the water, to swim a bit farther, and farther still. Much later, when I swam the 300 metres across to Saysutshun and back again, she applauded me as if I had broken an Olympic record.

~

I had a return ticket to England booked for the beginning of August. I didn't want to leave, and Dag made it clear he wanted me to stay. So I made some decisions, fast. I took a year's unpaid leave of absence from my teaching job in Manchester and got a position as a nanny in Vancouver, starting in September, which allowed me to live and work legally in Canada. Hearing of my plans, some friends in England wrote to ask if they could rent my Derbyshire cottage for a year. Things were working out very well. Then I flew home and faced my parents.

"A *nanny*?" cried Mum. Her lips were drawn tight and narrow. I knew tears would soon follow.

I was sitting with her and Dad in the living room of their house, drinking tea. They were on the couch. I was in an armchair opposite them. I was trying to break the news gently. But there was no way to soften the fact that their little girl was about to disappear across the world, yet again.

"It's beneath you!" she continued, her voice breaking. "What about your career? We sacrificed so much for your education, and you're throwing it away to be a nanny?"

She sat very straight. Sixty-eight years old. Stoutly built. Her hair permed into short, tight curls. The strap of a much-treasured gold watch digging into the plump flesh of her wrist. She wore a summer "twin set" – a short-sleeved sweater and matching cardigan – over a knee-length, cotton skirt. Her style hadn't changed for years. She was always there for me, solid in her love. But so needy for my presence. When she started crying, I knew it wasn't just about the nanny job.

Please don't go far away again, the tears said. *Please stay, settle down, have a family.*

Dad sat next to her, silent. Tall and lean, high cheekbones, a bald head atop a long neck. He was a quiet man who kept his feelings hidden. These were among the qualities, my Aunty Madge once confided to me, that had drawn my mother to him and made their marriage work. She was determined not to repeat her parents' patterns.

"She knew he would never hit her, or shout at her," Madge had said, "and he wouldn't get drunk unless someone else was paying."

Dad and I had never really understood each other, especially since my teenage years. Now he looked bewildered. "You're upsetting your mother," he said hoarsely, then went to pull weeds and dig in his beloved garden.

I had been writing to them about how much I loved Canada. That I had met someone special there. I knew they were relieved to see me happy again. Mum pulled a handkerchief from the sleeve of her cardigan. She wiped her eyes and blew her nose.

"If it works out with this man, would you live in England? Or Germany?"

I couldn't bring myself to tell her we'd base ourselves in Canada. Dag was enamoured with the BC coast and already looking at job opportunities there once he got his PhD. And if things didn't work out between us, then what? My nanny visa was for two years, so I didn't have to make a decision anytime soon. In England, I'd felt like a mouse on a wheel, trapped in a cycle of grief, stuck in a job I didn't like. On first arriving in Canada, I'd been amazed by its beauty and vastness, but I'd also sensed a huge psychological space. Suddenly, life felt open-ended again, full of possibility and surprise. While I had no clear idea of what my future held, there was one thing I was sure of.

~

When I'd first left for Vancouver Island, friends from the climbing tribe had arranged a surprise farewell party in Derbyshire. Now they were welcoming me back with another big gathering, hosted by Brian and Louise Hall. Brian was an experienced Himalayan mountaineer. He had climbed with Joe on their Everest in Winter expedition in 1981. Louise had been Joe's girlfriend before me. It was a closeness akin to family.

Brian had just got back from Pakistan, where he'd been on an expedition to K2. The flare up of an old knee injury had forced him to leave his team early. A number of other teams were also trying to reach the summit by different routes, and there had already been eight deaths among them. He was thin and drawn; a poignant reminder for me of how Joe looked after his long climbs.

By late afternoon, people were starting to drift in, and Louise, always the nurturer, was producing plates of food. I couldn't stop talking about Dag.

"You seem so different now. Much softer at the edges," observed one friend. "This man's obviously good for you."

There was a lot of teasing about the job I was returning to.

"You, a nanny?" said one woman incredulously. "You've never struck me as the Mary Poppins type."

"It must be a rehearsal for you having kids," said another. "Hey, our baby's asleep in the back room. When she wakes up, you can go and change her nappy. Good practice for the future."

"You should have a child, Maria," said a guy with whom I'd once had a fling, and who was a new father. "It will complete you as a woman."

I gawped at him. "*Complete* me?" He was saved from my wrath when Brian walked into the room, his face clouded.

"I'm really sorry to spoil the party before it even gets started," he said. "But I've just received some bad news from K2."

Details were trickling in about a terrible storm that had engulfed the mountain. Several climbers had managed to struggle to base camp, frostbitten and exhausted, with reports of people still trapped high up. Among them was Al Rouse, a friend of all of us and particularly close to Brian. Al had last been seen in a tent, delirious and terribly weak, unable to descend. Conditions were worsening.

"There's no chance of him surviving," said Brian. The room went silent.

As more news came in, and was conveyed to arriving guests, my welcome home party turned into a wake for Al. We stayed up most of the night and got very drunk. I dozed fitfully for a couple of hours, fully dressed atop a sleeping bag on a bedroom floor. When I woke, it was still early and the house was quiet. I went out into the cool morning to my car, put on my running gear, and headed up onto the moorlands behind the village. Despite all the alcohol in my system, I felt strangely alert and clear-headed. I ran for a couple of hours across the Peak District landscape I loved, and where I had forged close and binding friendships with the people still asleep in the house far below me. They would always welcome me back. But Al's death was a breaking point. Whatever was going to happen with Dag, I knew I couldn't live here again, braced for the next tragedy. Or risk getting involved with another mountaineer. I had to leave for good.

~

I only had a few days with Dag on Protection Island before heading to Vancouver to start my new job as a live-in nanny. It seemed like a plum position, with weekends off and good pay. My boss, Owen, was a widower in his early 40s whose wife had died 18 months before. He was darkly handsome, square-jawed, and clean cut, with a level gaze and a remote air. The agency that put me in touch with him had told me there had been "rather a lot" of nannies since his wife's death. They explained that the 9-year-old twin girls, Tania and Tegan, and their almost 4-year-old brother James, missed their mother terribly, resented their father being away on business so much, and took it all out on their caregiver.

I met them the first time just after my interview with Owen, while he was showing me around their house. A family friend had gone to pick up the girls from school and had taken James with her. The front door opened, a high voice called, "We're here!" and there was a stampede of feet in the hallway. The girls ran in first. They were tall and willowy for their age, dressed in smart school uniforms of tartan skirts and red jackets. They threw their bags on the floor and dived at their father. Behind them was a little boy with short blond hair. "Daddy!" he shouted, and grabbed one of Owen's legs. While Owen wrapped his arms around the three children, the woman who had arrived with them stood in the doorway, staring at me. She was middle-aged, slight, with short brown hair.

"Owen, who is this?" she asked, without taking her eyes off me.

"She's the new nanny," he said. "Maria, meet Sandi."

The children, who hadn't noticed me before, turned around. For a couple of seconds they were silent and wide-eyed. Then one of the girls yelled, "We don't *want* another nanny!" and burst into tears. She rushed from the room, her siblings following.

At the start, the girls were routinely horrible to me, but after my experience with high school students, this didn't bother me. It was the household rules that wore me down.

Part of my job description was to buy food and cook for the children. Owen insisted on them following a very strict diet. He had handed me a vegan cookbook and told me to carefully follow the recipes.

"No meat, fish, dairy, eggs, or cheese," he instructed. "A minimum of flour and salt. Lots of raw, organic vegetables. No sugar. Absolutely no candies or chocolate."

Every night I made a salad, a soup, and a main course of rice, lentils, or beans with some sort of tofu or vegetable topping. Every night the kids pushed away the salad, tasted the soup, grimaced, and yelled, "Yuck!" It wasn't just my poor culinary skills. They hated this diet. So did I. Once I'd gained their confidence, occasionally I snuck in pizzas and ice cream. I swore them to secrecy, and even little James managed to keep his pledge. But when I brought him back from a visit to the dentist and his father happened to be home, he busted me for something else.

"Daddy, I got chewing gum from the man who looked at my teeth!" James shouted. Owen gave me a furious lecture. I explained it was sugarless gum, but that didn't matter to him.

"I'm trying to set lifelong patterns for my children," he fumed. "And now James will want gum again."

I was also forbidden to give the children any form of Western medicine. When James got an ear infection, Owen was about to leave for the States. "Put some drops of warm olive oil in his ear," he instructed. For a whole day and into the evening, the little boy cried with pain. I took him to bed with me – neither of us slept that night. By the following afternoon, it was unbearable. I drove him to the hospital. A doctor prescribed antibiotics, and within hours the pain started to subside. When Owen returned, I told him the olive oil had worked perfectly.

Dag urged me to quit the job. "The guy's a weirdo," he said.

I agreed. But it's my nature to see things through, the girls were warming to me, and I had developed a strong bond with James. When I arrived at the house each week, he would come running into my arms. Every afternoon he'd curl up on my lap with one of his favourite books, which I'd read to him over and over again. When he had nightmares, I'd carry him into my bed and soothe him until he fell asleep. I loved the way he trusted me, how I could make him laugh, how he was blooming under my care. I'd discovered I was good at mothering – and that, for all the frustrations, it brought me a unique and puzzling happiness.

"I'll try to stay for a year," I told Dag.

As the weeks went by, however, things in Vancouver got stranger. I never knew exactly where Owen was. I wasn't allowed to call him unless it was an emergency. The children would constantly ask me when he was coming home, and when I couldn't tell them, they would cry. A couple of times a rough-looking guy banged on the front door, demanding to see Owen, saying he owed him a lot of money. I began to wonder what kind of strange business Owen was running. He would walk in unexpectedly and go straight to the fridge to check on the food I'd bought. He'd sit and have dinner with us, and in front of me quiz the girls about how much I was helping them with their homework. He'd walk around silently inspecting the results of the "light housework" that was another part of my job description. Before I got up the next morning, he would be gone. When I was due to be paid, a cheque would appear on the dining room table. Almost always there was a mistake. The sum was too small, or my name was misspelt, or he hadn't signed or dated it. So I would have to wait until I saw him again to ask him to write out another cheque. I felt like I was walking on shifting sand. His presence was disturbing, whether or not he was in the house. The stress started to affect my health. I developed a recurring urinary infection, headaches, and back pain.

Sandi, whom I'd met after my interview, usually looked after the children on the weekends. We crossed paths very briefly. A couple of times I asked about her connection to the family, but she evaded the question. On one Sunday evening, however, she hung back and helped me put the children to bed. Then we sat at the dining table, drinking chamomile tea. Alcohol wasn't allowed in the house.

"How are you getting on here?" she asked.

I paused.

"You're looking drawn," she continued. "I've been getting worried about you."

"The kids are fine," I said haltingly. "But Owen..."

"You don't have to explain. You've been here, what, over three months? That's a record. Most of the other nannies only lasted a few weeks at most. The agency was about to give up on us until you contacted them."

"They forgot to mention that."

"Well, of course. Did Owen tell you anything about his wife?"

"Only that she died from cancer. He doesn't talk to me much about anything."

"She was 39. It was very fast. She was under a lot of stress with Owen. I'm sure that's what made her ill."

Another pause.

"There's something else he didn't tell you. Come with me."

She led me to a small room I'd only popped my head into before. It was a sewing room, and I don't sew. Now I followed Sandi inside and looked around. There were piles of fabrics on the floor, a sewing machine on a table, next to it a tissue dress pattern pinned to a swath of material. It was as if someone had just been working there and had stepped away for a break.

"Did the other nannies...?" My question trailed away. On the wall behind the open door was a painting of a woman's head and shoulders. She had greenish eyes, high cheekbones, dark hair to her shoulders, a long neck. A shiver ran down my spine. She looked like me.

"That's Owen's wife," said Sandi. "It's why I was so shocked when I first saw you."

I was spooked. Owen had never referred to the resemblance, nor had he ever acted inappropriately. But suddenly I knew that, for my health and sanity, I couldn't work the full year. Sandi read my thoughts.

"If you decided to make other plans, I wouldn't blame you."

I walked out of the room. I didn't want to see that picture ever again.

"What would happen to the children?" I asked her. "What if you couldn't get another nanny?"

"We'd manage."

I had some extra days off over Christmas. The night I returned to Protection, Dag made us a lovely meal, then we sat in front of the woodstove drinking wine.

"I've got something to tell you," he said. "I need to see my PhD supervisor. So I'm going to Munich soon."

I was taken aback. "Oh. How long for?"

"I'm not sure yet. Probably at least until March. I can stay in my old apartment."

Neither of us spoke for a minute. A log crackled and sparked as it fell onto the grate. I knew he would be seeing his former girlfriend. The shadow between us.

"What if you decide you want to get back together with her?" I asked eventually.

It felt like an echo of my mother's question after I told her I was returning to Canada. *Will you come back to me?*

He shrugged. "I'm sorry. Right now, I don't know."

Trauma has long tentacles. I felt one lightly touch me, the pain of loss. I shook it away and brought down my emotional shutters. I was strangely calm. If our relationship had to end, I told myself, better now.

After Dag left, I spent my weekends in Whistler, skiing and staying with friends. I started making enquiries about nannying jobs in the area. I didn't hear from Dag, and I didn't contact him. I wasn't interested in seeing anyone else, yet it was as if a big "Unavailable" sign was on my head and men came out of the woodwork. They approached me in Whistler on the ski hill, and on the bus back to Vancouver. A German guy contacted me from Australia. We'd had a brief, intense relationship during my first weeks in Canada, when he'd been passing through on his round-the-world backpacking trip. He'd been working, he had some money, he planned to go to Fiji. He asked me to join him. He said he would pay for my flight.

I refused all the offers. I was in a quiet, reflective place; it was like floating in an eddy, waiting for a current that would take me to the next stage in my life.

Almost a month into the separation, I still hadn't heard from Dag. I presumed it was over between us, but I wanted to know. He'd given me the number of the apartment he was staying in, and I decided to call him on his birthday. A man answered the phone.

"Ah, Maria!" he cried, when I introduced myself. "Hello, this is Olaf. Dag has said a lot about you. Please wait, I will ask him to come."

I was sitting at Owen's dining room table in Vancouver. The twins were at a dance class. James was watching a cartoon in the next room. I heard the clunk of the receiver being placed on a hard surface, footsteps, the creak of a door, Olaf's voice calling to Dag. Then different footsteps, ones I recognized.

"Maria," he said quietly.

"Happy Birthday."

"I can't believe it. I was just about to write. I've sorted everything out. I want us to be together. I can't wait to see you. I'll be back in a couple of months."

James ran into the room, demanding my attention. I promised Dag I'd call him back soon. Then I picked up the little boy and held him close.

~

Owen tried to change my mind. He offered me more money, better conditions. He said that if I left, I could never contact the children again. I didn't tell them until the last minute. First I sat down with the girls. They were aghast. They promised to never act up again; they said they would eat my food without complaining.

"We know we've been horrible," said Tania. "But we really like you. You're the best nanny we've ever had. Please don't leave."

I fought to hold back my tears. They had endured such a devastating loss; why was I now heaping this one on top of it? I couldn't explain that it was because of their father; that working for him was compromising my physical health and my mental well-being; that I couldn't make this sacrifice for them. Instead, I hugged them hard, reassured them it had nothing to do with them, and that I would miss them terribly. I didn't know how to explain things to James. When he realized I wouldn't be returning, his cries cracked my heart. I can still hear them now.

Four

You cannot swim for new horizons until you have the courage to lose sight of the shore.

—WILLIAM FAULKNER

7

We moved into a rustic waterfront cabin on Protection Island. Perched on a low bluff, it had a tiny kitchen and living room area with a big window and French doors facing over the Georgia Strait to the mainland mountains. There was a small, dark bedroom, but we used that for storage. We bought our first piece of furniture together – a futon mattress on a frame that folded up to become a sofa – and placed it in the living room. By day, we could sit and look over the water. By night, we could lie and watch the stars.

The cabin had no bathroom, only an outhouse in the garden, and no running water. We collected rainwater in a barrel for washing up. And we bathed in the ocean. Every morning, we rolled out of bed and headed down rocky steps for a swim, our eyes not yet fully open.

Dag always plunged straight in and away, his arms arcing through a strong crawl. For me it was a slower entry, feeling the silky water rise up against my skin until the moment of surrender, trusting my body to float, my limbs to propel. Immersing my head, then shaking drops from my eyes to see the luminous sky, the light playing across the ripples of the sea.

It was the first of several swims during the day, sometimes with an extra one at night. I had first witnessed bioluminescence from Dag's boat, when its movement through the water caused microscopic creatures to emit their light. That had been astonishing enough, but actually swimming in it was like being dropped into fairyland. I could see the outline of Dag's shape, as if enveloped by stars, while I was like a watery Tinker

Bell in a cloud of pixie dust. On clear, new moon nights, when the Milky Way stretched above us, sea and sky merged and I floated in both. To be swimming without fear in deep, dark water was a miracle in itself, but nothing had prepared me for such transcendent beauty.

Practical matters threatened to overshadow this bliss. I was now in Canada without a job. I still had a work visa, but it only allowed me to be a nanny. Even if I was prepared to do that again, nannying jobs in Nanaimo were few and far between. Dag's PhD grant had run out. Our rent was very cheap, but we needed money. First, my friend Jeff came to the rescue, offering Dag work at his fibreglass shop. Then one of our neighbours on Protection started a small business, selling coffee and burritos from a stand in Fisherman's Wharf. Would I like to run the stand?

At the end of each day, Dag returned covered in fibreglass dust and jumped into the sea to wash it off. I joined him, eager to shed the day's memories of nerve-wracking sales encounters. When I accepted my new job, I hadn't realized the stand would be on a harbourside walkway that led to what was then the Employment and Immigration Office. I was an illegal, nervously selling coffee to officials heading there to work. Sometimes one would comment on my English accent and ask me where I was from.

"Manchester, originally," I would say. "But I've been here quite a long time. People like an English accent, though, so I've tried to keep it." Then I'd change the subject.

I was too much of a recovering Catholic, plied with guilt, to be a lawbreaker for long. This was horrible, and I knew I risked being thrown out of Canada, all for a paltry minimum wage.

Another nagging problem had been transportation from and to Protection. Dag's outboard engine was on its last legs, and we couldn't afford to buy another. There was an irregular ferry, but we could barely afford that either. A few weeks earlier, Dag had had an idea. In Jeff's workshop he'd come across some kayak molds. He told Jeff he'd like to build a couple of boats that we could use to commute. Jeff got enthusiastic about the plan, and the pair of them started staying on after work, drinking beers and building kayaks.

"This will mean we can go to town whenever we want," said Dag. "We can bring our shopping in the kayaks, right to the shore below our cabin."

There was no store on Protection, and getting groceries was a hassle. But I barely knew what a kayak looked like, except that it was skinny, shallow, and liable to tip over. The prospect of paddling groceries – never mind myself – in one wasn't exactly appealing.

One evening, Dag paddled up to the rocks below our house in his newly built kayak, towing mine behind him. They were short – four metres long – and wide. Dag insisted this made them very stable. Perfect starter boats.

He showed me how to slide into the bucket seat and work the pedals that adjusted the rudder. As we floated away from the rocks, he demonstrated how to hold the paddle and some basic strokes. Then he set off. Tentatively, I followed.

"Don't sit back in the seat. And lean into your strokes," he said. "You'll go much faster."

A motorboat zipped by, and its wake threw up waves with curling crests that sped toward us.

"Point your bow into them," called Dag. I stiffened with fear, holding the paddle high as the kayak bow bobbed up, then slapped down on each wave.

"How are you feeling?" Dag asked after ten minutes.

I didn't want to admit that my shoulders ached, and arm muscles I didn't know existed were hurting.

I smiled bravely. "I think I'll get used to it."

"There's so much storage room in these boats," he said. "We can go off on camping trips in them for weeks on end."

"Oh," I said. "Really?"

I quickly built up my paddling muscles, but for me the hardest thing was carrying the kayak to and from the water. Right off the bat, Dag made it clear I had to be able to do this myself. Though I cursed him at the time, I became proud of being able to hoist a 50-pound kayak onto my shoulder and carry it across rough rocks and sometimes for a fairly long distance. As my strength increased, so did my confidence. Before long, paddling to Nanaimo was no problem. At Fisherman's Wharf, I would draw up alongside a dock, clamber out, haul the kayak up over the raised edge, lean it sideways, and stow the paddle underneath. It was summer, so I usually paddled over wearing a light dress or shorts and a T-shirt. I was dressed and ready to sell coffee and burritos.

We often bought prawns from a fish boat at the wharf. It was owned by Bill, a small, gruff man with a grizzled beard. He had a girlfriend called Sharon, much younger and taller than him, who helped him on the boat. Like me, she hailed from England, and we got chatting. She told me Bill was separated but not yet divorced from his wife. She had met him on a previous visit and had returned to be with him for the summer. She had applied for a work permit, without luck.

"How come you can work here, Maria?" she asked one day. "I've seen you over there selling coffee and stuff."

I muttered something about having got a visa for a job in Vancouver, and that it was still valid.

"What kind of job?"

"A nanny," I said.

A few weeks earlier, we'd returned a half-kilo of prawns to Bill, telling him they weren't fresh. Even though we were still regular customers, he'd developed a grudge against us.

"Better smell them first, eh?" he'd say nastily, whenever we turned up to buy more prawns or fish.

Sharon must have recounted our conversation to him. They must have looked up the regulations for a "nanny visa." A couple of days later, right after lunchtime, I was at the stand serving coffee to a couple of men in suits.

"Cream and sugar?" I asked them, just as Bill hove into view. The men had their backs to him. As he started shouting, they turned around, coffee cups in hand.

"Ask her where she's from! And how she can work here when my Sharon can't! Ask her about her papers! Go on, ask her!"

One of the men started walking away. The other turned back to me, gave me a long look, then handed me money for the coffees.

"Keep the change," he said, and followed his colleague.

I closed up the stand. Wheeled it back to the office where it was stored each night. Put the perishables away in a fridge. Then I paddled back to the island and told the neighbour I was quitting. Immediately – no notice given.

When Dag got home, he found me sitting on the bench he'd built from driftwood on the edge of the bluff, staring over the water. My eyes were red from crying.

"Honey, what's wrong?" he asked, sitting down and putting his arm around me.

I told him what had happened. "I can't stay here," I said. "I just don't have what it takes to work illegally. I'll have to go back to England."

"No you won't," he said. "We'll get married."

I started in shock. And now he was staring ahead at the water. We'd had the "commitment" conversation a number of times. I'd told him I believed commitment was freeing. Already, by deciding I wanted to be with Dag, life seemed less complicated. I was ready to marry him in a second. He had said he wanted me at the centre of his life, sharing everything together, but, as a creature of avant-garde Berlin, formalizing that was another matter.

It was a calm evening. A small sailboat motored by. The mainland mountains were turning mauve against a golden sky.

"Did you just propose?" I asked.

He nodded. "I guess so. Although I'm not sure it was me. It felt like it was a disembodied voice."

We both laughed.

I thought for a minute. Did I want to get married just to stay in the country? Or marry a man who wasn't absolutely sure about it? Then I remembered something.

"I once heard about this couple, a climber in Calgary and his girlfriend," I said slowly. "They married so she could stay in Canada. They weren't sure if the relationship would work out, so they married in secret and agreed not to tell anyone for a year. That way, they could divorce if necessary during that year, without anyone knowing."

He turned to me. "And did it work out?"

"No," I said. "But I think it will for us."

~

It was almost mid-July. Dag was about to leave for Munich again for over two weeks to defend his PhD. We agreed it was important to get married as soon as possible, so I could start applying for residency. I arranged the wedding. I found a justice of the peace named Helen who lived on Hornby, one of the Gulf Islands scattering the sea between Vancouver and Vancouver Island. She was free the following Monday.

"Bring two witnesses," she said.

"That's a bit problematic," I replied. "We're eloping."

Immediately, I felt guilty. Would she guess we were marrying to keep me in the country? Would that be a problem? But she wasn't in the least bit fazed.

"Okay, I'll ask my neighbours to come over," she said. "They've done it before."

The day dawned clear, sunny, and warm. We stuffed our wedding clothes into a big plastic bag and set off in our kayaks to Nanaimo. Dag was ahead of me. He was shirtless, with the usual white silk scarf around his neck. His hair was getting bleached from the sun and sea. As he paddled, I could see his shoulder muscles moving under tanned skin. "I'm *marrying* this man today," I thought. I stopped paddling for a moment, amazed.

At the harbour, we carried our kayaks to the beat-up old car I'd bought the previous year. Dag hoisted them onto the roof rack and secured them with rope. Then we drove north to catch the first of two ferries to Hornby Island. Of course, we were late. Dag drove, gunning up the highway, while I fretted.

"Well, if we miss this first ferry, we'll miss our own wedding," he said with a grin.

On the first ferry, we hurried to the washrooms to get changed. I had brought two different outfits, because in our rush to leave Protection I hadn't been able to decide which to wear for the ceremony. One was my favourite dress, slinky and black with a recurring pattern of white writing. If you looked really closely, you could see the letters FCKYRASS. Despite that, it was really elegant.

I put it on in the bathroom, but suddenly my mother loomed before me. What would she think – when I eventually told her and showed her photos – about me getting married in black, never mind the message? I ripped off the dress, replacing it with a bright orange silk shirt and skirt. I raced back to the car. Dag was already in the driver's seat. He was the one in white: a loose cotton shirt and pants.

Helen was waiting for us with her neighbours. We walked through her house and onto a wide deck overlooking a beach of smooth rock slabs. The tide was far out. Seagulls were catching molluscs from the tidal pools, flying up high, dropping them to break open the shells, and swooping down to pick out the innards. Their flurry of white wings and raucous calls was the backdrop to our ceremony. Dag and I stood facing each other. There was no ring, only the promises, quickly made. Then Helen read Khalil Gibran's poem, "On Marriage." I had never heard it before, and at some of the lines I got teary.

Love one another, but make not a bond
of love:
Let it rather be a moving sea between
the shores of your souls.

I looked at Dag for his reaction. He had a strange, far-away, slightly puzzled expression. Helen pronounced us man and wife. Her neighbours clapped, and one of them went to get the champagne we had brought and glasses. Dag popped the cork and poured. We toasted and drank, then went inside to complete some paperwork. When it was done, and we were about to leave, Helen asked, "So are you off on a little secret honeymoon with your kayaks?"

"Actually, no, Dag's leaving for Germany in a couple of days," I said, immediately regretting it. I couldn't stop worrying about the implications of marrying to keep me in the country. What if she contacted the immigration office? What if the guys who had bought coffee from me put two and together?

Helen just smiled. "Well, I hope he gets back soon, and I wish you a very happy life together."

We drove to a nearby bay, unloaded the kayaks, and got changed back into shorts and T-shirts. Dag tied his white pants onto one of the roof racks.

"Why don't you put them inside the car?" I asked.

"They'll be fine there," he said.

For a couple of hours we paddled along an intricate shoreline, weaving through rock gardens. Kingfishers dropped from the sky in iridescent flashes, plummeting headfirst into the water, surfacing with little fish in their beaks. Bald eagles soared overhead and landed on the tops of trees growing from the cliffs. We pulled ashore for a break in a small cove, stripped off, and swam in the calm blue water. When we returned to the car, Dag's white pants were gone.

"Well, that's an interesting sign," he said.

We drove back to the ferry, giggling like kids. We'd just got married! No one knew! He'd lost his wedding pants!

"How do you feel?" I asked Dag as we waited to board.

"It was the weirdest experience," he admitted. "When we were making our vows, I had this ringing sound in my ears." Then he laughed, leaned over, and kissed me. "Hello, wife," he said.

Back in Nanaimo, we stopped at a supermarket – the one where I'd first spotted Dag – to buy some groceries. We were putting them in the back seat of the car when our friend Jeff appeared.

"Hey, you two!" he greeted us, looking at the kayaks on the roof. "What have you been getting up to today?"

~

Later that week, in the immigration office, we were shown into a room where a man sat behind a polished desk with framed family photos arranged on either end. I recognized him immediately. He'd bought coffee from me several times. While he examined our papers, I stared fixedly at the images of his pretty wife and three little children.

"Two girls and a boy," I commented stupidly. "How nice."

He looked up at me. "Thank you," he said. "Are you planning to have a family?"

"Ah, we don't know," I stuttered. "I mean, it's early days, I mean...well..."
As I trailed off, he gave me a puzzled stare. My heart thumped. *I've blown it*, I thought. Then he turned back to the papers. If he made the connection with the burrito and coffee seller, he never let on. Our marriage was accepted as bona fide.

"Congratulations to you both," he said. "And welcome to Canada, Maria."

When I was seeing Dag off at the Nanaimo airport, I had an anxiety attack and clung to him, weeping. I wasn't worried he'd go back to his former girlfriend. I knew that was over for good, that we were strong. I was afraid he would disappear. That, like Joe leaving for Everest, he would walk through the door to the security area and it would be the last time I'd ever see him.

"Maria, don't be silly, I'll be home with you in less than three weeks," he said. He had to peel me off him.

I cried all the way back to Protection. It was only when I sat on the rocks at the bottom of the bluff that the fear subsided. I had never lived next to the sea before. My fears had gone and everything about it entranced me: its moods and rhythms, the play of light on water, how the wind transformed its surface from the tiniest ripples to steep waves. Paying attention to all this, particularly to the tides, had brought visceral changes. Once crazily irregular, my periods had begun to arrive as if appointed, to the day and almost to the hour. And my mind had calmed. I saw life scrolling out ahead of me, full of possibilities.

I looked back at the territory I had crossed to get to this place. Five years before, Joe's sudden death had left me with deep hurts and unanswered questions about our relationship. These were like knots inside me. Suddenly, I realized I had to untangle them so I could move forward in my new life with Dag. In the little bedroom of our cabin, I hauled my suitcase from a dark corner, opened it, and rooted among my winter clothes to find the bag full of journals. The ones I had been carrying around with me for five years.

8

Not long after I got the news about Joe's disappearance, I started a journal. My first ever; even in childhood, I hadn't kept a diary. I went to the newsagent's around the corner from my house. The day was hot, and I wore a light cotton dress, short, with spaghetti straps. I'd bought it especially for Joe's return.

"Hello, love," said the newsagent kindly. "I'm so sorry about what happened. How are you doing?"

The story had been on the front pages of all the Sunday newspapers he sold: two famous mountaineers lost on Everest. I was a regular customer, and a neighbour had told him I was the girlfriend of one of the climbers. Haltingly, I explained what I wanted.

"Let's have a look on the stationery shelf," he said.

The only suitable thing we found was a big "duplicate book" with lined pages, each alternating one perforated so it could be ripped out, and sheets of carbon paper to be slipped between pages to make copies. That night I sat down with a glass of wine at my living room table and began to write.

Now, years later, at another table far away, I read the beginning of that first entry: "One week, two days after I've been told. Still the crazy half belief that they will be found. Tried to look at the date – it doesn't seem right to do so now..."

I stopped reading and thought about what it must have been like for Dick Renshaw, driving from his home in Wales to break the news to me. Parking on my street, walking up to the house. He had been on the Everest expedition with Joe but was forced to leave early after suffering a small stroke at altitude. He'd been home for almost a month and a half. Like the partners and families of the remaining team members, I'd been calling him, asking for his opinion on why, for the past three weeks, there had been no communication from the mountain. The letters had stopped, and so had the updates sent via the sponsoring company, Jardine Matheson, in Hong Kong. "Team leaving Basecamp" had been their last cryptic telegram.

"Maria, I'm sure they are all dead," Ruth Clarke, the wife of the team doctor, had said bluntly.

I couldn't let myself believe that. I went into full-blown denial. For the past year, using a government grant, I'd been having the ground floor of my house renovated. While the major work was happening, I'd lived with Joe. Now, just before he was due home, I'd moved back in. It looked lovely, a serene, light-filled space. I couldn't wait for him to see it.

To celebrate the last of the work being done, I threw an impromptu party. My parents and my sister-in-law Sue and her baby Laura were visiting, colleagues from work turned up, as well as several neighbours and my friend Sarah. The previous year I'd introduced Sarah to my lodger Alex MacIntyre. They had fallen in love and started living together in Derbyshire. He was also away in the Himalayas. We were both waiting for news. It was a warm afternoon, and the French doors were thrown open to my little backyard. There was an old green armchair out there; I'd been meaning to haul it away to the charity store, but I'd been too busy. As I moved between my guests, filling their glasses, I heard the doorbell.

～

Blue ballpoint pen on a lined page. Sloped, loopy handwriting.

When Dick said, "I'm afraid I've got some tragic news," everything stopped. The moment crystallized. I moved away, said something like, "I thought that's why you were here – come and tell me outside." I went to the fridge, got some wine, offered some to him....

I sat in the old green chair in the yard. His voice told me details, but I couldn't take them in. I felt in a void, an awful stillness, a numbness, a grip on my brain. Something anticipated for so long, feared, dreaded, spoken aloud to exorcise the fear.

I spent days curled up in that chair as a stream of people arrived with flowers, food, kind words. Sarah stayed with me for a week. I couldn't face sleeping in the bed I'd hoped to soon share with Joe again, so at night we unrolled sleeping bags on the new living room carpet. In the mornings, when I woke up, remembered, and started choking with sobs, she would hold me until I quieted. One day, she came back from work, sat down next to me, and took my hand. "Alex is on his way home," she said. "I have to go to him."

When I realized that even those closest to me had to draw away and attend to their own lives, I started the journal. It became a confidant, a receptacle for my anguish. I wrote in it obsessively. I filled it and started another; for some reason I felt it was important that it was exactly the same kind of book. Six months after I got the news, a journal came in my backpack with me to Everest.

Eighteen months after Joe's death, I stopped writing. I no longer felt the need to keep recording my days, my grief. But I was terrified of losing the journals. When I went away for a weekend, I took them with me, worried that the house might burn down or be burgled in my absence. The fears were irrational, but those journals had become totems, a symbol of my love for Joe as my life moved on and away from him.

That night on Protection Island, I read through them in one straight shot late into the night. Then I fell into fitful sleep. At dawn I went for a long swim. I had grown confident enough in the water to do this on my own. Dag had explained how currents work. That, when I was kayaking to Nanaimo, I should set my course according to a point on land and adjust my paddling to keep to it, otherwise a current could push me in the wrong direction without me realizing it. I'd started to do the same when I was swimming away from shore. Now I looked over my shoulder from time to time, checking the arbutus tree growing from the bluff, keeping it in line.

Sometimes it's helpful to look back before moving forward. I paddled into Nanaimo and bought some A4 notepads and a packet of ballpoint pens. Back on Protection Island, sitting on the bench my new husband had built, where he made his sweetly awkward proposal, I started writing.

On warm, still mornings, after my swim and breakfast, I took a pad to the bottom of the bluff and sat leaning against a rock. For a while I just looked and listened: the sucking of barnacles, the squeaky calls of bald eagles, the silver flash of a jumping fish. Seaweed undulating in a current. A ferry on its way to Vancouver, sunlit and tiny against the steep mainland mountains. Then I began the day's work. Expanding on my journal notes, I described the bewildering weeks and months after the news came through about Joe and Pete's disappearance. Going back to Joe's house, desperately needing to sit among his familiar things, lie in the bed we had shared, find his scent on the sheets. His family descending, stripping the place, taking away all his belongings, shutting me out despite my pleas. Meeting the other team members when they returned from the mountain. The two memorials. Hilary suggesting we go to the mountain. The discussion with Jardine Matheson, the shipping company that had sponsored the Everest expedition, which now agreed to help us with logistics and permissions. Raising money to pay for the outrageously expensive trip. And then setting off with Hilary to Hong Kong, mainland China, and onward to Tibet.

I wrote and wrote until my hand cramped. Sometimes I would look up and see a dark line across the water, the northwest wind moving toward land. When it reached me, I would go back up to the cabin and carry on writing.

By the time Dag returned, there was a neat stack of pages on one end of the table. It was the first draft of a long article, which I'd titled "Only His Girlfriend." During those early days, several people had implied – or said outright – that because Hilary had been with Pete for longer than I'd been with Joe, because they were married and had been trying to start a family, it was all much harder for her. I wanted to counter that, to show that a love cut short early on brings its own unique pain. That bereavement can't be evaluated and compared.

"I don't know what I'm going to do with all this," I told Dag, "but I just have to write it."

"It will help other people," he said. "You should try to publish it."

His parents came to visit and rented a house on the island. They seemed impressed by my writing efforts and bought me a typewriter. For days on end I pecked away at the keyboard, struggled with the ink ribbons, and kept a bottle of Wite-Out close by. It was painstaking work, but seeing the words typed up gave me confidence. I started thinking about contacting a national newspaper or magazine to see if they would like it as a feature.

"How about the *New Yorker*?" Dag suggested. I laughed at that.

Before I did anything, I had to check in with Hilary. She was a key figure in the story, and I needed her blessing and permission. I made Xerox copies of the pages and posted them to her home in Switzerland.

A few weeks later, I found a flimsy blue aerogram letter in our mailbox. The return address was in Cumbria, England. It was from Chris Bonington, the world's top mountaineer at the time, the author of several bestselling books, and the leader of the expedition on which Joe and Pete had perished. In the aftermath of the accident, he and his wife Wendy had provided an island of solace. In their quiet house, I could wail and rage for hours without feeling judged or embarrassed. When I was spent, they would tuck me up in bed, let me sleep for as long as I needed, feed me, take me for walks in the hills. Chris felt guilty at having survived. We often cried together.

His handwriting was terrible; it took me a while to decipher the whole message. He started by telling me Hilary had picked up my parcel as she was leaving her home in Switzerland for the airport on the way to visit him and Wendy. She read the article on the plane. When she arrived at their house, she handed it to him.

"No one has ever written about this side of mountaineering," he concluded. "It's an important story to tell. I strongly encourage you to continue. I'll be happy to introduce you to my literary agent."

I rang Hilary.

"Hasn't my letter arrived yet?" she asked. "Of course, I give you my blessing! Keep going."

Dag had got a contract at Nanaimo's Malaspina College for some teaching and research work, and the local school board informed me that, once my immigration papers were fully approved, I could start substitute teaching. Our cabin would be freezing in the winter, and bathing in cold sea water wasn't a good option. With "real" jobs on the horizon, we needed to look less salty and feral. By late September we had moved to another waterfront house on the island. It had a fireplace, carpets, hot water, a bathtub, a flushing toilet: luxury! There were two tiny bedrooms, but we put our futon in the living area, facing the view. One of the bedrooms became my office. Dag bought me my first computer, a Mac, and taught me how to use it. I wrote up and revised my work so far. Then I kept going. I described the long, dusty drives in the back of a truck over the high plains of Tibet. The trek up a remote valley on the east side of Everest toward the 3500-metre Kangshung Face, down which it was believed Joe and Pete had fallen to their deaths. The journey to the north side of the mountain, the base camp at Rongbuk, and from there our trek to the remains of their advance base at 6300 metres. Finally, the hardest part: turning away, heading down the mountain to start our journey home, knowing they could never follow us.

In November, I went to England. To see my parents, of course, but also to attend a prize-giving ceremony for the Boardman Tasker Award for Mountain Literature, which a group of us had set up in Joe and Pete's names. They had both been fine writers, and each had produced two books. Joe's second one, *Savage Arena*, was published after his death.

The ceremony was held at the Alpine Club in London. I was nervous; I was meeting Chris's literary agent there. I had a parcel to hand to her. A manuscript – 30,000 words.

Vivienne Schuster was petite and pretty, with dark hair and bright brown eyes. She wore a smart business suit and high heels.

"Chris told me all about you," she said. "I'm looking forward to reading this. Where can I reach you?"

As I wrote down a couple of phone numbers on the parcel, someone came up to talk to her. "I'll be in touch," she said, and turned away.

The following week, I drove with Mum and Dad from Wolverhampton to Manchester, to stay with my brother John and his family. We'd just had lunch at the big wooden kitchen table. From the hallway came the shrill ring of the telephone.

"I'll get it," said John. The family's red setter followed him, wagging his tail, hoping this signalled a walk. John reappeared.

"It's for you, Maria. Someone called Vivienne Schuster."

The ivory-coloured phone sat on an antique wooden table. Lying next to it, attached by a curly cord, was the receiver. I put it to my ear. "Hello?" I said hesitantly.

"Maria, it's Vivienne. I've just finished reading your manuscript. Chris was right, no one has written about this side of mountaineering. And you've done it so well. I would love to represent you."

I felt the dog's wet nose pushing against my other hand.

"How would you feel about that, Maria?"

I realized I'd stopped breathing.

"Of course. Yes."

"But it's only half a book," Vivienne continued. "The second half. Before I try to sell it, I need the first part, about your relationship with Joe. Can you write that? And do you have time to come down to London to see me before you return to Canada?"

～

My immigration papers arrived, and I started as a substitute teacher in Nanaimo's high schools. If I was needed to replace someone who had called in sick, I'd get a phone call around 6:30 a.m. Usually, I woke up before then and lay quietly in the dark, hoping there wouldn't be a call and I could spend the day writing. But it was the season of colds and flu, and often I was summoned. We'd get up in the dark, shower, have breakfast and coffee, and be ready to set off in our kayaks as it grew light outside.

Now that we both had work, we'd invested in some good paddling gear. Dry bags, lights for the kayak decks, head torches, pumps, and, in case we ever capsized, paddle floats to help us get back into the boats. Kayaking jackets, life jackets, rubber boots, rain pants, spray skirts that fitted across the cockpits of the boats, sou'wester hats with wide brims, and even "pogies" – neoprene muffs that fitted over our paddles for cold, wet days.

It was a lot of stuff to organize first thing in the morning. We'd waddle out, bulky in our life jackets, spray skirts flapping at our thighs. With the kayaks on our shoulders, at high tide we took a few steps across rocks – choosing ones covered in barnacles, as they were less slippery – before we dropped the boats into the water. If the tide was low, we had to slog through sucking mud. I was often grumbly about all this effort, but once we pushed off I always got a rush of elation. The sharp salt air, the oystercatchers scuttling over rocks on long pink legs, the splash of a startled seal: it still felt brand new, amazing. I wasn't getting into my car and driving 40 kilometres through increasingly heavy traffic to inner city Manchester. I was *kayaking* to work!

~

On the days when the phone didn't ring, as soon as Dag left I settled down to write. This time, I had no journals to work from, only memory. With my hands resting on the computer keyboard, I would close my eyes and sink into the past. It was like looking at a fire that had almost burned down. I reached in, stirred the cinders, and flames of recollection flared. My fingers moved, I opened my eyes, and the words were already forming on the screen.

During those days alone, memories spooled out, vivid and strong. Our first long conversation, as Joe drove me back to Manchester from Wales. It was a three-hour journey, and we talked nonstop. The beat of the car windscreen wipers, the rain caught in the headlights, our shy sidelong glances. We arrived in Manchester late. I had to get up early in the morning to do some lesson preparations, and he still had 50 kilometres to drive. He had a quick cup of tea at my house, then left.

A few nights later, he turned up on my doorstep. He had been at a meeting in Manchester, he told me. As he was leaving the city centre, he noticed one of his car headlights wasn't working. He was worried about getting stopped by the police, particularly as he'd had a couple of drinks. Could he possibly spend the night at my house and drive home early in the morning? Oh, and he happened to have a bottle of wine with him. I smiled at the story – on the way from Wales he'd told me his closest friends lived in Manchester, a few kilometres from my house. But I made no comment.

"Of course," I said. "Come in."

We spent more hours deep in conversation. He was intrigued by the woven wall hangings I'd brought from Peru. He was impressed I'd lived in South America, that I'd travelled a lot, that I owned this house and lived alone apart from the occasional lodgers. Then he talked about his mountaineering. I curled up on the couch, while he sat opposite me on a cushion right next to the gas fire. He was cold so often in the mountains, he said, he liked to be as warm as possible when he was home. His body was relaxed. He wasn't handsome, his features had a pinched quality, but his smile was merry and his blue eyes inviting. I couldn't deny the strong attraction. But when it was time for bed, I brought a pillow and sleeping bag from upstairs and put them on the couch for him.

Not long after that, we were back in my living room, him by the fire once more, me on the couch. We'd gone out for dinner, then to the cinema. Now we were talking about relationships. I hadn't completed my "hatchet job" on the man in Wales, but we were unravelling fast. My complications were slight compared to Joe's. He was involved with a married woman who lived overseas. He described it as "the best relationship I've ever had." She had been planning to leave her husband and move to England to be with Joe, but she had recently become pregnant with her husband's child. So Joe wasn't exactly sure how things were going to pan out.

"She might come here eventually with the baby," he said, then paused and ran a hand through his loose curls. "This won't sound exactly romantic, Maria. I know things are uncertain, and of course I'm away a lot, but I really like you, and, well, would you consider me?"

I recognized the signs. He had admitted he was impressed by my "fierce independence." I guessed he thought I was strong enough to deal with his other commitments – the biggest of which was mountaineering. And I had a boyfriend, of sorts. So, like his faraway, pregnant paramour, I wasn't fully "available," which made things easier for him.

If someone else had been in this situation and asked me for advice, I would have told them to run. I knew it was crazy. But I hadn't been able to stop thinking about him. He stood up, unfolding his limbs as lazily as a cat, and joined me on the couch.

The strong feelings that surfaced fast between us took him off guard. In the middle of one night, when we woke in the dark and reached for each other, he mumbled into my neck, "I didn't mean this to happen." I should have told him then that I loved him. That I'd never felt so sure about anyone. But I was afraid of scaring him away.

When he returned from K2, physically and mentally wasted, I cared for him tenderly. He kept saying, "Don't feel you have to do this," as I shopped and cooked for him. But I could tell he appreciated it all. And I felt a shift in him. One day, when we were driving, I hesitantly asked him about his lover overseas. He told me she was staying with her husband. It was clear he didn't want to say any more about it, but he reached over and put his hand on my knee.

Finally, it was clear we were a couple, and that I made him happy. But I maintained the pretense of fierce independence because I thought that was what he wanted. And I needed to protect myself: from the long, uncertain separations; from the fact that when he was at home he was so busy with writing books and articles, running his business, giving presentations, raising sponsorships, and preparing for his next expedition that he barely had time for me. I always came second. Or third. Or fourth.

Eventually, my feelings for him began to seep out in an unhealthy way. I became needy and insecure, questioning him about the other women he flirted with so easily, about my role in his life, how he felt about me. This wasn't the Maria he wanted.

"Why do I have to say the words?" he once retorted. "Can't you tell how I feel about you by the way I look at you and touch you?"

After two and a half years, finally, hesitantly, I admitted my hopes for a life together. I decided not to mention the crazy fantasy I'd had of being pregnant with his baby. I'd never wanted a child before, and having one whose father spent half his life in the Himalayas on dangerous expeditions, and who was far from ready to commit to me, never mind a family, was a ridiculous proposition. Perhaps this was a presentiment, a desire to have a part of him I could hold onto if the worst happened.

"I love you," I told him.

He took my hand and said simply, "Maria, I'm not ready for this." But when I cried, he held me tenderly. My admission opened things up between us. He still never said the words in return, but we were closer than ever before.

Twelve days later, I drove him to Heathrow Airport. It was the fourth time I'd seen him off on an expedition. This time, he didn't return. Among his personal effects that were sent back to me from the mountain, I found love letters from another woman.

∾

Why does anyone start to write? For me, it was catharsis. I had no choice, I was obsessed, driven to get the story out, to release pent-up emotions. Sitting in my little office on Protection Island, I recreated my relationship with Joe, mining my memory for details, moments, conversations, feelings. One day, as I sat at the computer, I felt his presence. It had happened before, just after I got the news of his disappearance, and again when I was trekking toward the east side of Everest. A sudden sense of him being all around me, the pressure of his hand on my neck. There were never any words, no vision, only an enveloping feeling of warmth and love. But those times were months after his death. Now it was years. I felt shocked, confused. I spoke aloud to him.

"Joe? Are you okay with me writing about you? Is that why you're here?"

The sensation gradually began to fade. I pulled on a coat and boots, walked down to the beach, and stared at the water. It lapped gently against the rocks. Seagulls landed and floated on the currents. I thought about why I needed to put myself – and Dag – through all this. We were less than halfway through our "trial" year of marriage, but he made me feel secure and loved in a way Joe never had. I was astonished by our happiness. Yet, to embrace it fully, I felt I had to close things with Joe, to validate the good times we had shared, to say all the things I never told him when he was alive. And to remind myself, by writing it down in stone, to never make the same mistakes.

Catharsis is exhausting. One evening, Dag gazed at me in concern.

"Your face looks like porridge," he said.

I went to the mirror. It was true. My skin was grey and lumpy. Aged.

"I think you need to take a break," he continued.

He needed it too. Shortly afterwards, he woke up one morning and recounted a dream he'd had about Joe.

"We were climbing together on a big mountain," he said quietly, staring at the ceiling. "We'd reached a difficult ice wall. I had to make a tricky maneuver, and I accidently knocked Joe off. He fell – it was a long slow-motion fall. Suddenly, there was ocean beneath him."

"Ocean?" I asked.

"You know how it is in dreams, weird things just suddenly appear. Anyway, at the last moment he righted himself and dived in. I could see him under the water. I saw bubbles on the surface, then his head appeared. I ran down the mountain as fast as I could. I found a wide, curving staircase, and I slid down on the bannister. I was going so fast my feet barely touched the stairs. When I reached the bottom, Joe was sprawled out, covered by a blanket."

He stopped and turned his gaze to me.

"He was alive, and you were sitting next to him. I took his hand and said, 'I'm sorry, man.'"

Both of us were blinking back tears. Now that Joe was worming his way into Dag's consciousness too, I knew I had to get this book finished.

Toward the end of February, Dag left for a field trip. I signed off on my supply work and put in a final push on the manuscript. On February 25, the eve of my birthday, I printed the final draft. Next morning, I sat on the floor of our living room, looking at the pile of paper next to me. On the top page, just my name and the title I'd only decided on the week before: Fragile Edge. It was five years and nine months since Joe had died. I was now 36 years old and married. It was time to get this thing sent off, to move on.

Outside, rain had set in hard, and a strong wind was blowing it sideways against the windows. Even in the channel there were small whitecaps. I thought about getting the ferry, but it didn't feel right. I wrapped up the parcel in heavy plastic and shoved it inside a dry bag. I put on all my gear. I hefted the bag and my kayak to the beach.

It was a frightening crossing. I focused on a high building in town, fighting the wind to keep on course. Waves hit me broadside, sloshing across my spray skirt, and I kept an eye out for bigger, breaking ones, ready to brace into them. The toughness of the paddling felt symbolic, a reflection of the personal journey told in the words inside the parcel. By the time I reached town, my kayak jacket was soaked through, and my hair hung below my sou'wester like rat tails. Hurrying into the post office, I hauled the parcel from its protective covers, placed it on the counter, and babbled to the clerk.

"I have to send this to the UK today by registered mail, it has no value, it's only paper, but it's valuable to me, it's my book, I've just finished writing it, and I have to know it will get there safely."

She looked at me wonderingly.

"Don't get it wet," she said. Looking down, I realized I still had the parcel in my grip, and water dripping from my sleeves was forming puddles on either side of it.

The clerk weighed it. "It's too heavy to send by registered mail. You'll need to take it home, make it into two parcels, and bring it back."

I'm not usually a crier. But at this I burst into tears. I can't remember what else I babbled, or what we sorted out, only that my manuscript somehow got sent off. I paddled home in the rain and wind, exhilarated. Each time I pushed one of the blades through the water, I had a sense of moving fully into the future. The ferry passed me; I was glad not to have taken it.

Although Vivienne had been talking to me about a book, although I'd told others I was writing a book, I didn't really believe it. I was untangling my past, chasing away shadows. As soon as the post office clerk stamped the parcel and took it away, I felt free of the work. Now I was pleased when the early morning call for supply work came. I was no longer distracted during the day, constantly thinking about my latest chapter. I had more energy, I was eager to socialize in the evenings. And I was with Dag, 100 per cent.

On a morning when I hadn't been called in to teach, and Dag had left for work, Vivienne called.

"Are you sitting down?"

I perched on a high stool, leaning my back against the kitchen counter. A heron flew past the window, landed on the beach, and stood very still, staring into the water.

"I got the news this morning, but it would have been the middle of the night there, and I didn't want to wake you up."

The first London publisher she had sent the manuscript to wanted the book, was offering a substantial advance, and on publication would bring me over to Britain for a promotional tour.

The heron contracted its neck into an *S* shape, then jabbed its long beak into the water and came up with a wriggling fish.

"Maria? Are you still there?"

"Yes...sorry...I can't believe it. But, of course. Yes."

"I'm so pleased for you," said Vivienne. "Congratulations. You deserve this."

Five

The ache for home lives in all of us,
the safe place where we can go as we are
and not be questioned.

—MAYA ANGELOU

9

The intertwining of our lives was marked by concrete things, shared possessions. A futon, the kayaks. A cat.

Dag returned from work one evening carrying a cardboard box that he'd stowed in the cockpit of his kayak. He placed it on the kitchen counter.

"I've got a present for you!"

From inside, a stirring. A meow.

He'd been telling me about the cat that had been coming to his lab for months. When she first arrived, she was healthy and had clearly been looked after, but she was never claimed by anyone. She slept on a bright windowsill, away from the sterile area. The staff would put her outside at night. When they returned the next day, or after a weekend, she would be waiting on the doorstep. Dag described how lovely she was, sleek and elegant. She was aloof, not much interested in people, but he'd been giving her lots of attention, and they'd formed a bond. She hadn't been named yet, so his co-workers decided it should be BKD, the acronym for a fish disease in salmon, the subject of Dag's PhD. He had shortened it to KD. He'd been hinting about bringing her home. I'd been hinting I wasn't so keen on the idea. I wasn't a cat person. Or a dog person. I'd hardly been around animals. Growing up, the only pets we'd had in our family were a budgie and a goldfish. My friend Sarah, in England, had acquired two cats. Whenever I visited her, I barely tolerated them, swatting them away when they crawled onto the bed at night, and fleeing from the kitchen when I saw one of them heading for the litter tray in the corner.

Like Sarah, a number of my friends had become avid dog or cat owners as a prelude to becoming parents. And while Dag continued to skirt around formal commitments – he had avoided conversations about "outing" our marriage – he had recently admitted to feeling a bit broody. So it was with some consternation that I watched him remove the lid of the box.

A grey face looked up at me. Green eyes, shaped like almonds.

"There are some tins of cat food in my dry bag," said Dag. "Can you put some out for her?"

He lifted the cat from the box and placed her on the floor.

"She's exactly the same colour as the carpet," I observed, watching her prowl across the living room, warily sniffing in the corners, peeking into my office. I opened a tin of cat food and spooned some of it onto a saucer.

"It smells disgusting," I said. "What's in this stuff?"

KD ran across to it and ate with sharp, efficient bites.

"Isn't she lovely?" said Dag. "It will take her a while to get used to the place. We'll keep her inside for now. I'm going to get some soil to use as cat litter. We can put it in this box lid."

"What? This place is too small for her to be shitting inside."

Dag ignored that. He picked her up and handed her to me. "Hold her while I go outside. Don't let her out of the door."

I carried KD to the futon and sat down with her on my lap. I stroked her back. She started to wriggle, then flail. She hissed and bared her teeth. She swiped at me with a free paw and scratched my hand. "Ouch!" I cried, as blood oozed. Leaping free of my grip, she headed for the kitchen door just as Dag opened it, and flashed past his legs.

We spent a couple of hours looking for her. Walking along the island's dirt roads and through the woods, calling her name.

"When we get back to the house, I bet she'll be there," I kept saying hopefully.

There was no cat waiting for us. We had a late dinner. We kept checking and calling. "I'll post some notices around the island tomorrow," said Dag sadly as we went to bed.

I woke first, feeling guilty. Dag was fond of this cat; why couldn't I have hung onto her, or shut her in my office? I walked a few steps to the kitchen and filled the kettle. While I was waiting for it to boil, I heard a sound from outside. Like a meow. Certain I was imagining it, I cracked the door open. As quickly as she had run out, KD slinked back inside and went straight to the place where, the evening before, I had set down a saucer of food. She sat on her back legs, curled her tail around them, and looked up at me expectantly. As I spooned more of the foul-smelling food onto a saucer, she rubbed against my calves and meowed again. I glanced over to Dag. He was still sound asleep.

"Shh," I whispered to her. "Let's surprise him."

While she was eating, I made two cups of tea and brought them over to his side of the bed. I sat next to him.

"Good morning," I said.

He turned over and yawned.

"Guess who's back?"

His eyes widened. "No?"

I pointed toward the kitchen, where KD was sitting by the empty saucer, contentedly licking her whiskers.

"Hey, KD!" he called, pushing up onto one elbow.

She stretched, then strolled over to accept caresses from his outstretched hand. She flopped onto her back, paws flexing, eyes shut, her body reverberating with purrs.

Suddenly, we were a little family. A cat was a commitment. It seemed a good time to raise that other commitment, the one we hadn't been speaking of much. It was a simple question. By the time July rolled around, would we still be married? When I asked Dag, he looked at me as if I'd gone mad. "Of course! What did you think? But let's wait until the anniversary to tell everyone."

There were a couple of people I had to tell before then.

～

I arrived in Wolverhampton on a warm May afternoon. Mum poured glasses of sherry. We took them into the garden, where Dad had set out three folding chairs on the little lawn. We'd first moved to this house when I was 7. In the summers, I used to cut blooming sweet peas that Dad grew on trellises at the end of the garden and take posies to my teacher. There was a small pond with fish. Beds of rose bushes. And clumps of lily of the valley. In the living room, Mum had a framed photo of me at my First Communion. I was standing against the brick wall of the church, clutching a bouquet of these tiny, fragrant flowers. I wore a knee-length white dress with a full skirt, a long veil, white gloves, white shoes, and ankle socks. A child bride.

It was from this house that I was supposed to set off toward the parish church for my big, lavish wedding. That's what Mum had dreamed of for so long.

I took a gulp of sherry. "I've got something to tell you."

They both leaned forward expectantly. Dad cupped a hand behind one ear. There was no way to break this gently.

"I got married."

"Married?" repeated Dad.

"When?" asked Mum. Her lips had narrowed.

"Last July."

A long silence while this sank in.

"Why didn't you tell us?"

It's awful to ruin someone's dream. To see it crumble and collapse in their eyes. I knew that – yet again – I was breaking my mother's heart. Not just because I'd denied her the wedding she'd longed for, but also that, as I explained about marrying so I could stay in Canada with Dag, get a work permit and, eventually, citizenship, she realized her only daughter would be moving for good to the other side of the world.

I'm sure she cried later, but then, in front of me, she fought the trembling chin and lips. She said that to see me so happy again after my heartbreak with Joe was all she and Dad could ever have wanted. She was relieved I'd returned to teaching. That Dag was obviously a good man and had a good job.

"Wait until I tell my friends my daughter got married to a veterinarian!" she said.

I felt weak with relief. But only momentarily.

"Does Dag want children?" she asked.

I stared at her. I remembered the day, very early in our relationship, when Dag told me he had always imagined starting a family, a large one, when he was in his 40s. How I'd laughed and told him he had better start looking for a woman much younger than me. Back then, it wasn't clear if our affair would go anywhere. But now we were married and starting to build the adventurous life we both wanted. He'd scrolled back on his expectations of a large family, but he thought we should have one child who could accompany us on our travels. I had told him about my fears around motherhood. And he regularly felt the brunt of my separation anxiety, worse than ever now, the eruption of terror when he left the house on an errand, that I might not see him again. If I was like that with him, how would I be with our child? Wringing my hands every time they set off on their bicycle or climbed a tree? Dag assured me he would balance all that. And I knew it was true. I'd watched him with other people's kids, how they were drawn to him, how he made them laugh like crazy, and emboldened them to do things they never thought they could do. He would make a fabulous father. I was the one holding back from parenthood. But I didn't tell my mother any of that, not then or ever.

~

The following July, we threw a party to announce to our friends in Canada that we had gotten married a year earlier. We'd sent out a teasing invite, saying we had a secret to share, offering possible answers. They included my book being optioned by Hollywood, Dag being made dean of the college, and me having dragged him down the aisle. No one guessed correctly. Almost everyone arrived at the party expecting to hear a baby announcement. I was astonished. I didn't look pregnant. But because we were living together, clearly committed, and in our 30s, our friends had made what seemed to them an obvious conclusion. When the real reason was revealed, the comments came thick and fast.

"You guys would make great parents."
"It's the most intense love you'll ever feel."
"Hurry up and get on with it, or you might regret it."
"Yes, and you'd be lonely when you're old."

It didn't seem to occur to anyone that I might not want a child. Or that perhaps I couldn't have one – something I had no idea about, as I'd always done my level best to not get pregnant.

Occasionally, I worried if there was something psychologically wrong with me. Six months after Joe died, I attended the christening of one of my nieces and the big party that followed at her parents' Manchester house. I was in the living room with a number of women around my age. We'd established I was the only one who wasn't a mother. Close to my chair, the door leading to the hallway was wide open. I was drinking wine, half listening to the women's conversation, which was mostly about children. Suddenly, a toddler appeared in the hallway and stood staring into the room. His face was red and crunched up, his mouth was wide open, and he was bawling angrily. As if by reflex, I leaned over and gently pushed the door shut.

The woman next to me jumped up. "No wonder you don't have kids!" she cried, opening the door, scooping the bewildered child into her arms, and heading off to find his parents.

The other women were staring at me in horror, as if they had just realized I was a pedophile. I wanted to explain myself. I was still in the daze of grief. I'd had too much wine. I wasn't thinking straight. Instead, I slunk out of the room and went to refill my glass.

~

It wasn't that I couldn't connect with babies. I comforted and rocked to sleep my nieces and nephew when they were newborns. I had loved breathing in the warm, milky smell of their delicate skulls; loved when they focused their eyes on me, gave me a gummy smile, reached up a hand to touch my face. While I could understand the love and joy they created in their parents, I was too set on my dreams to want one of these tiny creatures. But now I was married to a man who would be happy to have a child with me. Luckily, I had an excuse to delay the decision with him. I fell in love with a piece of land instead of a potential baby.

A couple of months before our big post-wedding party, I decided to check out an empty lot on Protection Island. It was about a third of an acre, cleared except for some tall cedars and Douglas firs around the perimeter, and overgrown with long grasses and ferns. As I waded through the vegetation, I wondered why someone had decided to cut down the trees. Were they intending to build a house and put in a big vegetable garden that needed a lot of sun? What had happened to their plans? My musings came to an abrupt halt when I reached the far side of the lot. The view from the low bank was stunning, across the Strait of Georgia to the snow-peaked Coast Mountains. I'd gazed endlessly at those mountains from the first cabin we lived in, and we could see them from the place we had moved to. But there was something different about this perspective. Framed by the northern ends of Saysutshun and Protection, the mountains looked huge against the sky. I knew I wanted to see this view every day. An arbutus tree was growing from the bluff. I sat down, leaning against its trunk.

"I'm going to live here with you," I said aloud to the tree. I laughed at myself. How west coast I had become! Then I hurried home and told Dag we were going to buy the lot.

I'd already been floating the idea of selling my place in England and buying a house on the island. But there was nothing suitable for sale. And Dag was reticent about owning property.

"None of my friends in Berlin or Munich own houses or apartments, they all rent," he'd said.

When I asked him why, he quoted a line from an old song in southern Germany: "*Schaffe, schaffe, häusle baue.*" Literally translated "work, work, build your house," among Dag's peers it was a derogatory phrase for people who were obsessed with secure, safe lives. We went over all this again.

"I own a house, and clearly I'm not tied down by it," I said. "In fact, it's the opposite. It's given me an anchor point from which I can easily leave, knowing it will be there if I ever need to return. The house has made me freer. We can carry on renting if you like, but I'm going to buy the lot anyway."

"It's not even for sale," he countered.

Except that soon after it was. A couple of weeks later, there was a real estate sign tacked to "my" arbutus tree.

"What kind of sorcery have you been up to?" said Dag when I told him.

I called the number on the notice and asked about the price. Then I called my brother John in Manchester. A solicitor, he had helped me buy my house there, sell it, and then buy the cottage in Derbyshire. The friends who had been renting the cottage were soon to move out. Could he help me again? John did some quick research on what I could ask for the cottage. I calculated that, after paying off my mortgage, I could buy the land outright. As Dag now had a steady position at the college, with luck we could borrow what we needed to build a house. But if Dag was still opposed, I was determined to get the land and see what happened next.

"Just go and sit there, imagine being in your living room and seeing that view every day," I kept telling him.

He was still resistant, so I held back until I discovered a neighbour was also interested in the lot. That galvanized me, and it changed Dag's mind. I made an offer. It was accepted. I used the portion I'd received of my book advance for the deposit, and my house in England went up for sale.

Of course, it was ridiculously impulsive. Dag was unhappy at the college. He was designing and running a new program to train technicians for the burgeoning fish farm industry, but the ideals he had started off with were already being eroded as he steadily discovered the dark side of fish farming. He kept muttering about giving in his notice. I had decided I wanted to be a writer, so I threw out my prospects of a secure teaching job with pension and benefits and instead did supply and contract work. But, thanks to my brother and my parents, unlike many people my age, I owned property. I'd put a lot of effort and money into renovating my Derbyshire cottage. I could ask a good rent for it. The sensible thing to do would be to sit on it and let it earn the mortgage payments while it increased in value.

Instead, I was selling it so we could buy a piece of land on a tiny island with no services, off a larger island, off the west coast of Canada. We were planning to build a house without any real idea of the complications involved, and no sense of how much it would ultimately cost, or how we were going to pay for it all. It was a hare-brained plan, but, as we would do so many times in the years ahead, we just plunged in not knowing where exactly we were going, or how things would work out.

The cottage sold quickly. I went to England to empty it and complete all the paperwork. On my return to Canada, we made an appointment with the bank. A woman with big hair and long, red fingernails sat across a desk from us. She'd been writing notes about Dag's salary and what our lot was worth. Now she was asking about assets that could help secure a loan.

"Do you have investments? Savings? Other properties? Private pension plans?"

Repeatedly, we shook our heads. None of those.

"Any vehicles?"

"We have a car," I told her.

"How much is it worth?"

"Um, about 800 dollars."

She gave me a steady look through heavy mascara.

"Anything else?"

"A couple of kayaks."

"Kayaks," she repeated. "And how much are they worth?"

"I built them," said Dag. "So I'm not sure..."

She pursed her lips.

"Shall we say, a thousand dollars?"

"Okay."

"Oh, I've got a book contract in England!" I blurted out.

"You're an author?" she said, her expression brightening. "How exciting. What's the book about?"

I rambled on about Joe and Everest, and how I'd come to Canada, met Dag, then wrote the book. Maybe she was taken by the bittersweet story of how I'd lost one man in the Himalayas and found another on Vancouver Island. But something worked, and we walked out of there with a loan, convertible to a mortgage when the house was built.

We designed the house around the shape of the land. It would be small but open, with an eight-metre ceiling and angled cathedral windows on the waterside to take in the views. There would be one main room – a kitchen and living room with a sleeping loft above it – plus a tiny extra bedroom and a spacious bathroom. Almost zero storage space, except for one narrow closet. We could have made life easier, and the whole process much cheaper, if we'd been happy with a normal, square house. It wasn't just the big windows that were set at an unusual angle – very few of the corners measured 90 degrees. We hired an architect to do the necessary drawings and nearly drove him crazy. In turn, he thought we were crazy.

"This design is going to make it impossible to build an extension. And why only one bedroom? What about when you have kids?"

"I'll build a funky tree house for them," said Dag.

The architect looked at me. I shrugged.

"It's going to seriously affect the resale value," he continued.

As usual, we hadn't thought ahead to this. I shrugged again.

"Builders aren't going to like it. It will mean a lot of extra work, and cost you a lot."

He was right in every regard. Dag did the contracting, and all the builders he talked to looked askance at the plans, with endless conversations and explanations ensuing. "What about when you have kids?" they kept asking.

I was doing a lot of shrugging. Eventually, Dag found a willing crew, and by late summer we had launched into the mind-boggling process of ferrying materials, equipment, and workers to the island. When the frame was up, I sent photos back to my family in England. During a subsequent call, I chatted with my 6-year-old nephew, Charlie.

"I saw the pictures of your house," he said. "It looks really small. Where will I sleep?"

We moved in on the following Valentine's Day. The exterior was still clad in tarpaper, and there were makeshift steps up to the doors. Once inside, the view just exploded: water, mountains, forest. It felt as if we were part of the nature all around us. We didn't care that the kitchen was just a sink and fridge with boxes piled around them. Or that – apart from our futon bed – we didn't have a scrap of furniture. We hauled in our few belongings, including KD. When I opened her carrier, she ran out, warily sniffed around, then ascended the open-plan stairs to the sleeping loft. Halfway up, she stopped and sat upright, with her tail around her paws, regally surveying her new kingdom. Below her, we danced together giddily on the gleaming wooden floor, amazed this was our home.

"You were right," said Dag. "I'm so glad you pushed for this."

~

With some of the money my parents gave us for a wedding present, we had bought a folding Klepper kayak. The wooden frame could be taken apart, the rubber and canvas skin folded up, and both stowed into a couple of large suitcase-sized bags. Dag loved the boat's history – designed over a century ago in Germany, along the lines of Inuit boats made from driftwood and seal or caribou skin. He loved the fact that, if part of the frame got broken, he could find a piece of driftwood and fix it. He kept telling me that in 1957 a guy named Hannes Lindemann did a solo Atlantic crossing in a Klepper. So we could go *anywhere* in ours.

For our "shakedown" cruise in the Klepper, that August we explored the Broughtons, an archipelago off Vancouver Island's northeast coast. It was magical – orcas cruised by us as we paddled, and we heard wolves howling at night. The big tidal range meant that, when we reached a new campsite, we often had to carry our gear and kayak what felt like kilometres up a beach. Then came the work of making camp, cooking dinner, washing the pots, and hauling the food bags into a tree, out of the reach of bears. Each night, I'd collapse into our damp sleeping bag, exhausted. But not always *too* exhausted.

One morning, I woke with a start, realizing I was on the tenth day of my menstrual cycle. Right on the edge of when I was most fertile.

"Shit!" I said out loud.

"What's wrong?" asked Dag sleepily.

The new regularity of my periods had allowed me to calculate when we needed protection. Usually, I was really careful. The previous night I'd slipped up. When I told Dag, he smiled, yawned, and stretched.

"That's okay," he said. He seemed rather pleased. "Let's have a booster on the next island. We can name the kid after it."

The next island was called Pearl. "The baby had better be a girl," I joked when we arrived. But before I joined Dag in our sleeping bag that night, I remembered to insert my cap.

During a restless sleep, I dreamed I was in labour. First, I was driving around trying to get to a hospital; then I was on a train, going to a TV studio for an interview about my book; and then in a school where I was supposed to teach a class, panicking because I hadn't prepared anything and the baby was on its way. Before I could give birth to Pearl, I woke up.

∼

The baby question still hung between us. But something else was in the mix. Some time before, a new scheme had been announced at Dag's college – faculty members could opt to work at two-thirds pay for three years, then take a sabbatical year on the same salary. Dag had been the first to sign on. We were already talking about going travelling for that whole year, taking the folding kayak with us. First, we decided, we should do another shakedown cruise, this time overseas. The following December, Dag was invited to a conference in Baja, Mexico. When it was over, I flew there to meet him.

10

We were stuck on a tiny desert islet. The Baja California Peninsula, and the airport where we soon had a flight to catch, was just a few kilometres across the Sea of Cortez. But for three days and two nights the notorious El Norte wind had been blowing full blast, churning the sea into a dangerous mess of 2.5-metre breaking waves. Being marooned on an islet might sound romantic, but there wasn't a scrap of shade, the sky was cloudless, and the sun beat relentlessly on our tent. Inside it, we slowly baked, listening to the maddening buffeting of the fabric walls, watching the poles bend with each strong gust. When we ventured outside, windblown sand filled our ears, scoured our skin, and half blinded us.

Dag kept telling me not to worry. "We'll make a break as soon as we can. And if we miss our flight, so what?"

Grimly, I reminded him we were low on water, and all we had left to eat was a bag of currants, a cup of rice, and some powdered milk.

"Oh, that." He ducked out to check on our kayak, which he'd tethered to a sturdy, tree-like saguaro cactus and weighted down with big stones. Minutes later, he returned, grinning.

"The kayak's okay, but guess what? There's a load of vultures flying around. What do you call that? A kettle? A committee?"

Irritated by his cheerfulness, I lay back, searching for something to distract me from the rumbling in my belly. Counting on my fingers, I calculated it was three years, nine months, and two weeks since I'd met Dag. In that time, I'd moved permanently from England to Canada, worked as a teacher, a nanny, and a burrito seller, overcome my fear of deep water, learned to kayak, written my first book, got married, bought land, and built a house. Not bad going, I thought. But there was something else during this stretch of time I had studiously avoided – and that was now looming larger. Along with our emerging plans to travel around the world with a folding kayak, Dag was talking about a baby.

"We'll get a bigger kayak for the trip," he said. "One with lots of room for a kid."

"I know you are joking," I'd retorted, knowing full well he wasn't.

I was on the cusp of 38. If we were going to create a child, we should get on with it. But any sense of urgency was drowned out by my anxieties. I recognized some of these as superficial. A few of my previously freewheeling girlfriends in Britain were now mothers. When I visited them, they were milk-swollen and sleep-deprived, surrounded by a clutter of baby paraphernalia. Our conversations were endlessly interrupted by crying, or feeding time, or naptime. I didn't want to become like them. And, stupid though it sounds, I had an antipathy to strollers and felt sorry for the women I saw pushing them around, loaded with shopping and a fussing child.

I knew I was only looking at motherhood from the outside, but I loved our unconventional life. I was still amazed we had a beautiful little house on a tiny island off the west coast of British Columbia and commuted by kayak to the nearest town. If we had a baby, wouldn't we need a motorboat, a bigger house? A move to town to be close to the right school? More money, both of us committing to secure jobs? It would change everything.

But these reasons masked the big one: the fear of loss. If we started a family, I was sure I would have to erect all sorts of safety nets. I couldn't face exposing a child to unnecessary risk; I'd have to take a different path through life – far more secure and settled than the one we were about to embark on.

∼

We'd come to the Sea of Cortez at the suggestion of some friends who were avid kayakers. They'd shown us charts of the body of water between the northwest coast of mainland Mexico and a peninsula stretching for over a thousand kilometres from its southern border with California. They pointed out a group of islands they called "a paddlers' paradise": uninhabited, with protected coves, desert landscapes, and clear blue waters teeming with fish. The sea was really a gulf, they explained, so its waters were fairly protected. Except when El Norte blew. The wind that can suddenly start blasting down the Sea of Cortez, too strong to paddle against. According to our friends, and to everything we had read, typically it lasts for about three days each time. On our trip, however, "typically" didn't always apply.

After Dag's conference, we'd met up in the old colonial town of Loreto, midway down the east side of the peninsula. We had a bout of sightseeing, eating fish tacos from street stalls, drinking margaritas, and provisioning with basic food supplies for ten days of paddling, then took a taxi out to our launch point, at Puerto Escondido.

"What's in the bags?" the driver asked us, as we heaved our luggage into the trunk.

"A boat," I told him, and he laughed.

"Very funny," he said.

By the time the taxi had dropped us at Puerto Escondido, El Norte was blowing strongly. Our original plan had been to make the four-kilometre hop over to Isla Danzante, then carry on to the much bigger Isla Carmen, which we wanted to circumnavigate over the course of several days before heading back to the peninsula and meandering north to Loreto. Instead, we spent two nights camped amid scrubby trees, pinned down by the wind. In the early hours of the second night it stopped, and next morning we crossed to Danzante. Dolphins leapt into the sunlight ahead of our bow, fish skipped over the surface of the water, and pelicans dropped beak-first from the sky in kamikaze dives. During that short stretch, I fell in love with the Sea of Cortez. The relationship was sealed when we arrived at Honeymoon Cove, a gorgeous, curving, sand beach protected by two rocky promontories that curled around like arms and dropped into azure water. This was some years before kayaking boomed in the area, and we had the cove to ourselves. We beached the boat and walked up the bluff behind it.

"Hello," said Dag, as we reached higher ground. To the north, a bumpy line of dark blue was stretching across the turquoise sea. The sign of strong wind. It moved fast toward us, and soon we were feeling the first gusts of El Norte.

Being stuck on Danzante wasn't a hardship. We spent all afternoon snorkelling in the cove, mesmerized by elegant moray eels, sinuous barracuda, and iridescent parrot fish nibbling on coral. Dag went spear fishing. As the day softened into evening, he marinated his catch in lime juice, garlic, and jalapeno peppers, and cooked it over a small fire of mesquite wood. We'd brought a stack of tortillas with us from Loreto, and we filled some of these with fish, onions, and salsa. We shared scraps of our food with a hermit crab, whose shiny black eyes popped up like buttons from its borrowed shell. It was a fastidious eater: one large claw held a piece of tortilla, while the other much smaller claw broke off tiny particles and lifted them to its mouth. When the three of us had finished dinner, Dag and I lay back and gazed at the planetarium sky, counting falling stars.

A couple of days later, the wind calmed enough for us to make the five-hour paddle to the south end of Isla Carmen. That night we set a pre-dawn alarm, so we could set off early on the first leg of our circumnavigation. Around one a.m., we were woken by a low howling and the tent walls shaking. Dag turned off the alarm.

From then on, El Norte blew erratically. Sometimes from the middle of the night until the following noon. Mostly for days on end. We made hops to new camps on Carmen, and from each one we explored parts of the island's rugged hinterland. The terracotta earth we hiked across crackled with dryness and was home to a dizzying array of cacti: tall as trees; squat as barrels; creeping along the ground; spineless and thick-leaved. After one dewfall, some burst with flowers, whose heavy petals resembled purple tissue paper and fine white muslin. Between the cacti grew spindly trees that looked as if they had been spray-painted ghostly white or bonbon green. We dropped down to exposed beaches, where we found whale bones and dolphin skulls. We swam and snorkelled in protected coves, then lay on the beach to warm up.

I was keenly aware of the isolation, of our precarious situation. After nine days, our supplies were running low. Near one of our camps we'd found an abandoned well, with potable water, but there was no guarantee we would come across another. And what if one of us got sick or injured? Dag was in his element: fishing, making fires, whittling pieces of wood into plates and cooking implements. He was endlessly curious. He spent hours wandering across beaches, exploring canyons, snorkelling over reefs. He was always keen to go further, to see what was around the next point when we were paddling, over the next rise of land when we were hiking.

Our last campsite on Carmen was a small beach with a narrow, winding canyon behind it. The smooth walls of the canyon were formed from a conglomerate of petrified shells, coral, and sand that had been scooped out by flash floods. Following its twists and turns to the end, we discovered a natural garden. Set amid sculpted rock were violet and yellow flowers, brittle bushes, and succulent cacti. It was silent and still, without a breath of wind. We stepped around carefully, fearful of damaging the delicate flora.

"I could stay here forever," said Dag.

"We might have to," I replied.

Our time on the islands had lasted almost twice as long as we expected. Unless we wanted to live off fish, find more wells for water, and risk Dag losing his job, somehow we needed to get back.

During the evening, the wind dropped. We got everything ready to be poised for a quick getaway. In the cold, surreal light of pre-dawn, we set our course toward the peninsula. We pushed hard. The sun peeked over the mountains, turning them mauve, pink, red, and gold. Eighteen kilometres later, it was bleaching them of colour. Still no wind. We were moving like a well-oiled machine. The coast was less than a 40-minute paddle away.

"Check out the horizon," I heard Dag say from behind me.

I'd been focused ahead. Now I looked northwards. A widening blue line.

El Norte wasn't going to let us get away so easily. Who else was there to tease out here? Within 15 minutes, we were fighting to keep moving forwards through chaotic waves that were building and breaking and threatening to flip us.

"We're heading for that islet," shouted Dag, swinging the kayak toward the only scrap of land between the peninsula and us. From my perspective, it was a cliff rising sheer from the water.

"There's nowhere to land!" I shouted back.

He was bent over the laminated map attached to the deck in front of him.

"There's a tiny beach on the far side, it should be protected."

As we rounded the islet, I saw it was shaped like a wedge of cheese standing on end. At the base of its sloping side, the beach was in a notch between two rock outcrops. We reached it just in time. After securing the boat, we scrambled to the top of the cliff and peered down. It was streaked in hues of rose pink, white, and yellow, and there was a strong acrid smell of guano. Cormorants hovered around our heads. Far beneath us, waves rolled in and smashed up against the boulders, sending spray high into the air. El Norte was getting into full throttle, making it quite clear that Puerto Escondido, a few kilometres away, might as well be on the moon.

~

I lay next to Dag, wide awake. It was our third night on the islet. The constant noise of wind whistling through guy ropes and rattling the tent walls was driving me crazy. I kept imagining El Norte ripping open the thin fabric of our shelter, sending it spiralling away over the water. Although Dag had checked the kayak again before we climbed into our sleeping bag, I was beset with worries about the vessel that was our only means of escape from this barren rock. What if there was an earthquake and a tidal wave? Would we have time to struggle with the boat up the cliff? The image kept looping through my brain, as maddening as the wind. Dag was lying on his back, very still.

"Are you sleeping?" I hissed, close to his ear. He moved slightly.

"I was trying to."

"What if there's an earthquake?"

"Huh, what?"

"An earthquake. Then a tidal wave. You, know, a tsunami."

I could sense his pained silence.

"Go. To. Sleep," he said finally, and turned over.

Despite everything, I did drop off. Until I opened my eyes to see Dag crouched at the tent door, unzipping it, and stepping out. I lay there for a moment, still half asleep, wondering what was different. Dawn light was seeping into the tent. And – wait a minute – the tent walls weren't moving. I sat up as Dag stuck his head back inside. "The wind has died down, and the sea is calming. Let's make a break for it."

We shoved things into dry bags, kneeled on our mattresses to press out air, dropped the tent, collapsed the poles. Carried all the gear, then the kayak, to the water's edge. Under a dawn-blushed sky, we paddled hard for Puerto Escondido. After half an hour, the wind came up, the waves started building again, but we knew we could make it.

"How are you feeling?" Dag called to me. Without breaking my rhythm, I called back that I couldn't wait to get to shore, eat a big meal, drink cold beer, and wash the salt and sand off my body.

"Really?"

He told me how sad he was that the adventure was nearly over, how much he looked forward to more kayaking trips like this, but for longer and in even wilder places.

"I've been thinking," he added, "that we could easily have a baby along on a trip like this."

I stopped paddling. I swung around to face him.

"A *baby*?"

"Why not?" He looked genuinely puzzled.

"Oh, just a few things, like baking heat, no shade, sandstorms," I retorted. "Not to mention running out of food and water."

"No problem!" he replied cheerfully. "You could breastfeed it. And, anyway, babies are tougher than you think."

"Have you lost your fucking mind?" I shouted, as a wave sloshed over my deck. "How could we risk having a baby along in these conditions? What if we capsized? What about all the stuff babies need?"

"What stuff?"

I flashed on a memory of watching friends with a baby pack for a weekend away. "Diapers, wipes, creams for skin rash, talcum powder, baby food, change mat, sterilizing stuff, clothes, toys, those spit cloth things – "

"We wouldn't need any of that shit," he interjected. "We'd do it differently. More naturally."

"OH, WOULD WE?"

And on it went. Despite paddling hard against the building wind, we managed to argue the rest of the way to Puerto Escondido. When we pulled into protected waters, I was overcome with relief, tiredness, and extreme hunger. I didn't want to think or talk about babies. I wanted to eat.

~

"I love the idea of us going off travelling like this for a whole year or more," I said, while we washed down big steaks with cold beers. "But, like I've said before, I know I'm not the kind of woman who could sling a baby on her back and head into the wilds. For me, having a child would mean a different path. Stability, some financial security. And, bottom line, we've both got to decide if it's something we really want to do."

We were calm now. After lunch we would pack up our boat and gear and take a taxi to Loreto. I gulped down more beer, then continued with my speech.

"Bringing a child into the world is probably the most profound experience of any woman's life. So deciding not to do it is a big deal. And it's a bigger decision for me than for you. I've only got a small window left to have kids. You've got years to become a father."

Dag started to protest.

"Hypothetically, that is," I interrupted him. "Hey, if for any reason I was out of the picture, you could find a younger model and have those five kids."

He thought for a minute.

"Let's wait until after the sabbatical to decide."

"I'll be 40 then."

He raised his glass to me.

"In every way, Maria, you seem so much younger than you are. I'm sure that won't be a problem."

I sighed. There were so many things that could be a problem. Especially at 40, when the risks of miscarriage and other complications shoot up. I clinked my glass with his and waved to the waiter for more beer.

~

The following February, I went to England for a short visit. My father had been unwell and was steadily losing weight. He was sure he had stomach ulcers. My mother took me to one side and broke the news that he'd been diagnosed with inoperable cancer. She had asked the doctors not to tell him; he was a hypochondriac, and she thought he'd find the truth too terrifying. So she kept up the pretense of "stomach problems," and the rest of us had to collude. It was in keeping with the tradition of family secrets, to which, of course, I'd added, hiding my marriage for almost a year. But I'd never found it easy; by nature I'm a truth teller, and now this was the hardest secret of all.

Back on Protection Island, I phoned my mother every few days for her whispered updates. He was eating less and less. The family doctor thought he should soon go to a nursing home with medical staff on hand. Mum flatly refused. She would look after him at home, right to the end, just as she had done for both her parents. When things got worse, she would get help; the council would send a caregiver once a day, and she would employ someone to give her a break at night. For now, she could manage. Her priority was to keep everything as normal as possible, not to worry him.

One day in late March, his condition suddenly deteriorated. Within hours of getting the call from my mother, I was on the first of several flights to England. At each layover, I phoned her with a sense of dread. When I was in Vancouver, Dad was still alive. By the time I got to Toronto, he had rallied. From London I learned he'd not only made it through the night, he'd had some breakfast and two cups of tea. Along with a great wave of relief, suddenly I felt undercurrents of a different worry. Apart from Joe, who had simply disappeared, I had no experience of losing someone I loved. How do you say goodbye? Were there things we should talk about? He'd never been a communicative man. And, since my teenage years, I'd increasingly become a mystery to him. His little girl with long plaits and a skipping rope had grown into someone who was always upsetting his wife. Should I apologize for that? Try to explain myself? I realized I had never really quizzed him about his early life on a farm in Ireland, moving to London for work, meeting my mother, joining the army when the war broke out. He'd only told me bits and pieces; it was my mother who was the talker. He had always just been my solid, reliable Dad, with a quiet but quirky sense of humour.

As soon as I arrived, my mother told me to go upstairs and see him. She poured a shot of whiskey to take to him. "You might have to help him with the glass."

He was sitting, hunched, in a high-backed armchair. Shockingly gaunt. He wore pajamas, a dressing gown, slippers. As I walked in, he slowly turned his head. His eyes registered surprise; bewilderment passed over his face.

"What are you doing here?" he asked me hoarsely. "Why have you come?"

It was a terrible moment. I had to swallow my anger toward my mother for yet another secret and find an explanation.

"Mum told me you weren't feeling well," I said haltingly. "I had been planning to come anyway at Easter as a surprise. It's so lovely to see you."

I leaned down and kissed his head. Laid my hand on his shoulder. His bones were bird-like.

"I've brought you some whiskey."

I put the glass in his hands, and he rested it on his lap. He stared ahead, glassy-eyed, his jaw slack.

"Can I help you with that? Hold the glass?" I asked him. He shook his head.

I stuttered out a few things: "Dag sends his love...he's dug a pond in our garden...I haven't seen your garden yet, I bet the spring flowers are up..."

He just nodded. I felt totally inadequate, out of my depth.

"I love you, Dad," I said, and then fell silent.

I saw his eyelids droop. I caught the glass just before he let go of it. His chin dropped toward his chest. I reached for his hand, convinced he was dying. But he had simply fallen asleep.

It was the last time he sat in a chair. He lived for six more days. My brother John drove up and down from Manchester. Mick flew in from Indonesia, where he was working, along with his wife, Eileen, and their children, 2-year-old Róisín and 5-month-old Tiernan. When they arrived, Eileen popped Tiernan next to my father on the bed. He smiled and weakly reached out a hand to touch the baby's tiny cheek.

Mum arranged for a night nurse. Princess was a young, voluptuous Jamaican woman with a sunny nature and a ready, loud laugh. She treated Dad as tenderly as she would have her own father. Since my teens, I had clashed with him about his racism. Yet whenever Princess swung into the room like a ship in full sail, and called, "Hello Tom, how you doing?" his eyes lit up.

Mum was sleeping with me in the next-door bedroom. In the middle of each night, I would get up and join Princess in her vigil.

"He's fine," she'd whisper. "He'll be here in the morning, don't you worry. I know when death is coming, the room fills with a scent like jasmine. If I smell it, I'll wake you and your Mum. Go get some rest now."

My mother knew the more tangible signs of approaching death: cold feet, fingers scrabbling at the sheets, a sudden bloom of health in the skin. All these started appearing. He could barely swallow and was only taking a little fluid. His mouth became terribly dry. We took turns to gently lay strips of cloth covered in ice against his lips. A priest came to give the last rites. While he murmured incantations and rubbed oil on my father's face, hands, and feet, gusts of March wind rattled the bedroom windows. I stared out at the trees, the swaying branches, the buds trembling at their tips.

On the sixth morning, my mother decided to go for a short walk. It was the first time she'd left the house since I arrived. Mick and his family were out shopping, John was back in Manchester. I was sitting alone with Dad when his quiet breathing changed to raw, rattling gasps. I saw a sudden flash of panic in his eyes. I grabbed his hand, leaned over him, talked rapidly.

"She'll be back soon, Dad, don't worry." I was trying to reassure myself as much as him. The thought that Mum would not be there when he died was unbearable. I told him I loved him, we all loved him, I begged him to hang on. His expression changed. The fear passed; he wasn't hearing me; he had withdrawn into a state of utter focus. He was unreachable then, as if he knew this was something no one could help him with. That he was heading into a territory beyond all our imaginings.

I heard the front door open. Several voices. I must have shouted out because Mick hurried into the room. He took one look and ran downstairs for Mum. Suddenly, she was on the other side of the bed.

"This is it," she said, reaching for Dad. "Oh, Tom."

He took several more gasps, his eyes wide open. And then, in an instant, his face fell in on itself, his skin drained of all colour, and he was gone.

Nothing had prepared me for the suddenness, the certainty, of that change from life to death. It was impossible to absorb at first, but the rituals of Irish Catholicism gave me some time. Aunty Madge arrived. With Mum, she prepared to "lay out" my father, something they had done for their parents, and for lots of people in their Irish community. I asked if I could help.

"It will be too upsetting for you," said Mum, but I insisted.

They brought in bowls of warm water, soap, and fresh towels. We bathed my father's body. We dressed him in clean clothes, changed the sheet beneath him. Following tradition, we placed coins on his eyelids. Gently, we inserted his false teeth. Madge wrapped a bandage round his face, chin to forehead, ribbon-like, and I tied it in a bow by one cheek, so that, when rigor mortis set in, his face would be in repose. We propped a book under his chin. Drew the covers up to his chest. Then we sat around his body, drinking tea and sherry and talking for about an hour and a half. At one point, I gazed at his bald head, his big ears, the bandage, and the bow like a gift wrapping.

"He looks like an Easter egg!" I blurted out, and we all laughed.

Mum stood up and opened a window. The time had come for his soul to leave his body, she explained, and we had to allow it an easy passage.

Mick and his family had gone for a walk while we were preparing Dad's body. Now their voices drifted up the stairs, then Tiernan started to cry lustily. Something in my mother's face changed when she heard the baby; it was like a cloud passing to let the sun shine through.

I sat in Dad's garden, looking at the rose bushes he would never tend again. I kept imagining him there, poking at weeds with a hoe. At the funeral, so many people had said, "You're just like your father." I couldn't see it. Nor did I want to be compared to someone with a bald head, big ears, and a large nose. But I knew I had his rangy body, his high cheek-bones, his thin lips. One woman I hardly knew had come up to me in tears. "Well, Tom Coffey lives on. You're the image of him."

It occurred to me that if I didn't have a child, no one would live on through me. I'd be the end of the line. There would be no little person someone would look at and catch reflections of me, then Dag, then me again.

From where I sat, I could see Mum in the house, cradling baby Tiernan. Having new life present in the face of death had given me some solace. I could only imagine what it meant to her.

My brothers and their partners had already provided Mum with six grandchildren. She was devoted to them, and they adored their "Nana." So to some extent the pressure was off. But over the years she'd often let me know that seeing a daughter becoming a mother was something very special, something she had looked forward to from the moment I was born.

A few months after I'd met Joe, I had a fierce argument with my mother over the phone. She was already upset about my new relationship. Then a good friend of mine and Joe's had been caught with a large stash of marijuana. I appealed to my brother John for help. He agreed to represent him, and got him off the charge on the grounds that the drug was for medical use. A neighbour of my mother's read about the case in the local newspaper and, of course, reported it to all their cronies. Her voice tense with anger, Mum told me I'd brought shame on her and our family. I was mixing with the wrong people; I was throwing away all the chances she'd worked so hard to give me. I tried to reason with her, to no avail. Finally, she cried, "You've never been the daughter I wanted!"

I slammed down the phone. I was stunned by her words, the pain of the attack. Minutes later, John rang me. She'd been on to him; she was hysterical. He begged me to call her back, to apologize.

"For what?" I asked, astonished. I told him what she'd said to me.

"She's in a state, Maria. She didn't mean it."

I called her. She repeated, calmly this time, that I had never been the daughter she wanted. Which, of course, I'd known all along.

After that, there was a wariness between us, unspoken anger. Things began to change after Joe died. To see me so broken was devastating for Mum. She was desperate to stop my pain, but that was beyond her power. Only then did she begin the slow journey of releasing me from the grip of her own dreams. Yet I never stopped feeling guilty. After I'd married Dag, occasionally I would try to imagine being the daughter she had wanted. I fantasized about flying from Canada to Manchester with Dag and our newborn. I'd even thought of names. Chloe or Phoebe for a girl, Noah for a boy. Mum would be waiting in the airport. The doors to the arrivals lounge would open, and I'd see her stout, reassuring figure, her snowy white, permed hair, her expression of pure joy as she caught sight of me and opened her arms wide, eager to hold the baby for the first time. Finally, I would have made her truly happy. But then, of course, we would leave again.

11

A friend on Protection phoned to say she'd found a stray kitten in her garden. "I've asked at the houses close by, and no one knows anything about her," said Margaret. "I think she's been dumped here. She's exactly the same colour as KD, so I wondered..."

I told her we didn't want another cat. Dag's sabbatical would start the following year, we'd be leaving for a long stretch, and so –

"Just come over and have a look," she interrupted. "I'll put the coffee on."

I left her house clutching a grey kitten. Dag was in our garden, digging holes and placing a small blueberry bush in each one. He smiled and scratched the kitten's head. He loved having animals around – the more the merrier as far as he was concerned.

"What are you going to call her?"

I thought for a few seconds.

"Blueberry."

Dag guessed her to be around five months old. "We'll keep her inside for a week to get her used to the place," he said. "Then we'll take her to town for her shots, and after that we'll get her spayed."

He was capable of doing this himself, but as he was registered as a vet in Europe, not Canada, he didn't have access to the necessary drugs to treat animals. Over the next few days, he watched Blueberry carefully. Unlike KD, who was regal and aloof, she was needy and nervous. One morning, he asked me to hold her while he palpated her belly.

"I thought as much," he said. "We won't be spaying her yet. She's pregnant."

"How is that possible?" I asked. "She's still a baby herself."

"She must be a bit older than she looks. At least six months. Some nasty tomcat got her on her first cycle. She'll be a teenage mum."

He calculated a birth date in early July.

Our garden bloomed. The raised beds filled up with salad greens and edible flowers – nasturtiums, marigold, and borage. Bulrushes and ferns flourished around the pond, lilies opened up from pads floating on the water. Meanwhile, Blueberry bloated. Her stomach outgrew her little frame. She waddled around the house, collapsing in corners. She grew so big she couldn't reach back to clean herself.

"She's your cat, you'll have to start wiping her arse," Dag told me one morning, when an unpleasant smell wafted from her rear end. But he took over the task, handling her as gently as he would a human baby.

One evening, when we were out for dinner, she produced four kittens. They soon grew into furry bundles of mischief, racing around the house, infuriating KD, who hissed and swatted at them. Dag adored the kittens, but he was also continuing with plans for us to leave on a kayaking trip to Haida Gwaii (at that time still called the Queen Charlotte Islands). A "practice run," he said. Something challenging, to start getting ready psychologically for next year's round-the-world adventure. I thought we should cancel because of the newly expanded family. Ridiculous, he said. The house-sitters would look after the kittens.

Just before we left, a friend from Vancouver came to spend a night with us, bringing her 4-month-old baby. She'd called me to say she desperately needed a quick break from the city, and from the baby's father – their relationship had hit a few problems. It was the first time we'd seen her since the birth, so, of course, we had to celebrate. She was sitting on the couch with her son, when Dag opened a bottle of champagne. The cork popped, flew up, hit a high beam, and dropped toward Susan, missing the baby's head by inches. Despite that near disaster, a little later she asked us to take care of the baby. She wanted to go for a walk, maybe stop for a swim along the way.

"I haven't had a minute to myself for – well, months. Just for an hour or so, okay?"

Before leaving, she fed and changed the baby. "He should be asleep soon," she said, handing me the little bundle as she headed out of the door.

For a minute the baby stared up at me with what seemed like curiosity. Then, as if sensing the exact moment when his mother went out of earshot, he began to cry. No amount of dandling, rocking, or back patting would soothe him. I tried to get him to suck on his pacifier, but he spat it out. The crying turned to frantic wails, and his face turned bright red.

"I've got an idea," said Dag. He went to the fridge, pulled out the half-empty bottle of champagne, filled a glass, and handed it to me.

"Where's that pacifier?" he asked.

"On the floor over there," I said, shifting the baby so I could take a glug. "Why?"

I soon found out. He dunked the plastic nipple into the champagne, and when the baby took a breath between wails, inserted it into his mouth.

"Dag, you can't do that!" I protested.

"Just watch, it will do the trick," he said.

The baby sucked with curiosity, then let the pacifier fall out of his mouth and gazed at Dag, who dipped it into the wine again.

"Stop it, Dag!" I demanded.

"Just one more. I bet your dad occasionally put whiskey on your pacifier and you turned out all right. Anyway, for the baby it's better than being hyper distressed for an hour."

When Susan returned, she was impressed to find her son fast asleep in Dag's arms.

~

Haida Gwaii lies 130 kilometres off the north coast of British Columbia. The archipelago is the traditional home of the Haida People, who had been fighting logging companies to preserve some of the most beautiful stands of old-growth forest in Canada. Their battles had been partially successful; the south part of Moresby, the second-largest island, had been made into a national park reserve, Gwaii Haanas. We planned to spend about three weeks exploring its eastern shore and satellite islands.

"We'll have to be totally self-sufficient. But there are lots of freshwater streams, and the fishing is supposed to be incredible," Dag had told me, pausing before the next bit of news. "Of course, it's a different climate zone up there, so we'll need to take good rain gear and wetsuits, and be ready for colder temperatures and storms."

On the day of departure, we were in our usual last-minute packing panic. Dag was down on the beach, loading all our stuff into the motorboat of a neighbour who would transport us to Nanaimo. From there, we would drive to Port Hardy at the north end of Vancouver Island, park the car, and take the first of two long ferry rides to Haida Gwaii.

I was in the house, writing instructions for the house-sitters. And I was in tears. The kittens were adorable. The weather on the south coast of British Columbia was hot, sunny, and still. The forecast in Haida Gwaii was for cold, stormy conditions. I didn't want to go. I felt like a barnacle being pried off a rock. I had gone into homebody mode, the opposite of Dag's default nomadic state. If I was like this with kittens, I thought, what would I be like with a child? I'd never want to go anywhere. Dag strode in.

"Maria, I forgot the – " He stopped when he saw my face. "What's wrong?"

"Nothing," I snivelled. "I'll be ready in a minute."

≈

My notes from the first week of that trip are full of recurring words and phrases: rain; storm; long crossing against the southeast wind; cold and wet; exhausted; grubby; more mosquito bites.

Just getting to Haida Gwaii had been arduous. A long drive, a night sleeping in our car in Port Hardy, 16 hours on a ferry, a night spent on the wooden floor of a picnic shelter in Prince Rupert, eight hours on another ferry, and finally hitching a ride with all our stuff in the back of a pickup truck to the place where we could assemble and launch the kayak. After all that, we immediately set off on a five-hour paddle.

The landscape was primordial. We kayaked through mazes of Zen-like rock gardens, past islets sparsely covered with windblown trees and heaps of honking sea lions, and along the shores of larger islands where mist drifted through stands of old-growth forest. Bald eagles swooped down to the water to grab fish in their talons; rafts of seabirds took flight. But I was too tired to properly appreciate anything. On our second day of paddling, the low pressure brought strong winds and heavy rain. We had a quick stop on Louise Island at an ancient village site. The resident Haida Watchman toured us around fallen totem poles and the remains of longhouses overgrown with moss, explaining his people's history and culture. I wanted to take it all in, but I could barely keep my eyes open. I squelched around after him in my rubber boots and my clammy wetsuit. Eventually, he took pity on me.

"The storm's going to get worse tonight," he said. "You should go and set up camp. There's an old cabin not far from here that kayakers sometimes use. I haven't seen anyone go there in a while."

I wanted to hug him. We paddled on and eventually spotted a small structure huddled beneath overhanging branches at the head of a steep, pebbly beach. Dag held onto the kayak, while I scrambled up to check the cabin. Its single window seemed to gaze at me as I approached. Hesitantly, I pushed open the door. Bunk beds, a table and two chairs, a rough wooden countertop, and an ancient wood stove. The room was dusty, cobwebby, and oppressive, but it was dry. I felt weak with relief.

By the time we hauled our gear and boat to the cabin, the rain was hammering down. I peeled off my wetsuit and changed into dry clothes. Dag brewed tea and added good measures of brandy. To my delight, I discovered a small pile of notebooks, filled with entries made by people who had stayed here over the years. Kayakers mostly, and a few fishers. The oldest entry, dated August 1976, was the most intriguing. In artistic flourishes, someone called Celia had written,

Nostalgic notes from the margins of my mind. I was here before, almost exactly a year ago. In glorious solitude, in anticipation of the arrival of Runnell and then onto Bagdad. Writing Arabic in the sand, eating orange cunt mussels, scanning the horizon. A full year has gone around like the tidal cycles. We came now from James Bay, with the airtight stove, with plastic for the windows, with kayaks to take us home again. Welcome to all who come after us.

While the storm raged outside, we made pasta, drank more brandy, and pondered over Celia. Who was she? Did she and Runnell really go to Bagdad? Where were they now? Did they have kids and stop their crazy voyages? Then we cuddled up in our sleeping bag on the lower bunk bed and fell into a slightly drunken sleep. I dreamt of our kittens, of our house being infested with fleas.

All next day, I brooded. I stared out through sheets of rain at mossy undergrowth, gnarled trees, long beach grasses, the sweep of grey stones studded with smooth black rocks, the tangled heaps of seaweed. It felt raw and inhospitable. I was miserable, wondering how I was going to fare on our planned worldwide kayaking trip, spending months on end in places and situations I couldn't even imagine. I wished I were home with our cats.

We stayed in the cabin for two more nights. Maybe it was because I had a chance to catch up on lost sleep. Or because Celia's adventurous spirit finally got through to me. Or simply because the storm passed, and the sun came out. But, suddenly, I was raring to go, eager to explore.

A high-pressure system settled in; the weather became hot and glorious. We wandered by kayak. We took our time to find the prettiest beaches to camp on. We always had them to ourselves and could hang out naked, well into the warm evenings. Dag got serious about fishing and caught salmon and ling cod. He snorkelled for abalone and scallops, which were still legal to harvest. He prepared sashimi and sushi – we'd brought lots of pickled ginger, wasabi, tamari, nori, special rice – and presented it beautifully on plates and with chopsticks that he'd fashioned from driftwood.

"You could star in your own cooking show," I told him. "You'd blow Martha Stewart out of the water."

We visited more Haida village sites, and talked to the Elders and their children guarding them. We hiked through old-growth forest, where the branches of huge trees were draped with long, beard-like strands of grey lichen. The ground was so deep in soft green moss I wanted to lie down in it and stay forever.

At night we would hear the echoing cries of loons – eerie tremolos, wails, and hoots. In the early mornings, we'd wake to raven calls. Their repertoire included sounds like a resonating bell, a deep booming, a constant clicking, and occasionally a disconcertingly human-like laugh. Once, when I crawled sleepily from the tent, a raven flew by so close I saw its bright eye registering me.

Our only contact with home was via VHF radio; we'd call the coast guard, give a phone number, and ask to be patched through. We did this a few times: to Dag's brother, to whom I relayed messages for my mother that he'd phone on to her; to our house-sitters; and to the wife of a commercial fisher friend who was on a boat in northern BC. The boat was due to head back to Vancouver Island in early September, and we had a vague plan to meet him in Haida Gwaii and get a ride across Hecate Strait to Port Hardy, where our car was parked. But so far we'd received just one message via his wife: the boat was still at the north end of the archipelago, and the captain didn't know their return schedule.

Life was simple and satisfying, and time went by in a drift. As I made my notes one morning, the import of the date suddenly struck me: August 30. Dag was due to start teaching in less than two weeks, and he had to be in his office several days before then. To get to where we could catch the first of two ferries to Vancouver Island, we'd have to paddle for several days. We had to leave immediately to have a chance of making it in time.

"Don't worry," said Dag. "I've been thinking about that, and I'm sure we'll find a fishing boat to take us across. Let's head back and visit Hot Springs Island again. Commercial fishers sometimes stop off there to soak in the pools."

By that afternoon we had set up camp in a nearby cove and were on our way to the island. The Haida Watchman, Alvin, welcomed us. He remembered us as the kayakers who laid around naked in the geo-thermally heated water for hours on end, only moving to go for cold ocean swims.

I should have guessed it was now Dag's turn to feel like a barnacle attached to a rock. This place was heaven for him; he had no desire to leave. We spent day after day soaking and swimming. After weeks of hardly seeing a soul, we had a social life, encountering sports fishers, people on yachts, and tourists taking day trips in Zodiacs. But no commercial fishers. Dag and I kept having the same conversation.

"We should be making plans to get home."

"Something will work out."

"Like what?"

"Like a boat turning up."

"If it doesn't, and we don't get back in time, what will happen to your job?"

"Maybe I'll lose it."

I'd already asked Alvin if he knew of any commercial fishing boats returning to Vancouver Island. He had said he'd keep an ear open for news.

"If you'd set off last week, you'd have been in Skidegate and on the ferry by now," he added unhelpfully.

Two days before Dag should have been in his office, I tersely suggested he try to get a message to the college, informing it he would be delayed.

"I'll do that tomorrow," he promised.

By mid-morning next day he still hadn't called. Instead, he'd gone snorkelling. I sat on the beach, fuming. If he lost his job, could we still go on our big trip? What about our house-sitters – I didn't know how long they could wait for us – and the cats? Would he be so laissez-faire if we had a child? What if we took the kid on a kayaking trip and got back late when they were due to start daycare or school? Dag emerged from the water, stripped off his weight belt and wetsuit, and lazily stretched out on the pebbles.

"Are you okay?" he asked, sensing my mood. It was hard to miss.

I said nothing; I knew it was pointless. He reached for the VHF radio and started fiddling with it. He dialled to an open channel, and a conversation crackled out. Someone called Bud was talking about winding up the fishing season and setting sail that night for Vancouver Island. Dag sat up, listening intently. Then the connection was lost.

"The boat must be in the area," he said. "Let's go and ask Alvin if he knows about it, and see if we can use his radio. It's got a much better reach."

We sprinted over to Hot Springs Island.

"I know Bud," said Alvin. "He's on the *Shady Lin*. I saw her go by a while ago."

We followed him to his house and radio. Dag got through to Bud straight away. Could he take two kayakers to Port Hardy? Bud asked for the coordinates of our campsite. Then he told Dag to stand by for a few minutes. We waited. I hopped from foot to foot.

"Kayakers on Hot Springs Island," barked the radio. "This is *Shady Lin*. Over."

"*Shady Lin*, this is kayakers on Hot Springs Island. Over."

"Kayakers on Hot Springs Island, can you be ready in 15 minutes? Over."

"*Shady Lin*, can you give us 45? Over."

"Kayakers on Hot Springs Island, okay, see you then. Out."

We almost flew back across the water and broke camp in record time. We were throwing bags into the kayak when a 21-metre aluminum seiner fishing boat chugged into view. As we paddled toward the *Shady Lin*, a ladder was lowered over the side. Three guys leaned on the gunwale, grinning down at us. Another man – who would turn out to be Bud – was in the wheelhouse.

"I can't believe this," I said to Dag as we came alongside and grabbed the ladder. "You must have horseshoes up your ass."

"I told you something would work out," he replied blithely.

The kindly crew plied us with beers and chocolate bars, offered us the use of the hot shower, showed us the berths we could sleep in for the overnight crossing, made us soup and sandwiches for lunch, and asked us if we'd like steak and chips for dinner. Dag joined Bud in the wheelhouse, and they were soon deep in conversation. Sipping a beer, I gazed at my husband: his tousled, sun-bleached hair, his long, tanned limbs. Sensing my eyes on him, he looked over, grinned, leaned out of the wheelhouse door.

"Bud just checked the weather. We're going to have a calm crossing."

I was relieved. Hecate Strait had a fearsome reputation, and I was prone to seasickness. He winked at me.

"Horseshoes, right?"

Indeed, I thought. We'll need lots of those in the future.

~

Deciding the destinations of our round-the-world trip was a bit like pulling ideas from a hat. We both agreed the South Pacific was a must. The Solomon Islands, southeast of Papua New Guinea, sounded really intriguing: the third-largest archipelago in the area, and the least developed, with few roads, erratic ferry schedules, barely any modern infrastructure, and next to no tourism. We decided to start there, reaching it via Fiji. I had always wanted to travel in India, and I'd recently read Eric Newby's *Slowly Down the Ganges*. He and his wife navigated the river by motorboat; we'd go by kayak. Dag thought this was an insane plan. I insisted. Meanwhile, we were talking about East Africa, which Dag had dreamed of exploring since his childhood. Ocean kayaking there posed too many challenges, including piracy and long stretches of exposed, surf-pounded coastline. There was a chain of huge lakes in the area, but the only one mostly free of the parasitic worms that cause schistosomiasis, a debilitating disease, was in Malawi. I wasn't too happy about the "mostly" bit. But Dag had agreed to the River Ganges, so I gave in on Lake Malawi. We felt we had to put Europe on the list, and Dag suggested the River Danube. We could fly into Munich and hang out with his mates there before setting off. Our last destination would be Alaska, where we'd paddle in Prince William Sound.

"Calving glaciers, grizzly bears?" I queried.

"Perfect way to end things off," Dag countered. "And far less hazardous than the Ganges."

The nasty subject of money came up. We estimated the cost of the flights, the equipment we'd need, including a more substantial folding kayak that would withstand months of continuous wear in a variety of different climates and conditions, and all our living costs along the way, with some extra for emergencies. It added up to quite a bit more than Dag's two-thirds salary.

We had a brief stab at getting corporate sponsorship. We produced a brochure about our "Jungle to Ice Expedition" and sent it to companies across North America. But as we talked to CEOs about our plans, and what they would expect of us in return, it became clear to us that what we wanted, what we'd wanted all along, was an independent, unfettered adventure. Which left us with money problems.

"Let's remortgage the house," I said to Dag one morning.

He looked at me blankly. "Can we do that?"

"I don't see why not. It's how I raised the money for my trip to Everest. Let's give it a try."

Soon we were sitting across from the woman who had approved the mortgage that allowed us to build our house. Along with her big hair and red fingernails, she now had impressive shoulder pads and lots of costume jewelry. Things didn't go quite so well this time. She was unimpressed by our forthcoming adventure. Her only suggestion was a loan against the mortgage, at an interest rate that made us shudder. We retreated to a nearby cafe to consider.

"It will take forever to pay it off," I said.

In the long silence that followed, we both stirred our coffee.

"We could forget the whole idea," said Dag.

I nodded. "That's one possibility."

There was another silence while we drank the coffee.

"Ready?" he asked.

I was. We headed back to the bank.

∼

Other things fell into place. The *Guardian* and *New York Times* expressed interest in stories and images from our expedition. I had a long chat with my literary agent and came up with a book proposal. To my astonishment, I quickly got a contract to write *A Boat in Our Baggage*. This helped us to get sponsored for lots of products, including a brand new, high-tech, folding kayak, paddling clothes, and camping equipment.

In the midst of all this, I went back to England to visit my mother. We were out shopping one morning when we ran into a friend of hers, Marianne, who was also originally from Ireland.

"Hello Maria, it's so nice that you're home," said Marianne. "Your mother keeps me up to date with your news, but it's years since I saw you last. You haven't aged a bit. You still look so young and fresh. How old are you now?"

"Would you believe she'll be 40 next year, Marianne?" said Mum.

She had a habit of answering questions for me, and discussing me with other people as if I wasn't there.

"I wouldn't have guessed, Bee! And how lovely and slim she still is. But, of course, she's never had children. That wrecks the figure early in life. Isn't that right?"

"It is indeed," Mum replied, taking my arm and giving me a nudge to signal it was time to leave. "I'll see you on Thursday at the Catholic Mothers meeting, Marianne."

When we were out of earshot, she said, "Take no notice of her, she's a bit of a busybody."

We were both silent for a while.

~

A few months before we left on the trip, Mum came to Canada for the first time. I was worried about what she would think of our house, especially in its unfinished state. But she loved it. She sat on the makeshift deck with me in the mornings, astonished by the hummingbirds that came to the feeder. I took her to the north and west coasts of Vancouver Island, where we saw whales and dolphins and sea lions. We went by train to the Rocky Mountains, and from Lake Louise we took a bus with huge wheels onto the Columbia Icefield. As she set foot on the glacier, she cried, overwhelmed by its majesty. She had always longed to travel, but my father had never wanted to venture further than Ireland, British seaside resorts, or my brother's timeshare apartment in Spain. It was lovely to see her soaking in these experiences, to be sharing my new world with her. This was the happiest time we'd had together since I was a child.

Dag's mother, Justina, now lived in Vancouver. On our return from the Rocky Mountains, Mum and I stayed with her in her apartment, then she came back with us to Protection Island. The two women became friends. They were the same age. Both of them had been nurses. Both had recently lost their husbands, one to death, the other to divorce. And there was something about Dag and me they definitely agreed on.

"Isn't this a lovely house?" Mum said to Justina one afternoon, as the three of us were having tea and cakes.

"It is, Bee, but there should be children running through it."

"I know! It's such a perfect spot for little ones. They could go and wade in the sea quite safely on their own. And Dag would have them swimming in no time. But I don't think Maria wants children. When she lost her boyfriend before Dag, she was badly shaken. I think it put her off wanting a family."

I stared at her, nonplussed. I had never discussed my fear of loss with her; I had no idea she knew about it.

"I think Dag would like children," said Justina. "The two of them would be wonderful parents."

"They would indeed. As long as they are happy is all that matters. But, of course, I'd love to see her have a baby."

"And it's time I had a grandchild, Bee. Maybe when they come back from this long trip."

"You never know."

I got up to make more tea.

∼

Mum was always brave about our goodbyes. Usually, I was the one leaving in a taxi, while she stood at the garden gate waving until I was out of sight. This time, she was getting on a plane, knowing she wouldn't see me for a year, with a lot of uncertainties during the months in between.

"As long as you're with Dag, I don't worry about you," she said at the airport, fighting back tears. "I know he will always keep you safe."

She had adored Dag from the moment she met him. Of course, it was because he made me so happy. But she also admired his strength and his practical skills. Their relationship was sealed one day when she broke the chain on the rosary beads she had inherited from Madge. Dag found her in the kitchen, in tears, clutching the chain. He whipped out the multi-tool he always carried on his belt and fixed it in seconds.

"I can't believe it!" she'd cried. "You're Mr. Wonderful!" I'd teased him with that name from then on.

Despite Mr. Wonderful's presence, I knew she was worried about our trip. And she wasn't the only one. When I let myself really consider what lay ahead, I was overwhelmed. The bald truth was that, while we had a general structure for our journey, we had no real idea of how the various components would work. Even people who had worked in the Solomon Islands, India, and Malawi – a variety of NGOs and doctors we had contacted – had been of little help. In our kayak, we'd be reaching areas they had never got to. They had advised us on health issues, cultural mores, and the best trade items and gifts to bring along. But they couldn't tell us what to expect. I kept reminding myself I had always wanted an adventurous life, and that no one was making me do this.

A few days before takeoff, we had a huge party. Some friends presented us with a book entitled *Shark Attack* and a card showing two crocodiles with swollen bellies lying on a beach surrounded by the remnants of a canoe, paddles, and life jackets. As the evening wore on, we were teased about the stunning sex we would enjoy on all those balmy tropical beaches, and what to do if we were disturbed in the act by a croc.

"Run around in circles!"

"Poke it in the eyes!"

"Whatever you do, don't try climbing a tree. Crocs can stand on their tails."

Everyone wanted to see the boat. Dag assembled it, with me handing him the various pieces. A press of people surrounded us, making comments – something we would become very accustomed to in the months ahead. Various friends took it out for a spin. Eventually, we laid it on the deck of the house, and the party raged on around it.

"Let's stay up and watch the dawn," said Dag. It was four a.m. The party had finally wound down. Friends and their children were curled up in our bed. Other guests had laid out sleeping bags on the carpet in the loft. I decided to join them. Some hours later, I woke with a start. Snoring bodies surrounded me, but Dag wasn't among them. I quickly found him. He was fast asleep in the back cockpit of the kayak, a peaceful expression on his face, the sea breeze ruffling his hair.

Six

Childfree or childless, if you're a middle-aged woman who isn't a mother, you're living a life that isn't for the faint-hearted....You *will* be judged, and you *will* be defined by your biological status, just as mothers are by theirs. It's just that yours is a little bit more complicated.

—NINA JERVIS

12

We were somewhere between Fiji and the Solomon Islands, beneath a great swath of the Milky Way and unfamiliar constellations. A warm trade wind filled the yacht's huge sails, pushing us steadily through the waves at ten knots. It was two a.m., and we had just started our first deck watch. The yacht was on autopilot; our job for the next three hours was to keep an eye out for any obstacles in its path. But beyond the lights of the boat, below the twinkling sky, there was nothing but deep darkness. It was like being in outer space.

We sat in the spacious cockpit, leaning back on comfortable cushions, sipping cold French wine from elegant glasses, listening to mellow jazz that drifted from an inbuilt speaker.

"This isn't quite what I'd imagined," I said.

"Could you get used to it?" Dag asked.

I thought for a moment.

"We'd have some explaining to do. And I'd need to change the book title. A Boat in Our Luxury Yacht?"

We'd flown from Canada to the Fijian island of Viti Levu, along with our folding kayak, our camping gear, Dag's weight belt for diving, and a pile of other stuff, crammed into two big – and now extremely heavy – bags. British Airways had kindly offered to waive excess baggage charges on our round-the-world ticket. But the flight we needed from Fiji to the Solomons, over 3000 kilometres away, wasn't included in that ticket. There was no agent for Fiji Airlines in Canada – and, back then in the dark ages of the early 1990s, no online booking. So we decided to book it once we arrived.

Outside the tiny arrivals building of Nadi International Airport, Dag had haggled with a taxi driver.

"These bags are too, too heavy," insisted the driver. "I take them, I will need new suspension, new tires, new everything."

"They're not *that* heavy," said Dag. "Look, I can lift one on my own."

"You must pay me much more!"

"How much more?" asked Dag.

"Ten dollars more!"

"That's ridiculous. Five, tops," countered Dag. He loves the cut and thrust of bargaining, and likes to make a game of it, but it always makes me feel heartless, something the driver clearly picked up on.

"Madam, I have a wife and five kids," he appealed to me. "They must eat! If my car is broken, I cannot work!"

Dag had already started walking away.

"Come back!" cried the driver and set off after him.

They disappeared around the corner, leaving me alone with our bulging red bags. I sat down on one of them. Despite my tiredness from the long journey, I was already feeling a buzz of excitement at arriving somewhere new and totally unfamiliar. The air smelled of sandalwood, frangipani, and jet fuel exhaust. From the foliage of lush trees next to the building came loud bird cries, then flashes of blue and red plumage. I jumped up. A flock of parrots!

Suddenly, there was another sound, guffaws of laughter, as Dag and the driver reappeared, sharing a joke. They stuffed our luggage into the car. We drove past startlingly green sugar cane fields, and through small settlements where lines of bright washing hung outside shacks built from branches and corrugated iron. We were wide-eyed, exclaiming at huge purple banana pods drooping on thick stalks, trees heavy with papayas, a mongoose running across the road. The taxi driver was amused.

"You are like my 3-year-old daughter when I take her on a drive," he teased us.

"We've never been to the tropics before," I explained.

"So you never drink fresh coconut either?"

He pulled up to a roadside stall, where a barefoot boy was selling green coconuts. With a huge machete, the boy chopped off the tops so we could drink the sweet, refreshing milk, then cracked open the nuts and fashioned little spoons from the shells for us to scoop up the gelatinous flesh.

"I could live on this," I enthused.

"You probably will," said Dag. "I'm going to buy one of those machetes for the trip."

As we carried on, Dag chatted to the driver about our plans to go to the Solomon Islands.

"Better you stay in Fiji," he advised. "No one goes to the Solomon Islands."

His opinion was echoed by the airline official we met the next day.

"Very few tourists go to the Solomons," she said. "The flights are too expensive."

"How expensive?" I asked, and the price she quoted made me gulp. We hadn't even started to talk about excess baggage charges.

That evening, drinking cold beers on the veranda of our hotel, we struck up a conversation with two young Englishmen who had been backpacking for months.

"This is a shithole place, isn't it?" said one who had shoulder-length blond dreadlocks.

I had to agree with him. Our room was like a cell, and we were sharing it with a family of cockroaches.

"Cheap though," said his friend, rubbing a hand over his shaved head, then tugging absentmindedly at a rather large nose ring. He gazed at us quizzically. "What are you doing here?"

He was probably referring to the hotel, but our story tumbled out.

"I've been trying to get to the Solomons too," he said. "You can sometimes get rides on sailing boats heading there. I was asking around at the marinas in Lautoka and heard about a big yacht that's on its way to the Philippines and needs a cook. But the skipper took one look at me and turned me down."

"Where is the boat?" asked Dag. "What's it called?"

"Max's Marina." The man rubbed his head again as he thought. "It's called Swedish something or other. You two look pretty respectable, you might stand a chance."

On the outside wall of the marina's small office building, a few notices fluttered from a corkboard. There were requests for people to do varnishing work, but none for crew. I found some pins on the board and stuck up the piece of paper on which I'd carefully printed our notice. "A couple and their folding kayak seek passage to the Solomon Islands in exchange for work," it read, along with contact details for our cockroach-ridden hotel. As I stood back, I noticed a tall blond man who had walked up behind us.

"Hello," I said. I pointed to our notice. "If you know anyone..."

"Yes, I just saw it. I am Soren, skipper of *Swedish Caprice*. We need a cook until we get to the Philippines, and we're going there via the Solomons."

"Dag is a wonderful cook," I offered.

"Can you come aboard now for an interview? My Zodiac is at the dock."

Stepping onto the immaculate teak decking of *Swedish Caprice*, we were greeted by another blond but much younger man, who introduced himself as Ole. He seemed surprised when Soren explained why we had come aboard.

"I'll make coffee after you've had the tour," he said.

We followed Soren around the 25-metre yacht. He showed us the computerized navigational system, electronically controlled sails, dive compressors, and water desalination system. We walked through the spacious salon, its walls lined with highly polished mahogany, its elegant furniture bolted to the deeply carpeted floor.

"Here's the all-important galley," said Soren. I gazed at the double sink, two fridges, two freezers, expensive cookware, a large stove, and every kitchen gadget imaginable.

"What are these for?" I asked, pointing to some belts attached to a railing that ran along the work surface.

"For the cook to strap into when the seas get rough," said Soren. "And, of course, the stove is hinged so it stays level when the boat heels."

Before I could ask what heeling was, Dag gave me a "no more questions" look.

Beyond the galley was a hallway leading to the cabins. "This would be yours," continued Soren, opening a door to reveal double-bed-sized bunks, a built-in wardrobe, and a "head" with a walk-in shower and marble wash basin with brass faucets.

Back on deck, while we drank coffee, Soren explained that a Swedish businessman based in London owned the yacht. His permanent crew sailed it around the globe, and he flew in every few months to join it.

"When the owner isn't here, usually we are five on board. Me and Ole, Pascale and Gael, who are on shore right now, and, of course, our cook. He plans to rejoin us in the Philippines, and ideally we'd like you to stay until then, but if you fit the bill, we'd consider you as far as the Solomons."

Then came the interview. Could we manage heavy-weather cooking? What was our previous sailing experience? Dag described his culinary skills, admitted his sailing experience was limited, but that he was enthusiastic, and, importantly, that he never got seasick. He would do the bulk of the work, and I would be his sous-chef. I kept quiet. Previously, I had only been out sailing on a couple of small boats for day trips. Both times I'd hunched in the cockpit, feeling nervous and nauseous. But I didn't admit this to Soren. Instead, I gazed out at the ocean, feeling the warm, tropical breeze on my skin, wondering what heavy-weather cooking entailed.

Soren offered us the job. No pay, only passage. We would set sail in three days but should move aboard as soon as possible. Along with cooking, we would have to provision the boat. In Lautoka there were some supermarkets stocked for sailors and expats. We were to buy the most expensive cuts of meat, good cheeses, and the best French wines we could find. The budget was open-ended.

"Oh, and one other thing," he added. "You'll need to take turns at night watch. We'll have the trade winds with us the whole way, and the sails are automated, so the watches are pretty straightforward. You could do them together. Is that okay?"

~

Initially, the crew was reserved toward us. They were tightly knit, and I presumed they didn't want to expend a lot of energy on "transients" who wouldn't be with them for long. But I quickly realized we also puzzled them. I was the oldest person on board. Soren was a bit younger than Dag; he had given up a career in architecture to become a ship's captain. The others were in their 20s, using crewing as a way to see the world before settling down to "real" life. They couldn't get their heads around the fact that we seemed to be doing things backwards.

At 21, Ole was the youngest. He was starting his second year on *Swedish Caprice* and hoped to do at least one more before taking over his father's automobile business in Denmark.

"It will be a shock, going from this to selling cars," he said, as we all had lunch on deck the day before setting sail.

"No kidding," said Dag. "If I'd discovered this life in my early 20s, I'd never have finished my veterinary training. I'd still be sailing around the world."

"It happens so easily," said Ole. "You are on a dock, someone yells, 'Hey, we need an extra pair of hands on board, are you interested?' And off you go."

"That is how it happened for me," said Pascale.

She had been crewing for four years, since she was 20. Her first job was helping to deliver a boat from France to Mauritius. She had no sailing experience, but she wanted an adventure. The voyage took five months. On arrival, she was offered a job on another boat sailing the Indian Ocean.

"It went on like that; it was two years before I got home to France. I couldn't settle. I returned to crewing again. But I won't do it forever. I want to have a family."

She leaned back against the cushions. She wore a swimsuit cut very high on the hips and low on the breasts, with a lace panel keeping the front sections together. Earlier, I'd watched her execute a perfect dive into the harbour, then climb back on board, goddess-like, water pearling off her toned limbs.

"Why didn't you have kids?" she asked, fixing me with a direct gaze.

"I haven't completely ruled it out," I said. "We'll decide when we get home next year."

"But you say you are 39, yes? Isn't that too old? I want to have children before I am 30, so we can grow up together."

"Well, I guess Dag and I haven't started growing up yet," I quipped, but in truth I was suddenly feeling very old indeed.

Before we set sail, I placed a call to my mother. It was 11 p.m. in England. "I'm sitting here reading a book," she said wistfully. I had a pang of sorrow mixed with guilt. I knew how lonely she'd been since my father died. I told her about the boat, its comfort. I stressed its safety. "It's like a floating hotel," I said.

"Maybe you should just stay on board for as long as you can," she replied.

That night, in our double top bunk, I dreamt about her. We were in a bus together, along with a small child, driving along a steep mountain road with snow slopes on either side of us. The bus stopped, and we got out to look at the view and take photos. Holding the child's hand, my mother stepped off the curb. Ignoring my frantic warning shouts, she began glissading down the slope, whooping with glee, heading toward a cliff. Then she and the child shot over the edge and started falling toward a glacier below. I raced down the road. A car came, and I waved frantically, but it drove on by. In utter panic, I kept running, my boots felt heavy and loose, they were slowing me down as my panic rose – then I sat up in the bunk and banged my head on the mahogany ceiling.

~

We cruised past islands covered with palm trees, ringed by dazzling white sand. Where the encircling reefs appeared, the water turned from aquamarine to a translucent, glacial green, as if lit from below. Soon there was no land in sight, and nothing to see except the occasional flying fish, or dolphins playing in our wake. By now, I'd learnt what heeling mean. The trade winds mostly kept the yacht leaned over on the same side, at the same angle. Unfortunately, the porthole in the galley was on that side, and always underwater, so it was like looking into the window of a washing machine on full cycle. This did nothing to help my ever-lurking seasickness. I peeled, chopped, and cleaned up until I had to run to the deck and stare at the horizon. Then Dag took over everything. He was able to whip up delicious concoctions even in adverse conditions, a skill honed on our kayaking trips. And now he had a wealth of ingredients to choose from and a generous space to work in. We feasted on coq au vin, crab pasta with bruschetta, steaks, and grilled fish. Everyone was pleased with his cooking. Soren floated the idea of us staying on beyond the Solomon Islands, as far as the Philippines. It was tempting.

After five days at sea, we arrived at the island of Efate in Vanuatu and tied up to the dock in Port Vila's marina. Suddenly, there was a social whirl around us. People yelled greetings from other boats. Happy hour at the thatched-roof clubhouse turned into a party. A local band belted out Western pop songs. The dance floor heaved. In the shouted conversations at the bar, I heard accents from England, Australia, North America, Scandinavia, France, and Italy. A guy from California – one of our neighbours on the dock – told me he had been "in investments," retired at 40, and now spent months each year sailing in the South Pacific. "I hope you got well stocked up in Fiji," he yelled in my ear. "There are no air conditioned supermarkets in this town. Want another drink?"

I wasn't in a party mood. I went back to the boat, poured myself a glass of wine, and sat up on deck. Next to the marina, there was an open-air market. Earlier, I'd seen women padding along, balancing baskets of pineapples and papaya on their heads, others sitting on the hard-baked mud arranging piles of taro, sweet potato, and cassava on banana leaves. Soren had told me people came from all over this island, and nearby ones, to sell their produce. The market was closed now, but some of the vendors were sleeping there. A couple of women lay side by side on empty sacks, their arms over their faces as if to block out the glare of street lamps. A stray cat rubbed against their bare feet. It seemed all wrong to be sitting aboard a multimillion-dollar yacht, while close by some women were too poor to afford a cheap hotel room for the night.

This feeling crystallized a few days later, when we stopped off in Espirito Santo, Vanuatu's biggest island, and anchored in a bay wrapped around with dense jungle. It was an ominous, brooding place, oppressively hot and humid. The sky was heavy with cumulus clouds; during periodic showers, fat raindrops bounced off flat, grey, silky water. Two fishers dressed in ragged shorts paddled past in a dugout canoe. At their feet were a few parrotfish. Dag and I called out greetings. Did they want to sell the fish? They just stared at us – and the boat – with blank expressions and carried on. Suddenly, I knew we wouldn't be going further than the Solomons on *Swedish Caprice*. Its luxury and ease were seductive, but the wealth it represented was putting a barrier between me and the places I was travelling through.

"Our fancy kayak will seem just as alien to local people," warned Dag. He was right, but he was also eager to get into the wilds. After six more days of open-ocean sailing, we woke one morning to see the southern-most islands of the Solomons slipping by. Steep forested ridges. Clouds of mist hanging in the valleys. For months we had stared at maps of this large archipelago, trying to imagine it. And now here it was.

13

Swapping a floating palace for a decrepit ferry with overflowing toilets was a severe reality check. Yet it was the only way for us to get from Honiara, the tiny capital of the Solomon Islands, to the first of a series of huge lagoons 200 kilometres to the northwest, where we planned to start paddling. We'd been warned to get on board the *Iuminau* long before departure, but even three hours ahead the passenger deck was packed. People reclined on mats chewing sticks of sugar cane, or leaned against sacks of coconuts. Heaped around them were stalks of bananas, live pigs trussed and wrapped in bright cotton, chickens in baskets. When we appeared, hands reached out to help us with our heavy luggage, and there was a flurry of shuffling to make space for us. As more passengers came aboard, the shuffling continued, until I was almost sitting on top of a small child who stared at me unblinking while her father searched through her hair for nits.

"What in disfela basket?" asked the man in Pidgin, indicating the bag I was sitting on.

My reply, "*Kanu*," was a conversation stopper. He looked at me as if I was mad and returned to scouring his daughter's scalp.

An hour after the *Iuminau* departed, a grey-haired man began picking his way through the crowd toward us.

"Where are your children?" he asked loudly, in a crisp English accent.

On hearing we had none, his face fell.

"I am so sorry. I will pray that God sends you a son."

Jim was a retired schoolteacher from the village of Mbili, in Marovo Lagoon, where we intended to disembark. He was also an active member of the Seventh Day Adventist Church, and when he'd spotted two foreigners on board, he decided to hit us up for a donation.

"Who has invited you to stay at Mbili?" he asked, as he wrote out a receipt for the money we gave him. No one, we admitted.

"But we will arrive at night! The people believe in spirits. They will be afraid when they see two white people appear from the darkness. I will tell them you are my *wantoks* from overseas, and that you have come to stay in my house."

Wantoks is a loose term referring to relatives and close friends. Custom demanded that Solomon Islanders always helped their *wantoks*, even if they turned up uninvited. "So my explanation will satisfy my neighbours," Jim concluded.

"*Em wantok bilong yu?*" asked the man next to me, pointing to Jim as he made his way back through luggage and people. "Is he your relative?"

"*Bilong me*," I replied, relieved that, in some senses, it was now true.

Around midnight, the engines slowed. While the anchor was being dropped, Jim came to get us. Two large motorized dugouts appeared from the dark. We followed Jim into one of them. Our bags were perched atop sacks and cloth-wrapped bundles in the other canoe, which slid away ahead of us.

Ten minutes later, we were standing on a beach. Fireflies twinkled in the trees. The air was damp and sweetly scented. Jim's house stood on stilts at the edge of the forest. One of its thatched window shutters was propped open with twigs, and through it we could see the soft glow of a kerosene lamp. When we walked in, Jim's wife, Linethy, started in alarm. But once Jim had explained our appearance, she smiled. "Lucky he found you," she said, then turned to me. "You want the toilet?"

She led me to a rocky section of the beach, where she turned to give me privacy.

"Where are your children?" she asked on the way back. It was too dark for me to see her reaction to my answer.

We slept on a mat in the corner of the main room. Mosquitos whined around our ears, and cats fought beneath the house. I dozed off for what felt like minutes, before awaking to roosters crowing, chickens squawking, dogs barking, a radio playing in a nearby house. A toddler appeared in the doorway, screeched in alarm, and fled.

Over a breakfast of pawpaw, coconut biscuits, and water from the rain catchment tank, we chatted with Jim and Linethy. Mbili was a Seventh Day Adventist village, so tea, coffee, and alcohol were forbidden.

"Sometimes your *wantoks* come in their yachts," said Jim. "They bring us many problems. They trade beer and whiskey for carvings, they give our young men bad ideas. They go with spears onto our reefs, and they catch our fish without permission, without compensation. You must tell your *wantoks* not to do such things."

Before we left Canada, we had learned that almost every inch of land in the Solomons was privately owned under a complicated system of customary tenure. Jim explained he was a primary landowner who gives secondary landowners the right to build houses, grow food, and to fish on the surrounding reefs. As 90 per cent of Solomon Islanders were living from subsistence fishing and farming, these rights were jealously guarded. It was clear that camping and fishing without permission would be akin to someone breaking into our house, sleeping on the sofa, and raiding the fridge. When we took out a map to show Jim our intended route, he swept his finger across the bottom end of Marovo Lagoon, including its islands and reefs.

"This is all my land. I give you permission to stay there. You have been very generous to our church, so there will be no charge."

In the shade of an enormous banyan tree, it took us an hour to assemble the kayak, and as long again to pack it. We hadn't yet established a system for what went where, so there was much discussion and rearrangement of dry bags and equipment. A crowd of villagers sat close by watching us. When we were almost ready, we smeared every inch of exposed skin with sun block and donned wide-brimmed hats and sunglasses. The curiosity of our audience was turned up several notches.

"They want to know why you are doing these strange things," said Jim.

We explained that, without the hats and cream, our skin would turn the colour of hibiscus blossoms, and without the glasses, the sun would blind us. The villagers gave us pitying looks, and we paddled off feeling rather foolish.

Marovo Lagoon stretched away before us for over a hundred kilometres. The temperature was around 34°C, the humidity almost 100 per cent. After less than an hour in the kayak, I had sweated off all my sunblock, my sunglasses kept sliding down my nose, and my hat felt unbearably heavy. After two hours, I was convinced we were paddling through treacle. After three hours, we finally reached a small island and the sand beach where Jim had given us permission to camp. Once we'd staggered ashore, unpacked our gear, hauled our kayak, and set up the tent, I collapsed under a tree and announced I was never moving again.

We woke at dawn to a pattering sound on the dome roof of the tent. Scattered over the beach all around it were fist-sized blossoms with pink petals cradling long scarlet stems. They were dropping from the trees above us, releasing a sweet, heady smell as they landed. The lagoon was still as glass. The sky was streaked with pink and violet, and there was an orange glow on the horizon. A shimmering lizard darted over my feet. Huge birdwing butterflies alighted on the kayak, which was lying next to the tent, attracted to its red colour. Parrots chattered in the branches above us; a white cockatoo with lemon tail feathers flashed by. I reached for my notebook, jotted down the date, and wrote, "This is nothing short of a miracle."

We spent two months exploring different parts of the Solomons. Sometimes we reached places far from any settlements, like the Arnavon Islands, a few uninhabited scraps of land sculpted by wind and waves out in the Manning Strait. Our campsite was on a soft white sand beach. Beyond it lay a picture-perfect lagoon with such a profusion of corals and fish it was off the amazement scale. At its edge was a sheer cliff where shafts of sunlight were swallowed up by shadowy depths, and huge parrot and grouper fish advanced curiously upon the two strange creatures entering their domain. I only peeked over the edge of the cliff, preferring to snorkel in the safety of the shallows. But Dag spent hours exploring it, using a weight belt, flippers, and great lungfuls of air to free-dive.

When I wasn't snorkeling, I moved from one shady spot to another. Weathered grey coconuts littered the sand. Hermit crabs busily crawled about. Gawky megapode birds crashed around in the bushes. The branches above me swayed as red parrots hopped from branch to branch, pecking at flowers and scolding each other. It was too hot to do much but lie back and think. I thought about Dag, swimming and diving beyond the reef in open water. What if a tiger shark attacked him? Or if he held his breath too long and lost consciousness? Where, in this expanse of sea and sky, could I go for help? How long had Dag been underwater now? Just as panic started to grip me, his head would pop up. Sunlight glinted on his body as it curved back into a dive, and finally his flippers slid beneath the surface of the water.

In other areas, when we thought we were in the middle of nowhere, a man would appear in a dugout canoe, on his way to a garden that was far from his home or to go fishing on a reef. We always fell into conversation, and inevitably we got an invitation to the man's village. I loved these arrivals. From a distance, we'd see leaf huts, often on stilts over the water. Then we were spotted, and children ran up and down the beach, their whoops of excitement carrying over the water. By the time we reached the shallows, a crowd of adults had gathered to help us unload and carry our gear and kayak.

Back in the early 1990s, the main form of transport in these villages was by dugout canoe, and most Solomon Islanders had learned to paddle before they could walk. The fact that we had arrived at a village by water, under our own steam, often from many kilometres away, gained us immediate respect and some shared understanding. And the men of the village were hugely curious about the kayak. They would gather around it, stroking the hull, putting their heads inside the cockpits to examine the frame and the rudder system, chattering excitedly about the double-bladed paddles. And then they would take turns going for a spin, the ones on shore laughing uproariously at the men navigating this strange boat.

Usually, we stayed with a family. But on Santa Isabel Island every village had a guest house for visiting dignitaries, such as church leaders, politicians, or NGOs. Foreigners in a kayak, though – we were the first.

In Samasodu village we were ushered to the guest house, where we sat gratefully in a cool, airy room, its floor made of bamboo and mangrove wood slats, the walls and roof covered in dried pandanus leaves. As usual, our privacy was short-lived, as an audience of little people gathered around us. The children were gorgeous. Due to a genetic trait in Melanesia, some of them had mops of blond hair contrasting with their brown skin. They tentatively touched the pile of dry bags heaped in a corner and our sandals lying next to them. When Dag spread out a map on the floor and started annotating it with comments about our route that day, they gradually surrounded him, taking turns to stroke his hairy arms, his beard, staring at him as if he just landed from another planet – which in a sense he had. And when we tried out our Pidgin English, "*Wefalas go lukim haus bilong yu?*" (Can we visit your house?), they rolled about, helpless with laughter.

The head man of the village came to see us, and we had gifts ready to compensate for our stay, precious things we'd brought from Canada – fishing lures and wires, sandpaper for carving, packs of needles and sewing thread. And, for the children, balloons. Aware of leaving plastic behind, we eked these out, just a couple per village. We blew them up, tied them, then handed them over. In seconds, the kids were outside, batting the balloons between them. When the first one burst, there was shocked silence. A boy ran in looking stricken.

"Baloon im no more!" he cried.

"No problem," we said.

He ran out to report this, and soon the cry was echoing across the village.

"No problem! No problem!"

Dag was a magnet for the kids. They followed him everywhere, and he had endless patience with them. He was in awe of the skills they acquired at a really young age. Little boys no bigger than toddlers fearlessly paddled tiny dugout canoes their fathers had carved for them, climbed trees to cut down fruits, dove into the lagoon and surfaced with sea cucumbers. Once, I watched in horror as a boy around 4 years old sat holding a machete as long as his torso and repeatedly smashed it on the ground between his outspread legs to break up twigs. I wanted to grab it from him; I was terrified he might chop off a finger, a hand, his penis.

Dag insisted I leave him be. He knew what he was doing, he told me; he'd probably been wielding a machete for two years already. This was all part of his learning.

"I love the way kids are so independent in these villages," he said, time and again. "It's the way I'd like to raise a child, instead of constantly instilling fears and insecurity."

Like I would, I thought.

For the girls, of course, things were a bit different. Toting their baby siblings on their hips, they went to the family's garden – a patch of earth in the jungle – to help tend the cassava and taro plants, and filled buckets of water from a stream and carried them back to the village on their heads. All practice for when they would marry and take on a big workload of growing food, cooking, washing, and childrearing.

At first, the women in the villages regarded us shyly, letting their menfolk quiz us and show us around. But, eventually, and particularly with me, curiosity overcame them. They invited me to their gardens, into their kitchens, and to collect water. Samasodu was one of the few settlements we came to that had a water system – a standpipe where women gathered to wash their pots and clothing, fill up big jugs to take home, and gossip. One morning, I joined them with our frying pan and sooty kettle, and it was clear the day's gossip was about me.

"What is the purpose of your journey?" asked one woman, scrubbing a handful of sandy soil over my kettle.

We'd been asked this countless times, and I'd never found a satisfactory answer. The concept of deliberately seeking adventure was alien in a place where people's lives revolved around the basics of survival.

"Is it true you left all your children behind in your country?" asked her companion, who had commandeered my frying pan and was busily removing its nonstick surface.

"I have no children," I told her.

She stared at me, aghast. "No children? Why not?"

The reasons were too complicated to explain, so I gave my usual shrug in reply.

"What about your *wantoks*?" she asked.

I told her about my two brothers, living far away from me in England and Ireland, and my six nieces and nephews. This seemed to cheer her greatly.

"I have five children," she told me. "But only three are with me. You must ask your *wantoks* to help you. I gave my sister my two youngest because she is barren like you."

I tried to imagine how my brothers and their wives would react to such a request. I was about to explain that adoption was far less casual in my home country, but she was so obviously satisfied with her solution to my dilemma that I thought better of it.

Gradually, I began to see why Dag was so taken by how children were raised in the Solomons. They flowed in and out of houses and through extended family groups. Though they were clearly loved and cared for, they weren't endlessly fussed over. They were given responsibilities early on. In another village, I helped a woman called Merver prepare dinner in a smoky cooking hut next to her house. While she wrapped taro and cassava roots in banana leaves and laid them on hot stones, I worked on the slippery cabbage, discarding each stem and shredding the leaves. Just outside the door, Merver's son sat astride a log, vigorously grating the insides of coconut shells. He heaped the flesh into a bowl and, with his hands, squeezed out its thick, white juice. Merver stirred this into some warm water, added the cabbage and the contents of a tin of tuna I'd given her, and let the mixture simmer over the open fire.

"How old is your son?" I asked her. I was guessing about 9. She looked vague.

"He was born in the season of the ngali nut," she said. "And I have another, younger, who was born in the season of the pineapple."

The sun set, fast and dramatically, lighting up great thunderheads that bubbled from the horizon. After eating dinner on the deck, built on stilts over the water, the family retreated, and we laid out our sheet sleeping bags. Around dawn, I was woken by an archerfish that missed its insect prey and squirted me through the split bamboo floor. For a few minutes I lay listening to the gentle slap of waves against the stilts, the snuffling of a child inside the house, a gecko rustling in the thatch above my head, the pops and trills of birds in the jungle. Opening my eyes, I peered down through the floor slats to where our kayak bobbed peacefully next to the family's dugout canoe. The sky was streaked with pink and violet. I felt completely happy. We'd been in the Solomons for over two months. I didn't want to leave.

∾

Like Dag back in Haida Gwaii, I kept putting all thoughts of departure to the back of my mind. We were on Vaghena Island in the northwest corner of the Solomons when he reminded me it was less than a week until our flight to Australia. We had missed a ferry that would have taken us to Honiara, on Guadalcanal Island, via a fairly direct route. There was another option, but it was on a "milk run," and I couldn't bear the thought of five days aboard a decrepit, cockroach-infested ship.

"Let's paddle to Noro on New Georgia," I suggested. "From there, we can get a boat or bush plane to Honiara."

Dag looked at me, wide-eyed. "Paddle there? Are you kidding? We'd be on open ocean for about 65 kilometres, and then there'd be another 30 or so kilometres along the coast."

"We can set out before dawn," I said.

"What if bad weather moves in? Do you realize how committing a crossing like that is?"

"We're fit and acclimatized," I said breezily. "It will nicely round off our time here."

"It might round us off as well," Dag retorted. Later, he admitted that, because of all his crazy plans I had agreed to, he felt he couldn't say no.

∾

When we paddled away from Vaghena, the moon had set, the sky was inky black, and the sea so flat and calm it was a perfect mirror for the stars. Dawn brought a cloud cover that kept the morning relatively cool. Around eight, there was a short burst of rain, then the sun burned off the clouds, and our shirts steamed dry. Behind us, Vaghena was a faint line on the horizon. Far ahead, across a vast expanse of cobalt blue water, we could see the peak of the volcanic island of Kolombangara.

It's one thing to paddle a few miles offshore – although being in striking distance of land is not a guarantee of safety, psychologically, it is reassuring. But an open ocean crossing, I discovered, is quite a different matter. You simply have to keep an eye on the compass, keep paddling, and, if you're lucky enough to have good conditions, hope they hold.

We had no storms to contend with, no strong currents, no headwind. In fact, there was no wind at all. The air was so still it felt like the day was holding its breath. Heat hung from the sky, a heavy, damp, oppressive curtain. I was desperate to go for a swim and cool down. But this part of New Georgia Sound was renowned for its tiger sharks. We'd heard that fishers came out here with rattles made of giant clamshells and coconut shells strung onto thick vines and shook them in the water to summon up the sharks. "Sharks are always watching and listening out there," one man had told us.

All morning the memory of his words had stopped me going overboard. When I needed to pee, I hung over one side of the kayak, while Dag stabilized it by leaning over on the other side. Finally, neither of us could resist. We scrambled out of the cockpits and swam under and around the kayak. The water was around 28 degrees, but compared to the air temperature and humidity, it felt refreshingly cool. Suddenly, from the corner of my eye, I saw something long and white below me. I knew that splashing attracts the attention of sharks. Panic overrode this knowledge and propelled me to the kayak in a frenzy of flailing limbs.

"There's something in the water!" I yelled at Dag, as I hauled myself on board.

He was floating on his back, his arms behind his head, his chest puffed out to give him buoyancy. "It's a length of toilet paper," he said calmly. "It came out of your shorts pocket."

Around one, the sun began its serious torment. Heat was a physical entity. It hammered on our heads and sucked the moisture from our bodies. Our shirts stuck to our salt-encrusted skin. My arms felt like pieces of machinery that had been programmed to paddle and paddle and paddle. Every hour we went overboard for a short swim; I no longer thought about sharks.

During the afternoon, the islands of Kolombangara and New Georgia gradually eased up from the horizon and began to loom large. By six o'clock, we could make out individual trees on the ridges of New Georgia. We planned to find a beach where we could camp, then set out at dawn for the last stretch to the settlement of Noro. With the end in sight, everything in my body started to hurt, the water felt thick and viscous, and pushing a paddle through it was a terrible effort. As the sun slipped away, the clouds shrouding the summit of the volcano turned a vivid orange. Darkness fell fast. It shrouded the jungle on the slopes ahead of us, but a warm wind blew offshore, bringing with it the heavy scent of tropical flowers. We could hear breaking waves, a sign we were approaching a coral reef. Once we were close enough to see the white foam of the surf, we inched along, hoping for dark patches where the coral was still submerged and we could cross. There were no dark patches.

In the cockpit behind me, Dag cursed. "Of course, it's December 20. Almost the lowest tide of the year."

And the tide was still dropping. We had no option except wait for it to rise. We carried on paddling in the direction of Noro.

My vision was playing tricks. When the moon rose, I kept seeing a gargantuan standing wave rearing up from the sea that would then transform into Kolombangara. Of more concern was the enormous flickering light bulb, low in the sky, moving around us about a kilometre away. A thunderhead cloud, illuminated by flashes of forked lightning.

"What will happen if we end up in the midst of that cloud?" I asked Dag.

"We'd be toast. Literally."

Of course. Our metal mast, the highest point on this whole stretch of water, was a perfect lightning rod.

There was nothing we could do. Around midnight, Dag dropped a sea anchor to stop the boat drifting too far, then we wriggled down into our cockpits, folding our legs around the bags of gear stored under the decks. Exhaustion overcame worry, and we both slept for a couple of hours while the cloud moved away.

Shortly after dawn, we crossed the reef and headed toward a beach. All I could think about was getting out of the boat and finding a place to lie flat. As we got closer, I thought I was hallucinating again. The rocks were undulating and making strange clicking sounds. Abruptly, Dag stopped paddling.

"No way are we getting out there," he said.

Covering the shoreline, from the water's edge back to the forest wall, was a deep, writhing layer of large land crabs. There were thousands upon thousands of them, clambering and scuttling over each other. At a safe distance, we floated and watched. Each crab had an egg sac on its lower abdomen, and when it scrambled down to the edge of the rocks, it raised its pincers, wriggled its body in a comical hula-hula dance, and released the eggs into the water. Then it turned and fought its way back against the tide of oncoming crabs. The water was murky with eggs, and colourful fish were milling about, enjoying the feast.

We kept paddling, sure that the crab layer would soon peter out. But it went on for a couple of kilometres and what felt like a lifetime. Finally, we anchored the kayak in shallow water and staggered onto a beach of sharp volcanic rock for a short break. Behind it, a patch of jungle had been cleared and planted with cassava. I lay on a fallen log, while Dag opened a can of tuna and spread it onto biscuits.

"We've got company," I heard him say. "They just paddled up."

I opened my eyes to see two boys standing a short distance away, staring at us. Dag asked them how far it was to Noro.

"Too far," replied one.

Thirty hours after leaving Vaghena, we arrived at Noro, a small settlement dominated by a large Japanese-owned fish processing plant. The workers who ran down to meet us were astonished to learn where we had come from. They plied us with questions, but we could barely hear them over the noise: the clanging of skips being loaded onto cargo boats, machines pounding inside concrete buildings, trucks revving their engines. It was like emerging from one strange dream and going straight into another. Close by, a man was holding a large hose, spraying a skipload of fish with fresh water. He attached it to a hook on a wall, and we took turns standing under its strong, cold gush. It was the nearest thing I could imagine to pure bliss.

14

"Kayaking along the Ganges?" cried Mr. Gupta, a government official. He stared at us across his desk, which was piled high with dusty files and papers. "You must be potty!"

We had flown to India with a grand plan. We would transport our kayak to Haridwar, where the Ganges leaves the Himalayas and enters the great northern plains, and paddle to Varanasi, thus travelling along the most revered part of the river, between two great pilgrimage sites. But we'd been unable to find maps or any information about our route; we hoped to source these once we were in New Delhi. And we expected to find encouragement there. We'd read that Hindus regard the Ganges as the holiest of rivers, embodying a goddess, Mother Ganga. That its waters offer pilgrims the chance of spiritual purification, of escaping the endless cycle of reincarnation. But as we climbed one dank stairwell after another, and sat in gloomy government offices, we heard the same story. Everyone thought we were crazy. We were warned about bandits, unsanitary conditions in villages, polluted water. No one could advise us on the levels of the river, or distances, or anything that might help us along the way. Until we met Mr. Koli. He ran an adventure tour company. He estimated the paddling distance was at least 1500 kilometres. "But Mother Ganga floods her banks and changes direction during every monsoon, so you must ask her," he said.

"The journey will spiritually uplift you," Mr. Koli continued. "And it will be a great adventure. I know of no one who has kayaked on this part of the Ganges. You must take someone to assist you. I will send you my best man."

His "best man," Bapi Sankar, agreed to accompany us for at least three weeks. A Bengali in his early 20s, he was small and wiry, with a mop of black curls, a dazzling smile, and heaps of self-confidence.

"I've done a wilderness survival course," he told us. "I can catch fish and turtles and make shelters in the woods. I've guided white water kayaking tours, I've led treks in the Garhwal Himalayas, I can identify wildflowers, and I was once charged by an elephant and almost killed!"

It was highly unlikely that any of these skills or experience would be needed on our trip. But what really impressed us was that, despite being from a wealthy urban family, Bapi loved rural life and was as eager as us to engage with local people.

$\sim$

Right from the start, the trip was mind-bending. We inched our way through the maze of channels the great river shrinks to during the pre-monsoon season. We would paddle for hours, seeing only sand, soil, and water. Rounding a bend, suddenly there would be a bright splash of colour across this monochrome landscape: a field of marigolds, or a group of women that had just finished washing and were holding up saris to dry, the wind transforming them into bright, fluttering flags.

We paddled past floating corpses and saw dogs swimming out to chew on them. We stepped ashore next to human bones we sometimes had to walk across. Initially, these sights were deeply shocking, but soon we came to acknowledge them as part of the cycle of life and death on the Ganges. Ironically, it was here that my fear of loss began to diminish. For the first time, Dag and I talked to each other about our own deaths. If one of us perished on this part of the trip, we agreed, we wanted to be burned atop a pile of dung and wood, our ashes put into the river. The possibility wasn't too remote: banditry was rife along the river, and a man brandishing a rifle had already chased us. Sometimes we spent nights out on the flood plain, never sleeping well, aware of how easily we could join the bodies floating downstream.

As we were travelling during a holy month, we came across many encampments of sadhus and their followers, living in temporary huts built from straw. They always welcomed us to stay with them. Sleep was also difficult here, as they chanted and rang bells throughout the night. But we felt safe. They told us that, because our boat was red – a holy colour – and because we were travelling between Haridwar and Varanasi, we were on a pilgrimage ourselves. So the sacred river would protect us. We took this to heart and started bathing every day in the river like them, and other pilgrims we saw along the way, fully immersing ourselves three times to receive the blessing of Goddess Ganga.

Occasionally, we stayed in villages. One morning, the current took us close to a riverside cremation. When the men standing next to the pyre waved us over, Bapi insisted we go ashore. I was hesitant at first; it seemed like an imposition.

"Maria, we have to, they are requesting this," he said.

The body lay inside a burning pile of wood and dung. Two men tended to the blaze with bamboo poles. About 15 others stood to one side. They wore *dhotis* and were wrapped in blankets, with only their faces and thin legs showing.

"*Namaste*," I greeted the men, pressing my palms together and raising my hands to my forehead.

"*Namaste!*" they delightedly chorused.

Our bow hit the shore with a soft bump. Something on the funeral pyre cracked and popped; flakes of windblown ash pattered onto the deck of the kayak and against my face. There was an acrid smell, with disquieting overtones of fat left sizzling too long in the pan.

We were invited to sit and watch as the fire burned down. Normally, only men were allowed to attend cremations, but an exception had been made for this Western woman who had appeared in a strange boat. Lumps of *gur*, crude sugar cane, were passed around. An old man with wizened skin handed me one as big as a tennis ball and watched intently as I started to nibble it. Eventually, the charred remains of the body got swept into the river, and the chief mourners followed it for a ceremonial bath. Through Bapi, we learned the body on the pyre had been an 85-year-old man who had died only hours before in a village five kilometres away. His remains, and the fuel for the fire, had been brought to the riverbank in the tractor-trailer parked behind us. The mourners believed our appearance was auspicious. That it had brought them a blessing they wished to carry to their village. The matter had already been decided for us – several men were hauling our fully loaded kayaks up to the tractor-trailer. Before long, we were heading away from the river along a bumpy track through fields of yellow mustard.

Gessapur was a village of about 800 people. We rumbled past flat-roofed houses crowded together along lanes of deeply rutted mud. A gate swung open. We drove in and parked next to a manger of tethered buffalos. Beyond was a courtyard, with a few rooms leading off it. A *chapoy* – a wooden bed frame with a base woven from rope – was pulled out for us to sit on. Beakers of milky chai were thrust into our hands. A crowd of people formed around us, staring and firing questions at Bapi. It was decided that Dag needed a shave, and he was led off to find a barber. I was left in the courtyard, surrounded by women. While the men were there, they had covered their faces with the ends of the scarves draped over their heads. Now they let these fall, and their inhibitions with them. They squatted on the ground around me, giggling at my attire. I couldn't blame them – it was a ridiculous mishmash of dusty clothing. The nights and mornings on this part of the Ganges were cold, and at our campsite that day I'd dressed in pink thermal leggings under shorts. Before joining the crema-tion, I'd pulled out my faded yellow South Pacific *sulu* – a long length of cotton cloth – and wrapped it around my waist. On top of that were my pink thermal top and an orange kayak jacket. The women had a discus-sion, then one slipped away, quickly returning with an armful of fabric and a brass bowl filled with warm water. Six of the women led me into a cool, dark, mud-walled room off the courtyard; the others crowded the doorway. Their glass bracelets tinkling, they removed my clothes, right down to my underwear. They washed my face and feet. They dressed me in a short bodice that left my midriff bare, and a long cotton petticoat tied at my waist. Then came metres of fine, magenta silk, which they expertly folded, wrapped, and tucked into a sari. My hair was combed and oiled, a small, red, plastic disk was stuck onto my forehead to indicate I was mar-ried, and bangles were pushed over my hands onto my wrists.

The women stepped back to admire their handiwork, and their friends clapped with delight. I was reunited with Dag, who was equally spruced up – clean shaved except for a moustache, and wearing a new *kurta* – a long, loose shirt – over his jeans.

"How do you like your husband, Maria?" asked Bapi. "Isn't he so handsome now?"

Then we were led around the village. We managed only a few steps along the narrow street before a man came flying though a wooden doorway and dragged us into his courtyard, offering tea and snacks. And so it went on for several hours. Everyone was curious about us and anxious to invite us into their homes. There was no real privacy in Gessapur, as the flat roofs of the houses allowed views into neighbouring courtyards. When one family treated us to potato pakora, word quickly spread, and the next-door family would serve us potato and onion pakora, along with milk curd. This wasn't just competition, it was also the matter of *atithi devo bhava* – the belief that guests have to be welcomed and looked after, as if they are reincarnated gods. We, in turn, felt duty bound to force down the great quantities of food and drink offered to us, as any refusal was met with open dismay.

During the course of this long afternoon, I got a sense of the average workload of the women in the village. They carried dung from the fields to make into patties for fuel, or to mix with water to form mud that they smeared onto the walls and floors of their houses. They washed clothes by hand, and pressed them with irons filled with hot coals. They milked buffalo, spun and carded wool, winnowed lentil seeds, and chopped up fodder for their animals. They cooked and cleaned, cared for children, and tended to demanding husbands.

On our first night in the village, we stayed with Sidraj, the son of the man who had been cremated, in his small house at the edge of the village. He lived there with his wife, Durta, and four children. It was clear they were one of the poorer families, but it seemed a matter of pride that he hosted us. While he sat outside with Bapi and Dag, sharing chillums of marijuana, I joined Durta in the kitchen, where she was squatting on the mud floor, preparing dinner. She was pale, scrawny, and pregnant with her fifth baby. She bent over the fire, feeding it with twigs and dung, and blowing on it to keep the flame strong enough. While the curry bubbled, she mixed maize flour with water, kneaded the dough, and rolled small balls of it into flat rounds on a stone slab. She cooked the rotis one at a time in a dry pan, transferring them to some hot coals and leaving them there just long enough to puff up without burning.

When it was time to eat, I was called to join the men in the courtyard. Durta kept darting from the kitchen to replenish our bowls of curry and bring us more rotis. The children were nowhere in sight.

"Will Durta come and eat with us?" I asked Bapi. "And the children?"

"In the villages, the women and children must wait until the men of the family have finished," Bapi explained. He registered my horrified expression. "This is the tradition, Maria."

I quietly finished my bowl of curry and refused more, hoping Durta and her little ones would have a decent dinner.

We slept in the room and on the *charpoy* where Sidraj's father had died the night before. A small oil lamp set in a wall niche threw weird shadows on the thatch ceiling. The previous night, we'd been camping on the riverbank, worried about bandits. Now, despite the morbid situation, I quickly fell into a deep dreamless sleep.

Next day, we were moved to stay with another family. We weren't consulted about this, or if we wanted to spend longer in the village. These were executive decisions, relayed to Bapi who shared them with us. I was relieved on both counts. I didn't want to leave Gessapur yet, and I knew we were stretching the means of Sidraj's family and putting extra burdens on Durta. Sidraj was gracious about our departure. He insisted we were now part of his family, that we could wander where we wished, but his house would always be our home.

What we thought would be one more night turned into five. Our new host was Shiv Kumar Choudhary, who lived with his mother, Ewartadevi, his wife, Reeta, their 1-year-old baby girl, Ritika, and his younger brother, Rahul. Since their father had died three years earlier, the two men had been looking after the family business. They had over a hundred acres of farmland that was worked by labourers. Their house had two courtyards, several rooms for living and sleeping in, and, to my great relief, a latrine. Although it was only a hole in the ground below a mud brick wall next to the manger, it offered more privacy than I'd had the previous night, when under cover of darkness I'd gone into a field beyond Sidraj's house, found a thicket of bamboo, and almost stumbled over a man who was squatting there. This would be embarrassing in any circumstances, but a woman trespassing onto the men's toilet area was breaking countless taboos. Now, by comparison, I could relax, watched only by a tethered buffalo with pieces of grass stuck to its nose.

As an official "auntie" of the family, I was expected to stay in the courtyard with the women, while Dag and Bapi went off on forays, to hunt wild boar, take motorbike rides, and visit other villages. This was fine with me; I was happy to hang out with Ewartadevi, Reeta, and baby Ritika. One day drifted into another. In the spacious main courtyard, an old servant in a thin cotton sari used ash to scrub pots to a shine. Reeta filled buckets of water at a hand pump, and Ewartadevi stoked a fire to warm the water so I could wash, while I held Ritika. As I bounced her on my knee, the tiny bells hanging from silver chains around her plump ankles tinkled prettily. She stared at me through dark eyes ringed with kohl to ward off evil spirits. When she started to cry, Ewartadevi scooped her up, took out her wrinkled breast, and let the baby suck on her nipple. Women from other houses arrived, via the system of interlocking roofs and courtyards, to sit, watch my every move, and discuss me. They picked through the contents of my toiletry bag, paged through my notebooks, watched in amazement when I inserted my contact lenses. The boldest ones sat very close, lifted up my sari to look at my body, feel my breasts, and pat my stomach. I was learning more Hindi words; I knew what the burning question was: *bachche*, children.

Bapi was brought in to help explain. He already knew where Dag and I had grown up, where we lived, our professions, and the reasons for this journey down the river. But when it came to how old we were, and information about our family, he had to check with me first. I took a deep breath and told him bluntly.

"I'm 39, and Dag's 34. We don't have children."

Bapi was too flabbergasted at first to translate.

"Maria, you are 39? How can this be? My mother is not so old as that!"

My age, my being older than my husband, and being childless became the village scandal. I was discussed, pointed at, and given long questioning looks. I was taken to the temple for pujas to Parvati, the Hindu goddess of fertility. I felt thoroughly confused. In comparison to these women, I had huge freedoms and opportunities. I had chosen my husband, I could earn my own living, direct my destiny, control my fertility, travel at will. And yet I lacked the one thing that, in their view, gave life purpose – a child. Through Bapi, I could have tried to explain that, in my culture, it was possible to find other means of status and fulfillment, other insurances for old age. I could have admitted I had chosen to be childless. But I said none of those things.

"Reeta is praying you will come back to Gessapur with a baby son," Bapi told me shortly before we left. I knew the subtext. Everyone was feeling sorry for Dag. How did he get stuck with an older, barren wife? He just laughed this off. But I had been rattled by my time in Gessapur. Why was I dragging a kayak around the world instead of being at home and raising a family? What was wrong with me? I was about to turn 40. I kept thinking about something Mum had said during her visit to Canada: "Women have too many choices now. It was easier in my day. The path was more obvious." She hadn't been directly referring to motherhood, but of course I knew what she meant.

～

Bapi left us, and we continued on alone. We missed him, but we had learned some of the local mores and enough Hindi to get by. Fed by tributaries, the Ganges got wider, deeper, busier. Camel trains plodded along carrying sand being dredged from the riverbed to be used in construction. We passed electricity pylons, fort-like pumphouses, villages set on cliffs high above the flood plain with television aerials on tiled roofs, boats ferrying passengers across the river. Warnings about banditry increased. One night, we camped with a gang of rough, heavily armed fishers, figuring – and hoping – this was safer than being alone. The next night, we just kept paddling, too afraid to go ashore. Dawn found us frazzled, fed up with this long journey, wanting it to end. Then we arrived at the *ghats* – the steps leading into the river – of a beautiful village called Sultanpur. We were invited to stay in the courtyard of its temple, even though a wedding was starting. It went on for three magical days; the guests simply gathered around our tent and boat, enfolding us into the lengthy celebrations. When it was over, a woman from the village invited me to her house. She insisted on massaging my feet and calves with oil, an honour usually accorded to elderly women. I thought I was off the hook as far as the children question was concerned. But after the massage she accompanied me back to the temple and made a puja asking that I be granted a son.

After six weeks on the river, we reached Varanasi. From there, we took a train back to Delhi and found a letter waiting for Dag. It was from his college. Due to funding problems, his program was being discontinued. There would be no job for him to return to. We sat in our hotel room, staring at each other. Already on the trip, we'd sold articles and photos to the *New York Times* and the *Guardian*, and I was confident I had excellent material for my next book. We'd been talking about reinventing ourselves as a freelance photographer/writer/adventurer team. We'd acknowledged how dependent we'd become on Dag's monthly paycheques and the medical and dental benefits of his job. Giving those up was a daunting thought. After teetering on the edge of a diving board, afraid to jump, finally we'd been pushed. It was exhilarating. And my chosen path – opting for adventure instead of a family – was once again clear.

~

From India, we flew to Malawi and set off to kayak the eastern side of the third-largest lake in Africa. Along those 600 kilometres, there were no large towns, only small villages and farms. The water was warm, potable, and teeming with fish. It was also home to crocodiles, hippos, and lake flies that hatched in the millions under the surface and rose up in dense, choking clouds. Because the lake was the size of an inland sea, it was often beset by strong winds, storms, big waves, and waterspouts. The fishers we met at our first night's campsite thought we were crazy. "You go all the way in that boat? No engine? Only paddling? You like death?"

They couldn't understand why we would seek out such danger. For them, daily life was dangerous. The country was in the grip of a repressive regime guilty of appalling human rights violations, including suppression of free speech and the press. Prisons were full of political detainees. There was a network of spies, informers, and paramilitary that had everyone on edge, even in the smallest settlements. One of the worst droughts for decades was underway, causing crops to fail. People were going hungry. About a quarter of the population had AIDS, which was referred to as "Slims Disease" – you catch it, lose a lot of weight quickly, and then die. And we constantly heard stories of deaths caused by hippo and crocodile attacks, and by the tiny malarial mosquitos.

Almost every beach we camped on had a village close by. We would seek out the headman, ask permission to stay the night, and give gifts of fishing lures and line and carving equipment, which were always accepted with sheer amazement. We'd pitch our tent on soft sand beneath baobab trees. By dawn next morning, there would already be women and children waiting for us, watching as we made pancakes with flour and milk powder.

"*Mzungu*," the children would whisper. White people. "*Mzungu* food."

The staple diet here was maize or cassava flour mixed with water to form a bland paste, called *nsima*. Salt was rarely added – few could afford it. Sometimes the *nsima* was eaten with relish made from tiny fish boiled into a mush.

The children asked us for everything: discarded tea bags, empty tins, the soup packet from last night's dinner, our clothes, our sunglasses, our watches, soap, flour, sugar, salt. And medicine. Soon we were eking out our medical kit, as Dag treated the people who came to us with suppurating cuts, septic wounds, burns. Those telling us they had headaches, gonorrhea, or stomach ache we had to turn away.

Early one morning, on the beach close to the village of Sanje, a woman walked past our tent on her way to collect water in the lake. We'd met briefly the day before, and on learning we had the same name, she had laughed in delight. But now she was sombre. She whispered that a baby had died in the night.

"Come with me," said Maria.

Outside the house of the bereaved family, a group of woman sat singing hymns and swaying from side to side. From inside came the low insistent wailing of the mother as she grieved over the body of her dead infant. He was her seventh child, Maria told me, and the third she'd lost to malaria. Later, the family would bury him with his siblings in the shade of a giant baobab tree. I was speechless. I felt desperately sorry for the woman in the house, for Maria, and all her neighbours. They couldn't stop having babies. They couldn't stop them from dying. They were trapped by poverty; this village was the start and end of their lives. Then Maria leaned over and asked me how many children I had.

"No children," I said.

"Ooh," she gasped, her face clouding with renewed sadness. "I am so sorry for you."

~

When I returned to our tent, Dag was heading out in a dugout canoe with Herring, Maria's husband, to go fishing. I sat staring at them as they paddled away across the lambent water. Several children had followed me, bringing gifts of baobab tree nuts covered in soft green fuzz. They showed me how to break them open and suck off the tart yellow sherbet coating the seeds. Then the boys practised somersaults and handstands. Two of the girls crept close to me and started stroking my hair and looking through it for nits. Thinking about their fate, I put my arms around them for a hug. Squealing in alarm, they retreated to a safe distance, staring at me through wondering eyes. The boys began jostling about, obviously daring each other to go closer to the *mzungu* and risk being grabbed by her. It turned into a game. Soon I was a snarling monster, chasing the laughing children around the beach. Finally, exhausted, I sprawled on the sand, while they excitedly tugged at my hands, begging me to carry on playing. This is how Dag and Herring found me when they returned from their fishing trip.

"You should take one of these children to your country," said Herring.

I laughed. In the Solomon Islands and India, we'd often heard the same comments, made by parents who jokingly thrust their alarmed offspring at us, exhorting us to make room for them in our kayak. But Herring wasn't joking.

"Why not?" he asked. "Your husband just told me you have no children. Take one of these. Give him a good education. A good life."

I tried to explain that such adoptions were not recognized in our country. We couldn't just turn up with a child; it wasn't possible –

"For *mzungu*," Herring interrupted me, "anything is possible."

15

Arriving in Germany from Malawi, we got a huge culture shock, everything seeming so shiny and orderly and organized. We spent a few days in Munich, getting ready to paddle down the Danube as far as Budapest. Before setting off, we went to see some old friends of Dag's from university days, Marcie and Peter. They were climbers, hikers, and cyclists who liked to go on long trips. I had met them a couple of years earlier, when they visited us in Canada. They had told us then they were planning to have a baby they would take with them on their future adventures.

"We want to spent six months trekking in the Himalayas," Marcie had said. "It would be so cool to have a kid along with us."

Unlike me, she had no hesitation about the prospect of slinging an infant on her back and heading into the wild. "Dag is right," she said, when I recounted the furious row we'd had in the Sea of Cortez. "Babies are tougher than you think."

Now they had a son who was 11 months old. Dag was really looking forward to the visit. He's a talker, a discusser, a big thinker. He loves to have long debates about world affairs and future plans. In Canada, he'd stayed up until the early hours with Marcie and Peter, excitedly discussing ideas for expeditions and creative endeavours. On the way to their apartment, I warned him that things might be different, that he should be prepared for a domestic and baby-centred scene. He didn't seem to be listening.

"Hello! Welcome!" Peter greeted us at the door. "Come in, we are just about to feed the baby."

Their son was strapped into a small chair fixed on the edge of the kitchen table. Newspapers were spread all over the floor. Marcie and

Peter stood on either side of the chair, each with a bowl and spoon in hand, taking turns coaxing the boy to eat. We soon understood the need for the newspapers, as he spat out most of the mush, or, reaching his fingers into his mouth, flung it across the room with impressive strength. Between mouthfuls, he wailed furiously, drowning out any attempts at conversation. I stood back, observing this tableau – the angry baby, the food flying about, the adoring parents, and Dag, gazing in horror at his role models in not-letting-babies-rule-your-life-or-change-you-in-any-way.

There were no long discussions that day about adventure and creativity. Peter and Marcie barely managed to complete a sentence. And when they did, it was about the new family member. Dag had planned to invite them out for dinner, bringing the baby along. But that wouldn't work with his feeding and nap schedule – or theirs. He still woke them several times during the night. And he was teething, which made everything worse.

"We take him out for walks when he is crying a lot, because that helps to calm him sometimes. And we have gone to my parents' place in the countryside for weekends. But, otherwise, we have been nowhere. Really, it is just too complicated," said Marcie.

Their plans to hike in the Himalayas had dissolved. In a year they would start trying for another baby. "Maybe we will travel again when the kids are bigger and can appreciate it," said Peter.

We left before dinnertime. "Feeding a baby in a kayak, we wouldn't need newspapers," I said on the way back. "The food would end up in the sea. The fish would love it."

My joke fell flat.

"I honestly thought that wouldn't happen to them," said Dag.

He soon got another dose of reality.

~

At the end of our paddle trip along the Danube, we received the sad news that my Aunty Madge, who had been dealing with cancer for the past few years, had died. As we arrived in England for the funeral,

Dag developed symptoms of the malaria he must have contracted in Malawi. We stayed with Mum while he recovered. By the time he was well enough to travel again, it was too late for us to go to Alaska, as we would risk running into its storm season. Instead, we decided to take a quick trip to the west coast of Ireland to see my brother, Mick, who had moved to Kerry with his family. And then, to fill the Alaska gap in my book, paddle around the Beara Peninsula, which was bound to produce good material. I suggested to Mum that she come with us as far as Mick's place, and we'd meet up with her after our trip. First, though, I wanted to visit some of my old friends.

As we charged around England and Wales, we kept making last-minute arrangements, often changing these at short notice and turning up later or earlier than we'd promised. Some of our friends, especially those with families and demanding jobs, were exasperated.

"For almost a year you haven't had to keep to anyone's timetable but your own. Now you have to adjust to real life," said Sarah, when we turned up at her house hours late. "It's not fair to expect people to wait around for you."

She was doubly cross because she'd just phoned my mother to ask about our whereabouts.

"She told me no one knows where you are, that John has been trying to contact you. That she's exhausted after her sister's death, sorting out all the paperwork on her own, going to the graveyard alone. Honestly, Maria, it's not on. You should get back there."

We'd been invited to dinner in Sheffield the next night. After that, I decided we'd cut our trip short and return to Wolverhampton. Our hosts, Paul and Janet, had a 3-month-old baby, Will. When we arrived at their house – late – we were introduced to another couple who lived next door. Before coming, they had put their two small children to bed, set up a baby monitor in the room, and brought the speaker with them, so they could hear if either child woke up.

"It's so good to get out for once!" the woman said, knocking back a glass of wine. She turned to me. "Our parents don't live close by, and it's hard to find trustworthy babysitters."

"God, I know what you mean," said Janet. "These days I'm beside myself when I see the inside of a pub."

Dinner was a takeaway from an Indian restaurant, and Janet was handing round a large plate of samosas and onion bhajis.

"Are you going to have a kid, Maria?" she asked, just as I bit into a samosa. Without waiting for a reply, she pressed on. "If you do, for God's sake opt for a Caesarian. Giving birth to Will was bloody awful."

She jumped off her chair and squatted on the floor, making a grimacing face.

"I started to push, like this, and Paul said, no, it's not time, don't push yet, wait."

Paul shook his head. "That's not exactly what I –"

"But I *couldn't* wait," Janet interrupted him. "I just *had* to push, and it was like the parting of the Red Sea. I was torn from here to here, it was like shitting an enormous coconut."

She paused for breath. The other mother was nodding, Paul was wincing, and the rest of us were focusing on our food. Then a gurgling sound came from the speaker.

"Shush!" chorused the neighbours, even though we were already silent. We all listened intently to the snuffling and breathing.

"I think it's okay," the man surmised.

"Turn up the volume, so we don't miss anything," said his wife.

As we helped ourselves to curry, Janet returned to the birth theme.

"My theory is women are supposed to have children between the ages of 17 and 20, when they're all stretchy and pliable *down there*, so they don't rip apart. And afterwards everything springs back into shape. But for us 30-year-olds, well, we're all hardened up, and this ripping happens and then the stitching. Ooh, it's gruesome. How old are you now, Maria?"

This time, it was a mouthful of naan bread that stopped my response.

When the meal was over, we gave our profuse thanks and excuses and headed for the pub.

"Does that happen to everyone?" asked Dag on the way there. "Would it happen to us?"

"Yes to both," I replied.

~

I knew things were going sideways with Mum when I called her the next morning to give her our ETA.

"You better have lunch before you get here," she responded coldly. "I've had no time to shop, and there's no food in the house."

This was a first – feeding her children was the biggest symbol of her love. I called my brother John. It turned out the problem was more than me going away for a few days after the funeral.

"You know how you suggested she could go with you to Ireland?" he said. "She seems to think she's going to follow you the whole way, taking buses and staying in bed and breakfasts and meeting up with you in the evenings."

"I never said that. I meant for her to come as far as Mick and Eileen's house and stay with them."

"Unfortunately, I pointed that out to her and got an earful."

Sitting in Mum's living room a couple of hours later, I tried to explain that our itinerary would depend on weather and tides. That we couldn't predict where we'd end up each night. Sometimes we might be camping on a beach, far from a road.

"So you don't want me to come with you," she responded, and fell into a hurt, bitter silence.

"Of course, I do," I insisted. "But following us on the kayaking trip just won't work."

The next few days were an emotional rollercoaster. In the space of hours, Mum's demeanour switched from hostility to sweetness and back again. She decided she would come with us, packed a bag, and seemed excited. Then she phoned Mick, learned that I hadn't been in touch with him about exact details yet, and blew up. I had left everything to the last minute, I'd treated her very badly, I was thinking about no one except myself. She unpacked her bag. By the next morning, she'd changed her mind again; she was coming. She cooked us a big roast dinner, and made an apple pie.

"What *is* going on?" said Dag in bed that night. "I can't keep up."

I explained that Mum's grief for Madge had dialled up her neediness to maximum. And that I hadn't exactly been a dutiful daughter.

"The problem with having kids," he said, "is that it creates a hole in your heart that can't ever be filled. No matter how often you visit your mum, or how long you stay with her, it will never be enough. She will always crave more."

He yawned and wrapped his arms around me. "I'm glad we're not having any."

"So..." I wriggled in his embrace to keep him awake. "It's off the back burner now?"

"What is?"

"A baby."

"I guess so."

It wasn't a complete shock. He'd been talking about his fears around having a severely damaged child. "I just don't think I could cope," he said now, when I pressed him on the subject. "I'm scared I'd be one of those guys who abandons the family to do his own thing. And then spends the rest of his life feeling guilty about it."

"At least you'd feel guilty," I joked.

"No, honestly, Maria. It's something that haunts me. And, well, I guess I realized you were right. All the crazy stuff we've done on these last trips – they wouldn't have been possible with a kid."

"That's putting it mildly."

"But if we're not going to have kids, we have to keep taking advantage of the freedom that gives us. We've got to keep doing interesting things. Even more interesting."

I thought about the open-ocean crossing in the Solomons; the hippos that grazed around our tent in Malawi while we lay inside, holding our breaths; the floating bodies we bumped into along the Ganges. I wasn't sure I needed life to get any more interesting than that. But I knew what he meant. We could get secure jobs and settle into middle age. Without children, we'd be able to live well, pay off our debts, build up some savings for old age, and still afford nice holidays in boutique resorts. Which was exactly what neither of us wanted.

~

The Beara is one of five peninsulas that reach out like fingers from Ireland's southwest coast. We made our way around it in weather that varied from what the locals called "fine soft days" – steady, light rain – to a big storm that caused us to pack up our kayak and hitchhike along one section of the coast. We camped on beaches where sometimes we woke to find visitors close by – long-bearded goats, cows, a huge bull. We stayed in a room above a tiny pub, where the drinking and music sessions went on until the early hours, and breakfast wasn't served until 10:30 a.m., as well as a hostel that was like a shrine, the walls covered with religious pictures. We consumed so much Guinness I don't know how we managed to paddle.

I kept calling Mick, giving him updates on our progress, and when we expected to return to his house. We arrived there to another frosty reception from Mum.

"What's the problem now?" I asked Mick.

"No idea," he said. "She was fine while you were gone."

She said little during our journey to Dublin, and as we boarded the ferry. We had a four-hour night crossing ahead of us, followed by a long bus ride, and then only a couple of days in Manchester before Dag and I flew back to Canada. I decided to try to clear the air.

"Mum, can we talk?"

She turned to me, her mouth a narrow line.

"Talk about what?"

"About what's upsetting you."

"You should know what's upsetting me," she said tersely. "I shouldn't have to spell it out."

I sighed. It was an old refrain.

"Look, I'm sorry about the muddle over the trip. And I know you were hurt when we left after Aunty Madge's funeral."

Finally, she opened up. "Is it any wonder? I'd just lost my sister, I was dealing with everything, you could have helped, but, no, you had to go off and see your friends instead. It's always been the same."

"My old friends are important to me, Mum. They saw me through some very hard times; they're like family to me."

She swivelled around to face me. "They are not your family! Me, John, and Mick, and their wives, we're your family. We've always been here for you, we always will be. Look at all we've done for you! But you care more about your friends than us."

On the other side of me, Dag had taken out a book. I could sense him trying to shrink in his seat.

"Mum," I said wearily. "I wish you and I could be friends."

She stared at me in shock. Her chin wobbled; behind her glasses, tears welled up and started to flow.

"I thought we were friends!" she cried brokenly.

Instinctively, I knew I had to seize this moment. That if I didn't finally set some boundaries, our dance of guilt would go on endlessly. I had to break something in our relationship in order to rebuild it.

Gently, I reminded her of what she'd said to me on the phone all those years ago. "*You've never been the daughter I wanted.*" That I knew in some ways it was true. That I loved her greatly, but I couldn't bring myself to sacrifice my dreams for hers. I had to make my own life, and fate and circumstances had brought me to a place far away from her. I reminded her of how often I came back to England – up to three times a year. I promised that in the future I would spend more time with her on my visits, but I wanted her to try as well. That the guilt and recriminations were creating an ever widening gulf and preventing us from being friends, as well as mother and daughter.

While I said all this, she wept. The weeping continued for the rest of the crossing, and on the bus ride to Manchester. It was almost five a.m. when we arrived. My brother John met us at the station. He looked at Mum in alarm. She had finally stopped crying, but her eyes were red and her face swollen from all the tears.

"Everything all right?" he asked, as we piled into his car. He gave me a questioning look. I answered with a "tell you later" face.

As soon as we got to his house, Mum had a cup of tea, then went straight to bed.

"What happened?" asked John, once she was out of earshot. I gave him a short synopsis of the hours on the ferry.

"How could you say those things to her?" he retorted. "That was cruel."

And maybe it was. But around 11 o'clock that morning, Mum reappeared in the kitchen. She looked rested and cheerful. She announced she was hungry. Gail cooked her a big breakfast and made soup and sandwiches for the rest of the family. Mum laughed with her grandchildren. She never mentioned our row on the ferry, not on that day or in the years to come. But it changed everything between us. It was as if a festering boil had been lanced, the poison allowed to seep away. I would never fully escape her guilt trips – she was, after all, a master at creating those – but now I could put them into proper perspective. Finally, we were friends. She lived for 19 more years, and our relationship entered a whole new era.

~

In late August 1992, at the end of our year-long trip, we flew back to Vancouver. Our plan was to spend a few days with Dag's mother before kayaking across the Strait of Georgia to our house on Protection Island. When Justina met us at the airport, and I reached to hug her, she placed her hand on my belly. After so many months of paddling, it was flat and hard. She looked disappointed.

"I was hoping there would be a baby in there," she said.

She and I had a talk on our own. When I was a teenager, my mother told me several times that married couples who didn't have children were selfish. The nuns in the convent school said the same but went further: the whole purpose of marriage, they claimed, was to procreate. I had always laughed this off, but I wondered if the remnants of such indoctrination were what kept me from coming straight out and telling Justina that I simply didn't want a child. Instead, I told her that Dag and I had decided that mixing our newly freelance, adventurous lifestyle with babies probably wouldn't work for us.

"Maria, just go ahead and get pregnant, and tell Dag later," she advised. "Then he will have to get a job and settle down. I'm sure the college will take him back."

"He'd hate that," I protested.

"At first, maybe. But he'd get used to it."

What about me? I thought.

"And I will look after the baby while you write your books," she continued.

"We're really happy as we are, Justina."

She gave me a long look.

"When you have a child, happiness and love grow," she said gently. "And with each child that comes, the love expands to encompass them. Having children is hard sometimes, but it's better than anything else in the world."

It was a version of what I'd been hearing for years. As usual, there was nothing to say. I knew Justina would make a wonderful grandmother. But it was something I just couldn't give her.

Seven

If you do not expect the unexpected,
you will not find it, for it is not to be
reached by search or trail.

—HERACLITUS

16

The small passenger ferry from Haiphong to Hong Gai was like a rusty bucket, listing to one side. We wheeled our bikes up its wobbly gangplank, parked them on the lower deck, and hauled our bags inside. There were two seating compartments, their floors strewn with lychee and banana skins, chewed-up sticks of sugar cane, and empty cigarette packets. The first had large wooden benches that extended families were quickly commandeering. As we moved through it, a woman leaned forward, pointing back to the abandoned bikes.

"*Nhieu ke trom*," she warned. "Many thieves."

It had been my idea to buy the bikes. My idea to cycle them over a thousand kilometres along the coastline of Vietnam. I didn't care if someone stole them. In fact, I'd be happy.

The previous year, when I'd learned that Vietnam was finally opening up to tourism, I persuaded Dag we should go there for our next long expedition. At first, he wasn't keen. The coastline was highly restricted; foreign sailing boats weren't allowed, so kayaking would be impossible. I suggested finding a local sailing boat, and that caught his interest. He started researching wooden sampans, the traditional long, narrow watercraft of Southeast Asia. Larger versions of them are called junks, named after their type of sail rigs, which have bamboo battens across them.

We got a bit carried away. Within weeks, we had decided we would try to buy a sampan in southern Vietnam, find an intrepid guide, and sail up the coast as far as Ha Long Bay. We'd have ducks on board, maybe a little pot-bellied pig. I wrote up a book proposal. My agent loved it. I had a contract, an advance, and flights booked before I'd even looked into the legalities of what we hoped to do.

Once we got to Vietnam, the whole plan crumbled. Buying a sampan was impossible. We did manage to travel across the Mekong Delta, and then to Phu Quoc Island and back, aboard a variety of cargo boats and small fishing vessels. But we spent quite a bit of time stuffed into engine rooms, hiding from police. We got arrested once. We realized we were putting the owners of the boats in danger. And our intrepid guide gave up on us. "No safety," he said, so many times it was like a mantra. So, in Da Nang, I came up with the brilliant idea of cycling the thousand kilometres to Haiphong, and from there, taking a ferry to Ha Long Bay where, maybe, we could get out onto the water again.

"When were you last on a bike?" Dag had asked.

I had to think for a while.

"When I was 12."

"That's 30 years ago," he said. "Coffey, you have lost your mind."

Before long, I agreed with him.

Despite being brand new, from day one the bikes' brakes and gears started to fail, the frames rattled alarmingly on downhill stretches, and parts kept falling off. For weeks we pedalled them north up Highway One. Back then, it was riddled with potholes and so narrow we were often almost taken out by the manic trucks that passed dangerously close, squirting us with scalding oily water from their rudimentary cooling systems. In towns, we navigated crazy rush hours, weaving through masses of scooters, cyclos, bikes, and buses. Every night in some grim guest house, we scrubbed layers of sweat, grime, and dust from our bodies. I got giardia along the way. By the time we reached Haiphong, I had enough material to fill several books, and I was done with cycling.

The second passenger compartment of the ferry had rows of upright seats, mostly taken, and the aisle was rapidly filling up with boxes and sacks. We grabbed a couple of places, and, when the engines started, Dag went to the upper deck to take photos. I stayed with our luggage, gazing through the glassless window at the cranes and smoking factories of the port. From the corner of my eye, I registered a movement and turned to see a boy sitting on our bags. One of his legs was missing from the upper calf. The end of the stump was bare and misshapen, with rough folds of skin. His shorts and shirt were worn and dirty. He held a wooden crutch and a cloth bag. He gave me a sidelong smile. Dag returned and clambered to his seat.

"Hi buddy," he said to the boy, who just nodded back.

"Keep an eye on him," I muttered. "He might be waiting to pinch something."

Dag gave me a wry look. "Since when have you been so suspicious?"

From his bag, the boy took out a soft straw hat and a pair of aluminum spoons. He put on the hat, stood up on one leg, and tucked the crutch under his opposite arm. Then he held out the bag to me.

"Madam?"

"He wants you to look after his stuff," said Dag. He turned to the boy. "Careful, kid, she might pinch something."

As the boy headed into the other compartment, I peered inside the bag. There were a few thousand dong – several dollars' worth – and several sets of postcards. Each set sold for the equivalent of a dollar, and getting rid of one or two a day meant good business for street children. Shame washed over me. This boy, who I had taken as a thief, had entrusted me with his money and some of the means of his livelihood.

"Hey, do you hear that?" said Dag. "It must be the kid."

A pure, high voice, accompanied by rhythmic metallic tapping, carried through the ferry. The boy reappeared, leaning on his crutch. He closed his eyes as he sang, lifted his chin, and expertly ran the spoons across his fingers. Though we couldn't understand the words, the song was haunting. Our fellow passengers grew silent; a man sitting across from me wiped his eyes. The boy went along the aisles, holding out his hat for money. We added some notes to the pile, and he sat down next to us, counting his takings.

"What's your name?" I asked him, guessing that, like most street children, he could speak a few words of English learned from tourists.

"Vinh," he replied, still focused on the money.

"How old are you?"

"Twelve."

"Where are you going?"

It occurred to me that I was subjecting him to the same rote questions that had driven me crazy for the past weeks as we'd cycled the coast. He looked up, puzzled.

"Hong Gai, madam."

Of course, he was going to Hong Gai. The ferry didn't stop anywhere else.

"Your family in Hong Gai?" asked Dag.

"Father Haiphong." He held his hands over his eyes. "Father no see."

Retrieving the bag from me, he carefully placed his newly earned money, the hat, and the spoons inside it.

"Thank you, madam," he said, and left.

The ferry chugged along the industrial Red River Delta, past sprawling warehouses, shipyards, huge cargo ships at anchor, and barges heaped with coal slurry. As the river met the sea, the colour of the water changed from milky red to a deep green. We heaved our bags onto the top deck, anxious to get our first glimpse of some of Ha Long Bay's fabled islands – an estimated 2,000 of them, spread across 1000 square kilometres of protected water. Vinh was asleep in one corner of the deck, curled up in the arms of another boy. His head rested on his bag and his crutch lay next to him. The stump of his leg was hooked over his friend's thigh.

Ahead was a fog bank, with the jagged peaks of Cat Ba Island easing above it. Dag fitted a zoom lens onto his camera.

"Holy smokes!" he cried, peering through it. "Maria, look."

Strange shapes were materializing from the mist. Limestone rocks rose sheer from the water up to several hundred feet. They were humped and angled, patterned with fissures, caves, and arches, and cloaked in tropical vegetation. As we moved past them, more and more appeared, in serried ranks reaching back into the fog. I was so enchanted by this otherworldly landscape, I forgot about Vinh. When I looked for him again, he was gone.

Hong Gai's harbour bristled with fishing boats, some with patched junk sails and bamboo canopies over the decks. Our plan was to find the skipper of such a boat, who would take us out into the bay. First, we needed to find an interpreter who could help us with this. There were no hotels in Hong Gai where foreigners could stay, so we headed straight to the seaside town of Bai Chay, a few kilometres away. It had a huge curving beach and a spectacular view of the islands, but its hinterland was a mess, the land chewed up by an army of earth diggers, and tall, skinny hotels, mostly half built, rising like a concrete forest. The one we chose at random was finished – but only just. Six stories high, it had four rooms to a story. Our room smelt of wet plaster. It turned out we were the only guests in the place, and by the owners' deliriously happy reaction, we guessed we were the first.

Bai Chay was a new destination for Vietnamese tourists. Lining its beach were kiosks selling drinks and snacks, billiard tables under flimsy thatch roofs, and karaoke stands. Despite the rain setting in, families wearing plastic ponchos wandered along the main street of single-story buildings, browsing the paraphernalia hanging in shop doorways: buckets and spades, rubber rings, beach towels and mats, bathing suits, flip-flops, and shell souvenirs. They far outnumbered the foreign tourists who, like us, were sheltering in small restaurants. We ducked into one owned by Mr. Song, who spoke English with a French accent. He was a handsome man, with thick hair swept back from his forehead, kind eyes, and a genial nature. He told us about his childhood in Bai Chay, during which time the US military was supporting the South Vietnamese Army in what was locally known as the American War.

"It was so different then. The village was bombed, all the buildings destroyed. My family had to hide, sometimes we ran to the mountains, other times we went to the islands with fishermen and lived in caves and grottos."

While he talked, a parade of large wooden boats was motoring across the bay toward the nearby jetty. Brightly coloured, square wheelhouses and junk-rigged masts, the decks filled with people.

"These boats are new, they take tourists to the islands, twice a day," he said. "They go to some of the caves where we hid. Every day, more and more boats, in the morning and the afternoon. It is good business for the owners."

"Why are there no fishing boats?" I asked him.

"The authorities moved them away from the eyes of tourists," he explained. "Now they have to stay a couple of kilometres south of here."

We told him we were interested in exploring the bay in a traditional fishing boat. He didn't seem to think this was a strange idea.

"I have a French friend, Denny, he lives close to where the boats are now, and he knows the fishermen. He will help you."

Once the rain eased, we cycled along a beachside road until we spotted the fishing boats, about 20 of them lying at anchor. Beyond a huddle of small shops and food stands, we reached the long concrete building where, according to Mr. Song's instructions, we would find Denny. Outside sat two battered ultra-light planes. A man was bending over one, tinkering with the engine.

"Ah, the Canadians," he said. "Mr. Song, he telephoned me you are coming."

Denny was in his 30s, but he had the weary air of someone who had lived a long, hard, and disappointing life. He told us he'd had the planes and a couple of rowboats shipped from France for the fledgling tourist business he had set up in partnership with a local man. They had also built a 14-metre wooden boat to take out groups of tourists on day trips.

"My partner, Mr. Dang, this company was his idea," he told us. "I bring the money for the land, this building, and the junk. Now I have no more money, and nothing is working. Mr. Song, he call me, he say I send you two Canadians. But he tell me you look for an original boat. So I know you won't like my junk. My partner, instead of wood he put everywhere plastic, how do you call it, Formica? And plastic flowers. The Vietnamese tourist, they love this. But it is horrible."

I smiled. He was a hopeless salesman, but I was charmed by his honesty.

"One of the fisherman, Mr. Hoi, last night I drink rice wine with him, and he said he wants business with tourist," he continued. "He will think I am very clever when I bring you so quick."

Denny rowed us out to a weather-beaten boat. Squatting on the deck was a small, wiry man. When Denny explained what we wanted, he sprang to his feet, helped us aboard, and proudly showed us around the nine-metre-long vessel. It had a very shallow draught, a centreboard that dropped through a well in the hull, and a rudder that could be hauled up. There were two long oars for rowing, two masts, and junk-rigged sails patched together from different-coloured cloth. Mid-deck was a low canopy, just big enough for the four of us to crouch beneath. Mr. Hoi lifted a plank to get at a bottle of rice wine, some tiny cups, and a length of bamboo with a pipe inside it. While we sipped the wine, he stuffed tobacco into the pipe, lit it, and inhaled deeply, watching us through the smoke.

"Mr. Hoi wants three dollars an hour to take you on this boat," said Denny. "He ask when you want to go."

"Tomorrow, early, for the whole day," said Dag. When this was translated, Mr. Hoi grinned in delight.

We had dinner that night at Mr. Song's restaurant and shared the news with him. He had taken our orders and gone to the kitchen when I spotted Vinh and his friend walking past. The friend saw us first and alerted Vinh to the two foreigners. He smiled and held up postcards. We went outside and bought a pack from each of them.

"See you tomorrow," said Vinh. "I go sleep now."

"Where?" I asked. He pointed in the direction of the bus station and market, then took his friend's hand and left.

When Mr. Song came with our food, I asked him if he knew an amputee boy called Vinh, who sang beautifully.

"Everybody knows him. They call him Vinh Mot Chan; it means Vinh with One Leg. He got hit by a train on the track in Haiphong."

He told us most of the street children had families that sent them to Bai Chay to beg and sell cards to tourists.

"Where do they live when they are here?" I asked.

"Where they can. These kids, you know, they look after each other."

~

Mr. Hoi was waiting for us next morning, his boat floating in the shallows. We waded out and climbed on board. He rowed for a short distance, then raised the sails by pulling on frayed lines. And we were off, moving nicely through a light breeze. We cruised past weirdly shaped rock outcrops and close to natural arches that framed the islets beyond them. Mr. Hoi was in his element, steering the tiller with his foot, drinking his way steadily through a bottle of rice wine, and smoking one pipe after another. He chortled to see Dag fiddling with the rigging and getting such delight from his simple boat.

Around mid-morning, a light fog rolled in. An hour later, this had been replaced by heavy rain. Buoyed by rice wine, Mr. Hoi was all for carrying on, but we decided to call off the trip and try again the next day. We drifted back, sheltering as best we could under the leaky canopy. Denny was waiting for us on the beach, and he helped us sort things out with Mr. Hoi. We paid him for the day and arranged to meet again the following morning. He set off cheerfully toward the shops.

"I think he need more rice wine," observed Denny.

By late afternoon, the skies were clearing. We left our damp hotel, and as we turned onto the main street, we spotted a familiar figure ahead of us.

"Hey, Vinh!" called Dag.

The boy swung around.

"Sir, you play billiard?"

He led us to a couple of billiard tables. Despite being so small, he skillfully wielded the cue stick and played fast and competitively. He won the first game, Dag the second. They high-fived, and we moved to a food stall and ordered some snacks and drinks. Vinh took out his spoons and absentmindedly tapped a tune.

"Your song on the ferry? Will you sing it?" I asked.

Vinh understood. He nodded.

"One minute," I said. I wanted to record the song and later have it translated. I hurried back to the hotel and quickly returned with my Walkman recorder. Vinh seemed perfectly at ease with the microphone, which I held close to his face. He lifted his chin, closed his eyes, and sang like a choirboy. Twelve, I was thinking. How long before his voice breaks?

"Brilliant, buddy," said Dag when the song ended.

"I go," said Vinh. "See you later."

~

From Denny's beach next morning, the only boat in sight was a tourist junk. It was newly painted in red and blue and had a large square wheelhouse and some red furled sails. Denny emerged from the concrete house, looking embarrassed.

"Mr. Hoi and all the other fisherman go squid fishing," he explained. "They leave late last night."

"When will they be back?" asked Dag.

"Maybe some days."

Another man appeared, nattily dressed in a suit.

"He is my partner, Mr. Dang," said Denny wearily. "He suggest you go in our junk. He say you can stop and meet fishermen in old boats in the bay."

Mr. Dang was nodding. He handed each of us a business card.

"He invite you to breakfast."

In a close-by shack, a woman was preparing *banh cuon*. She spread a thin layer of rice flour batter onto a muslin screen over a large pot of boiling water. When each pancake was cooked, she sprinkled it with fried meat, onions, and garlic, rolled it up, and chopped it into bite-sized sections, which she served with a sauce of *nuoc mam* – aromatic fish sauce. Mr. Dang ordered portion after portion, which we washed down with bottles of warm Festi Cola. Denny didn't eat; he chain-smoked and resignedly translated for his partner.

"He say on our junk you can sleep comfortable on deck, the crew make the food, bring ice, so you have cold drinks."

"How much does Mr. Dang want?" asked Dag.

"Fifty-four dollar a day. I really think the fishermen will not come back soon, so perhaps it is better if – "

A scooter drove past the shack, drowning out the rest of his sentence. It did a sharp U-turn and screeched to a halt. Its driver was a short, chubby man, with dark curls tumbling into his eyes and an assortment of cameras hung around his neck.

"My god, the little planes!" he cried, rushing into the shack. "Who owns the little planes?"

I soon learned that wherever Son Nhu Hoang went, a whirlwind of energy followed him. He switched his attention from the ultra-lights to the food and, between mouthfuls of *banh cuon*, gave us a potted version of his life story. In 1975, at the end of the American War, he fled Vietnam and ended up in California, where he became a realtor. Nine months earlier, with government sanctions lifting, he had been able to return to his homeland, and since then he had divided his time between California and Vietnam, trying to set up various business schemes.

"But the government here is always napping," he complained. "I call up some department at two o'clock, and they say, 'Sunny, we taking a nap, call back later.'"

"Sunny" was a nickname he had acquired in California, and it suited him perfectly. His round face was constantly wreathed in smiles, and his laugh was infectious.

"I'm so lucky!" he cried. "I wake up in Haiphong early this morning in the house of my cousin, and I think, I need a holiday. So I get on my motorbike, and I drive here. And now I meet you guys. Hey, Denny, can I video the planes?"

Mr. Dang followed them outside.

"Why don't we take the junk for a couple of days and invite Sunny along?" Dag suggested. "He could translate for us. And he's good fun."

Before I had a chance to respond, Sunny raced back inside.

"Mr. Dang just told me about your trip on the junk!"

"You want to come with us?" I said.

"Yeah! Let's go!"

~

The boat's wheelhouse was strung with plastic flowers. A few cane chairs were scattered across the deck, and a tarp was strung from the mast for shade. As we headed into open water, Luong, the deck hand and cook, pulled up the sails. These were mostly for effect, as there wasn't much wind, and the engine was pushing the boat. Sunny raced around, apoplectic with delight, recording everything.

"Fantastic! Maria, stand by the sail so I can get a shot!"

I posed dutifully.

"What do you do for a living, Maria?" he asked, from behind the lens.

"I'm a writer."

"Really? Hey, I have lots of stories for you!"

Just then, Kiem, the captain, walked past us holding several burning joss sticks, which he wedged between two planks in the prow.

"Wait, I ask him what he is doing," said Sunny.

Kiem patiently answered his questions.

"He says we are coming through the Gate of the South Sea. So he must pray to the spirits in the four corners of the sea." He paused for a moment. "I think it is like paying a toll fee on a highway in the States."

We motored slowly all day through mazes of islets. Dag spent a lot of time in the wheelhouse with Kiem, and every so often he called to Sunny to help translate as they discussed a route. The place they chose to anchor for the night was divine. Limestone walls towered high above us. Long vines trailed down from gnarled trees that had somehow taken root in fissures of the rock. The water was still and the deepest, darkest green. There was silence save for the echoing calls of unseen birds, the squeaking of bats, the steady whirr of insects – and Sunny's cheerful whistling as he sat on deck chopping up potatoes, which Luong would turn into French fries.

"I feel like a billionaire," he said happily. "This is why I came back to Vietnam, for the simple life. In the States, I work and play too hard."

He told us about his car collection in California and pulled out photos of the vehicles. In each one, a gorgeous girl in a swimsuit struck pin-up poses against the hood.

"Look at her!" he said, pointing to one girl. "She wants to be a model. She's hot! But my real girlfriend is in Saigon. Her name is Bich Hoa. I lost her for 15 years. Maria, I tell you!"

As Sunny's story unfolded, the night crept over us. Luong took the potatoes away to be cooked. Kiem placed candles on the deck. Their flames flickered in the soft, warm breeze. I put on a headlamp and bent over my notebook, trying to keep up with Sunny.

"I met Bich Hoa when we were 12 years old, in Dalat, at the Catholic high school. I loved her from the first minute. But when she was 16, her family moved to Saigon. She wrote me a long letter, told me she cared about me. I wrote back, told her I loved her. She kept writing, why didn't you reply? I always replied, but she never got the letters, her family hid them. So she stopped writing. But I never forgot her. Three years later, she came back to Dalat, and I saw her in the marketplace. She wore silk; she looked like a movie star. She was on a motor scooter with a tall man in a sharp suit. She told him to stop, she ran over to me, she was crying, she said, 'Too late, too late,' and ran back to the scooter. I didn't see her again. Then, in 1989, my sister in Vietnam phoned me. She had heard Bich Hoa was in Saigon and had a beauty shop. She said she would go there for me, so I sent presents and a letter. I was careful what I wrote, maybe she had a husband, he would be angry. So I just ask after her family. When my sister met her, she told her I was still single and had been thinking of her these past 15 years. Bich Hoa said that after we met in the market, she broke off her engagement to the man in the suit. Because of me! But her parents were angry. They made her marry another man. She had children, but the marriage was unhappy, and they divorced. When I found out, I wrote to her again, nonstop, for 40 pages. Like a whole book. I said everything in my heart. Can you imagine, Maria?"

"Yes, I can," I replied, still scribbling.

"When she read the letter, she had to cover it in plastic because she cried so much. We kept writing for three years. Then, last Christmas, I came back to Vietnam. I surprised her. I knocked on the door of her beauty shop. She opened it."

He took a long drink of beer. He stared into the night. Scribble, scribble, scribble – I caught up.

"Then what happened?" I asked. I should have known.

"I took pictures," he said dreamily. "Lot of pictures. She was so happy. I stayed with her one week. When I went back to the States, I called her all the time. Since then, we have only been together 20 days, but it is like forever. Next week, I will see her again. Our story is so beautiful. Maybe you write it in your book, Maria, and someone in Hollywood makes it into a movie!"

Kiem and Luong came with plates of food to share and set them on a mat on the deck. Beer and rice wine went around. When we'd finished, we helped to clear everything away. Kiem and Luong would sleep in the wheelhouse. We were happy under the stars.

We were just starting to settle down when I remembered Vinh's song. I told Sunny the whole story about meeting him.

"Would you mind translating the song for me tomorrow?"

"Sure," he said. "You got it with you? I'd like to hear it now."

I pulled out my Walkman, Sunny put on the headphones, and I got my notebook ready. Moths flapped around my face, attracted to my headlamp. A bat flickered by. From the recorder, I could hear the faint, tinny sounds of Vinh's singing. Sunny listened for a couple of minutes, then ripped off the headphones.

"My God, I don't believe it! This boy is fantastic. And his song is like my story. Play it back from the start!"

The peace of the night was broken as Sunny shouted out a translation:

In the suburbs, I had a hut, small and simple. A girl lived close by, in the wealthy area. I'm not a good musician, but my lovely neighbour used to listen to my song, and she always applauded and made my heart tremble. I had no chance of a future with her, so I went far away and tried to forget her. But I thought about her all the time. One day, I received awful news that she had married a rich man.

"Stop the tape," said Sunny. "This is breaking my heart."

It took a bottle of beer to compose him sufficiently to carry on.

And now I wonder if she remembers the poor musician. Just the other day, I had a good life, like everybody. But today I have to go out on the street and sing for a living. Thanks to you all, giving me a few pennies here and there, I can survive in the rain and under the sun. For the rest of my life, I'll remember your help. Maybe in the next life I can pay you back. I wish you always to have happiness and wealth. I wish you luck in your travels, near and far.

No one spoke for a while. Into the silence came the whirr of cicadas.

"I am sure the boy wrote this song," said Sunny eventually, his voice unsteady. "He is special."

"I wish we could help him," said Dag. "Send him to school."

"It's not too late," said Sunny. "It just costs money."

"Is there some way we could make it happen?"

"How long you stay here in Vietnam?" asked Sunny.

"Just a few more days."

"So why don't we go find him tomorrow? Take him out on this boat, away from people listening. Talk to him about his whole situation, discuss what we could do."

"Is it okay to take him on the boat?" I asked. I'd seen all the warnings about sex tourism in the south of Vietnam, and how the government was taking steps to protect vulnerable street children. Surely, three adults heading off with a street child into Ha Long Bay would be misconstrued?

"No problem," Sunny assured me. "I will explain to the kid, and to the authorities if they ask."

Next morning, when the sky began to lighten, we roused Kiem and Luong and instructed them to return to Denny's beach and wait for us there.

∼

In Bai Chay, Sunny called out to local people, asking about Vinh Mot Chan. We soon found him outside the bus station. He greeted us with a delighted grin. When we sat down with him at a food stall, about 15 other street children gathered around us, laughing excitedly and teasing Vinh. He handed his can of Festi Cola to the boy next to him, and soon it was being passed around, each child taking a tiny sip. Meanwhile, Sunny quietly asked him questions.

"Vinh sleeps here with the other kids," he said, pointing to the space between the row of food stalls and the brick wall enclosing the bus station. "He says in the summer it is okay, but in the winter they have to find cardboard and paper to keep warm."

Vinh put his hand on Sunny's knee and added something.

"He says he has a big brother and a little sister here. The sister sings too. He wants Maria to meet her."

Vinh led us to a parked bus. It was packed with people, some struggling to get on board, while others were trying to get off. Dag and Sunny started taking photos of the equally confused scene on the roof, as sacks of rice, live pigs, roosters, and crates of ducks were passed up and down. Vinh nimbly climbed on board, indicating I should follow.

I was on the top step when a tiny girl appeared, wiggling through the bodies, singing in a high breathy voice and holding out a hat for money. Tousled dark hair fell into her eyes and framed a sweet, heart-shaped face. Her long, loose pants and flower-patterned blouse were dusty; her feet were bare. Around her neck hung a pink cloth bag, roughly stitched with brown thread. Vinh lunged forward to grab her. She looked bewildered as the three of us backed down the steps and stood on the gravel.

"Name, Bac," Vinh told me, hugging her.

I squatted down so we were eye to eye.

"Name, Maria," I said, pointing to myself.

"Ma-ri-AH," she repeated slowly. "Ma-ri-AH."

Holding my gaze, she fished around in the pink bag, pulled out a dirty plastic comb, and dragged it through her hair.

17

How can you explain love at first sight? I'd met and hung out with countless children during our three-month journey up the coast of Vietnam: the kids of the families who took us across the Mekong Delta aboard their cargo boats; the children who always appeared from nowhere when we stopped at roadside cafes during our endless ride along Highway One, mistaking the tan on my legs for dirt and trying to rub it away; and in any tourist place, the street children trying to sell us postcards and chewing gum. When I'd first met Vinh, once I got past the idea he could be a thief, I was drawn to his special qualities. He was self-contained, measured, and proud, aware of but not cowed by his circumstances. What I felt on meeting Bac was completely different. Friends of mine had described the "love rush" they experienced after giving birth to a baby. Yet there was nothing hormonal to explain why, when I stood up and Bac slipped her hand into mine, I was besotted, with all my protective instincts suddenly roused.

At a food stall, Bac hungrily slurped soup, while Vinh was more restrained, carefully chewing on a baguette and breaking off pieces to share with his friends, who were again crowding around us. After about ten minutes of general conversation, Sunny broached the subject of Vinh and Bac coming with us on the junk. As he spoke, Bac's face brightened, but Vinh looked serious and answered with downcast eyes.

"He says they have to work to earn money for their dad. The dad is 60 years old, he is blind, and has no teeth."

"We'll make up their earnings and a bit more," said Dag.

At this news, Vinh smiled shyly.

"He says he has to ask their big brother," Sunny translated.

The brother arrived within minutes. Seventeen-year-old Hung looked 13 at most. He could read and write a little. He organized the street children in Bai Chay, deciding which sections of town they worked and sorting out any problems or arguments. He took a cut of their earnings, which in turn he had to share with the provider of the postcards. He told us if we made up his losses incurred by Vinh and Bac being away for a couple of days, they could go with us.

"He's a middleman," said Sunny. "He would do well in the States."

We set off toward the boat, Bac sitting in front of Sunny on the scooter, and Vinh perched on Dag's bike rack, holding his crutch crosswise. When we arrived at the beach, Sunny told us he needed to charge the battery for his video camera in Denny's house.

"See that hair salon across the street?" he said. "Let's take the kids there while we wait, get their hair washed."

The salon was in an open-fronted shack. Bac stood gawping at the photos of models, the two gilt-edged mirrors hanging from the rough wooden walls, and the small glass-fronted counter filled with bottles of bright nail polish. Sunny gave some instructions to the women inside.

"They will do you too, Maria!" he said. "I go for beer with Dag."

One of the hairdressers led Bac to a reclining chair in front of the only sink in the place. She climbed into it and lay staring fearfully at the ceiling. But as the woman began massaging her scalp and gently washing her face, neck, and hair, Bac relaxed, closed her eyes, and smiled. Meanwhile, Vinh and I sat side by side in front of the mirrors, with a hairdresser apiece. They took greasy combs from jars of grey water and began yanking them through our wind-tangled hair. They poured a little water on our heads, added some shampoo, and worked it into lathers, vigorously scratching with their long nails. Vinh took it stoically; I winced in pain. When Bac was led into the yard behind the shack to have her feet and hands scrubbed in a plastic bowl, Vinh and I took turns in the reclining chair. By now, my scalp felt like someone had run a garden rake across it, and I feared worse was to come. But the soap was gently rinsed out of my hair with cool water, and then I too got a soothing face and neck wash.

"Ma-ri-AH," said a voice in my ear, and I turned my head to see Bac. Her hair was clean and combed, and the skin on her cheeks was buffed to a shine.

"*Dep lam*," I said approvingly. "Beautiful." Her face broke into a wide smile.

Once on board the boat, Bac became wary. She stored away her spoons and her pink cloth bag in the front compartment of my holdall and carefully zipped it shut. Then she sat close to Vinh, frowning and constantly pushing back the hair that fell into her eyes.

For a couple of hours, we slowly motored through the shape-shifting landscape. What seemed like a rock wall straight ahead of us would magically open up, revealing itself as myriads of islets divided by narrow channels of still, emerald green water.

Reaching a larger island, we pulled up at a jetty close to some caves that Kiem had told Sunny about. Vinh had a quick discussion with his sister.

"She doesn't want to go into the caves," said Sunny.

"No problem, I'll stay here with her," I said.

Dag, Sunny, Kiem, and Vinh went ashore. Steep stone steps led up to the high cave entrance. Bac and I watched as Vinh mounted them faster than the able-bodied adults. When he disappeared into the cave mouth, Bac gave a little cry of alarm and pressed herself against me. To divert her attention, I took out a bottle of nail polish I'd bought at the hairdressing salon. Looking at me expectantly, Bac placed both her hands on my knee. She sat very still while I painted her tiny nails. Once they were dry, she insisted on painting mine and smeared polish all over the tops of my fingers. Pulling up one of her pants legs, she revealed a makeshift dressing on her calf, made from a wad of toilet paper tied on with string. She ripped off a bit of paper and used it to wipe off the surplus polish. When I tried to see what was beneath the dressing, she pulled away.

To distract her, I took out our Lonely Planet guidebook of Vietnam. It had proved useless so far, but Bac loved it. She pored over the images of places and people, and pointed to photos of fruits and vegetables, telling me the names of each one in Vietnamese. When I pointed to some Vietnamese words in the dictionary at the back of the book, she shook her head. Like Vinh, she was illiterate.

We were playing a game of noughts and crosses in my notebook when the cave expedition returned. Vinh was triumphant, glowing from the adults' praise.

"You should have seen this little guy, climbing up and down rock walls," said Dag. "He went places I wouldn't go. He's totally fearless."

From then on, Vinh and Dag were inseparable. They sat together on the deck, Vinh resting his leg stump on Dag's knee. When Dag treated Bac's injury, Vinh was his helper, holding bandages and ointments. As Dag carefully removed the toilet paper, cleaned the wound, and dressed it, Bac clung to me, quivering and mewing.

"I'm sure I'm not hurting her," said Dag.

"She tell me she got this burn from the exhaust pipe of a scooter on a ferry," said Sunny. "She remember the pain, and she is scared."

Bac was 7, but she looked barely 5. For half of her life she had been motherless. And now she seemed intent on making up for the nurturing she'd missed over those years. She wasn't in the least bit interested in the islets, grottos, sea caves, and arches we were cruising past. She wanted to be cuddled and fussed over, and I was more than happy to do that. Unlike Dag, I'd never had much patience with kids, and after playing with them for a while I would grow bored. But I was willing to sit with Bac on my lap for hours and give her all the attention she needed.

As the day got hotter, Kiem anchored the boat in the shade between a couple of towering islets. Vinh clambered onto the gunwale, balanced on his one leg, then dived in. Dag followed. Together, they swam to some water-level caves and disappeared from sight. This time, Bac wasn't worried, and she helped us lay out a picnic lunch. When the swimmers returned, we all sat around a mat with the food spread over it. The children insisted on serving the adults. Vinh gave everyone drinks, and Bac solemnly handed out bowls of rice and vegetables, baguettes, triangles of soft cheese, lychees, and slices of fruit. Then they asked each of us in turn, starting with Kiem, who was the oldest, "*Moi ong, an com? Moi ba, an com?*" "Sir, may I eat? Madam, may I eat?"

"This is the tradition in Vietnam," explained Sunny. "We learn to respect our elders."

We all snoozed after lunch, then set sail again. We'd seen few other boats all day, but soon more sampans appeared, and when we rounded one islet we found many more, rafted up together at the base of a cathedral-like cliff. Echoing off the walls were the sounds of puttering engines, radios, barking dogs, and the laughter of children.

"Kiem tell me the people spend all their lives on these little boats," said Sunny. "They born here and die here. Bigger boats come from the town to buy their fish."

We passed the evening playing card games with the children, until it was time for dinner. Darkness dropped quickly over the bay. Lights twinkled on boats. Some generators chugged. By nine o'clock, tiredness overcame me, and I stretched out on the deck behind our group. Bac joined me, snuggling in close. She began to sing in a high, breathy voice, pausing every now and then, as if trying to remember the words. Sunny leaned over to listen.

"Maria, she makes a song for you. She says, 'Tomorrow I will pick purple flowers to hang in your hair.'"

I dozed off. At some point, with Bac still attached to me, I shuffled onto the mat Dag had spread out. A sheet was gently laid over us. Then I was conscious of nothing more, until I woke to a hazy dawn and birdsong. As usual I had been sleeping on my side, my back spooned against Dag, who had his arms around me. Gently wriggling free of his grasp, I propped myself on one elbow. Something stirred behind Dag, then a little hand appeared above his shoulder.

"Ma-ri-AH," said a sleepy voice.

∾

Luong served us strong coffee, boiled eggs, bread, and fruit.

"I didn't talk to the kids yesterday about their education," said Sunny as we ate. "I wanted to wait. I think now they trust you; they know you wouldn't promise something, and then go away and forget them." He paused for a moment. "I know that too."

When Bac finished eating, she crawled onto my lap and handed me a comb. Gently, I started to tease the tangles of the night from her hair.

"What will happen if they don't go to school?" I asked Sunny.

"Now they are okay. They are cute, they can sing and beg, and people will give them some money. But soon Vinh will grow up, and it will be hard for him to get a job. And Bac." He stopped and sighed. "Maria, men come across the border from China and Taiwan. They pay a lot of money for a pretty young virgin, maybe two or three hundred dollar. For a poor family, it is a big temptation, but for the girl it is the end. Afterwards, she can only be a prostitute."

I looked down at little Bac. The thought was unbearable.

"Okay, I talk to them now," said Sunny.

At the news we wanted to send them to school, Bac's face lit up. Vinh reacted more soberly.

"He says it is not possible because of their father. If they go to school, they can't work, and he won't eat."

"Maybe we could support their father," suggested Dag.

"You must be careful," cautioned Sunny. "You don't know what the dad will do. Maybe he is a good man, but maybe he take the money, and still they have to work. I think we have to go to Haiphong and meet him."

"But we're flying out of Hanoi on Sunday," I said. "And today is... Thursday."

Our original plan had been to give away our bikes in Bai Chay and arrange for a car to take us directly to the Hanoi airport for our afternoon flight.

"So we go to Haiphong tomorrow with the kids and see the father," said Sunny. "We stay in the house of my cousin, and you can go from there to the airport. If we can agree something with the father, I can help with everything after you have gone."

"Sunny," I said, "You are an angel."

Bac leaned up to pat my cheek, wanting to regain my attention.

"Ma -ri -AH," she whispered.

I dropped my face to the top of her head, breathing in the scent of her scalp.

~

The last day of our little idyll stretched ahead – until the authorities arrived. Dag and I were sitting with the children, teaching them to write their names in English, when a black motor launch zoomed toward us. As a policeman boarded, Vinh pushed his crutch out of sight and covered his leg stump with the edge of a mat. The policeman talked to Sunny for a few minutes, then asked for our passports. He told Sunny, Kiem, and Luong to go to the launch, where another policeman was waiting. Then he questioned the children. Bac cringed against me, but Vinh sat up straight and quietly gave his answers in a cool, collected manner. The policeman switched his attention to Dag and me.

"Canada?" he asked, pointing to the children and then to us.

"No," said Dag. "Haiphong. Father."

Of course, this looked suspicious. I appreciated the concern of the police. But I was afraid of the possible repercussions; that they might take the children away, and we'd never see them again. Sunny came bouncing back with reassurances.

"The problem is this boat has no registration for the tourists, no proper safety equipment, and no permission for foreigners to stay overnight. And they are worried about the children. But I explain everything. They are cool. But we must go straight back to Bai Chay."

During the journey, Vinh and Dag lay on the deck, practising writing. I caught up on my notes, while Bac sat next to me, singing and playing her spoons. When Denny's concrete bunker was in sight, both children carefully collected up their new belongings – notebooks, pencils, nail polish, and chewing gum. Luong gave them the leftover food, and they squirrelled this away too.

"The kids should stay in their usual place tonight," advised Sunny, as we wheeled our bikes and his scooter to the road. "Otherwise the police might think we have bad intention."

He went ahead to find Hung and talk about our new plan, and we followed with Bac and Vinh on our bikes. Sitting on my luggage rack, Bac clung to me like a limpet. I cried all the way into town. This little urchin had drawn out mothering instincts I never knew I had, and the prospect of leaving Vietnam without her was awful. But what could I do? Spirit her away from her family and the world she was familiar with? And even if it were possible, would I be doing that for her or for me?

By the time we reached the bus station, I'd composed myself. Sunny and Hung were there and had already made arrangements to travel to Haiphong the next morning. Other street children instantly surrounded Bac and Vinh. We had to interrupt them to say goodbye – they were busy talking to their friends and sharing out the food they'd brought from the boat.

~

Inside the Haiphong ferry next morning, we took over one of the wide benches. Vinh and Bac squabbled quietly about whose turn it was to tug at Dag's beard. Then Bac curled up on my lap, while Vinh leaned against Dag, drawing in his notebook.

"Hey, you guys look just like a family," called Sunny, who was standing on deck videotaping us through the window. His comment hung in the air for few moments.

"When I was younger, I always used to think I'd like a big family," Dag told him nonchalantly. "Then I sort of went off the idea."

Bac tapped my arm, wanting my attention.

"Mar-ri- AH!" I looked down at her wide smile.

"Go Papa!" she cried excitedly.

~

In Haiphong, Hung hired a motor scooter and set off to warn his father of our imminent arrival. We dropped off our bags at Sunny's cousin's house. On the ground floor, there was a clothes shop, and we told Vinh and Bac they could each choose an outfit. For several minutes they gazed around at what was on offer. Vinh chose a pair of long grey pants, a T-shirt, and a belt. Bac went for a yellow dress with a full skirt, gold buttons, and red braiding. We bought both of them shoes and underwear. Sunny's cousin let them use her bathroom and bedroom to wash and change. After half an hour, we knocked on the bedroom door. Vinh sat on the bed combing his wet hair, while his sister danced in front of the mirror. Dag changed the bandage on her burn. This time, she was braver about it, singing quietly to herself as he worked.

~

A tiny ferry took us across the Red River. We stood crammed in among bicycles and scooters with their engines running. Bac patted my leg, indicating I should keep it away from the hot exhaust pipes; it was on this ferry she had got burnt.

From the disembarkation point, we followed Hung's instructions, taking a short stretch of road before turning onto a narrow sandy path on top of a dyke. Soon we saw a cluster of houses in the fields below, small structures with wattle and daub walls and thatch roofs. The children dismounted from our bikes, jigging with excitement. We'd been spotted: people were running up the dyke toward us.

"What happens to this place in the monsoon?" I asked Sunny, as we leaned our bikes against his parked scooter.

"It floods. The people move and come back later if they can. They are squatters, they have no rights."

A washing line hung outside Vinh and Bac's house, and some bright flowers bloomed in pots set on the dirt. We ducked under a low doorway into one of the two rooms. Their father, Mr. Le, sat on a low wooden stool, wearing a shirt open to the waist, patched pants, and dark glasses. He was gaunt, with a sunken chest. On the mud floor before him were small cups and a teapot. The room was empty save for a wooden bed base, where Hung sat with another brother, a year younger than Vinh. A few odds and ends – a comb, a pen, a pack of cigarettes – were stuck into the thatch ceiling. More stools were brought for us. We shook hands with Mr. Le, and he poured green tea, feeling for each cup before carefully and expertly filling it. As Sunny began quietly speaking to him, he listened with his chin upturned, like Vinh and Bac when they sang. They stood behind him, their hands on his shoulders. Sunny turned to us.

"It is traditional for a blind man to sing and get money, but he got too sick, so he taught his children to do this. Three years ago, his wife got influenza and died. So now one kid stays and helps him, and the others go to work."

The children went outside, where curious villagers had gathered. Through the doorway, I could see Bac twirling to show off her new dress. I asked Sunny to tell Mr. Le how impressed we were by Vinh and Bac's kindness and good manners, how well he had raised them.

"You know, he is overwhelmed," said Sunny. "They are the poorest family in this village. I told him you want to send Vinh and Bac to school. I warned him it might take some time to arrange. He says it doesn't matter, because someone thinks of him and loves his children. But I say nothing about money. We don't know how much this will cost, how we will organize it."

Mr. Le stood to shake our hands, and we slipped him some dollars. Then we headed back to the dyke. A crowd of people followed us to our bikes. Vinh and Bac were among them, busily answering questions.

"Let's say goodbye here, Maria," said Dag. "It will be easier."

In turn, we hugged both of them.

"I told them I will bring messages from you," said Sunny.

"And that we'll return," I reminded him.

"Yeah. I already say this."

Fighting back tears, I picked up Bac and held her close.

"Ma-ri-AH," she whispered in my ear.

"Bac," I whispered back. "Gọ Papa."

I cycled away as fast as I could. Some of the other children ran alongside me, yelling and laughing. Then, from behind, I heard another voice ringing out.

"MA-RI-AH!"

I stopped and turned to wave at the tiny figure in a yellow party dress, standing on a dyke with the vast expanse of the Red River Delta spread out behind her.

18

Before leaving Haiphong, we gave our bikes to Lai, one of Sunny's cousins. In return, he insisted on arranging our transportation to the Hanoi airport. His friend, he said, had a car. The friend turned up an hour late, driving an old Russian-built Lada. The back seat was ripped and held together with packing tape. The gears made sharp cracking sounds. All the windows were stuck open. We crawled along behind trucks belching out poisonous exhaust fumes and past roadworks where the smoke from drums of boiling tar filled the car. We reached the airport looking much like we'd done for much of the past three months: sweaty, dirty, and dusty, with wind-tangled hair. And way behind schedule.

"Hurry, hurry!" urged the woman at the check-in desk, handing us our boarding passes.

In passport control and security, we begged other passengers to let us go ahead of them.

"Run, run!" cried the man at the departure gate.

We had barely reached our seats before the doors were closed. As the engines whined, and the plane started to taxi, the thudding of my heart slowed down. Along with relief that we'd made the flight came the shocking realization that this long, crazy journey was actually over. We climbed into the low clouds covering Hanoi. The attendant handed us cool, sanitized, white cotton cloths. I wiped my face with mine, turning it a murky grey. Remembering how bedraggled I must have looked, I reached into the holdall at my feet, feeling around for a comb. In the corner of the front compartment, my fingers closed over something else. Even before I pulled it out, I knew what it was: Bac's pink cloth bag, childishly stitched together with brown thread, and inside it, two aluminum spoons. I sat staring at it for a long time, as Vietnam fell away beneath us, tugging at my heart.

~

A few days after we got home, I was standing in a checkout line at our local supermarket. Strapped onto the shopping cart in front of me was a bucket chair with a young baby in it. When we made eye contact, the baby chuckled and started windmilling his legs and arms. Leaning down, I cooed at him and touched his soft cheek. Suddenly, the cart was yanked forward. Alarmed by the motion, the baby started to cry. I looked up and met the mother's angry gaze.

What did she think? That I was going to snatch her son and run out of the store?

"I'm sure that didn't cross her mind," said a friend I talked to later, who had a child of her own. "But I can't say I blame her for not wanting you to touch the baby."

She railed about the women who used to lean over her daughter's stroller, making comments about her plump, rosy face. "Sometimes they'd even pinch her cheeks," she said. "It made me furious. It was so disrespectful. I mean, how would you feel if a stranger came up and did that to you?"

I'd forgotten where I was. In Vietnam, I'd grown used to having babies thrust into my arms. It was normal there – children got passed around between friends and neighbours, and sometimes to kindly strangers.

~

We were already trying to set things in motion for getting Vinh and Bac off the street and into school. Dag had told me about SOS Children's Villages, an organization he'd first learned about in his teens when his family moved to Germany. It was highly regarded there, as was Hermann Gmeiner, the Austrian founder. Gmeiner's mother died when he was 4 years old, but his eldest sister had stepped in to raise him and his six siblings. During the Second World War, he fought in Russia. The suffering of orphaned and abandoned children he witnessed during and after the war led him to give up medical studies and pursue his idea for a children's village. His mission was simple: children need a mother, siblings, a house, a community. He garnered supporters, and in 1949 the first SOS Children's Village was established in Imst, Austria. It was a model that, in the years to come, would be successfully replicated in many countries around the world. Each village comprises of ten or more family houses; each house has a "mother" caring for up to ten children of various ages. The children go to school and get medical care in the wider community. At age 18, they move into a single-sex youth house in the village, where they can live while they study or get jobs. But the original house and family grouping remains their home, even when they leave the village to start their own lives.

The first SOS village in Vietnam was set up in Saigon in the 1960s, because of all the children being orphaned by the American War. There was now one in Hanoi, and another being built in Haiphong.

While Dag was first telling me all this, my eyes kept drifting back to Bac's bag and spoons, which we'd hung on a piece of driftwood in our living room. I was sure she'd just forgotten them. I imagined her trying to find material to make another bag, bending over with it with a needle and thread. She was such a little mite, cast out into a big world. She desperately needed a mother.

The SOS village sounded perfect. But I couldn't deny the yearning I felt to have Bac cuddled up on my lap.

"If it was at all possible, even later, would you consider..." I began hesitantly. My voice trailed off.

"Adopting them?" said Dag. "Of course."

His certainty took me aback.

"It would change everything," I said, talking to myself as much as him. "It would transform our lives. I mean, they would have to go to school. We'd have to stop travelling, get regular jobs."

"I know all that," said Dag. "And, of course, it would be best for them to stay in their culture and close to their father. But if SOS doesn't work out, and there's no other option, and if it was what their father wanted... Well, we'd have to do it."

Thinking of how we would adjust to such a massive shift in lifestyle made me reel. And yet, in our minds at least, suddenly we had opened that door. I imagined telling my mother. Flying to England to see her. Walking into the arrivals hall of Manchester Airport, holding the hands of two Vietnamese children.

It was a short-lived fantasy. After a number of faxes and phone calls, we got through to Ms. Kim Duong, the director of the Hanoi SOS Children's Village, who spoke good English in a quiet way, with lots of pauses. She told us that SOS usually took in babies or very small children, so they could grow up used to the structure of the village. But it was clear that Vinh and Bac were at risk, particularly as their family was squatting.

"There is an organization in our government, the Vietnam Women's Union," she said. "It is for the protection of women and to empower them. It is at all different levels of government, including in villages. Normally, the Women's Union in a village would be aware of children being sent onto the streets; they would intervene. But this family has moved away from their original home. Where they live now is an illegal settlement. There is no Women's Union there. No level of protection for the children. So we might be able to look into the possibility of accepting them, depending..."

There was a long pause. I held my breath.

"We will have to visit the father, and he must agree to let them go, so they can become part of the family in the SOS village. You mentioned being willing to cover their earnings, but there cannot be any financial deals with him. We have learned that this never works. It only leads to more demands and children being used for bargaining."

We told her we understood.

"And there is something else I must tell you. In case you are hoping to adopt them, it would not be possible."

"Well –" I said.

"We hadn't –" Dag said at the same time.

"The children have a father. And, in any case, the policy in Vietnam is to keep children in our culture," she said firmly. "Overseas adoptions are rarely approved."

"Yes, yes, of course," we chorused, though my throat caught a little.

She told us Vinh and Bac would be expected to obey their house mother, do chores with their siblings, and keep up with school work.

"For street children, this is hard. They are used to being free and independent. We have taken a few street children into our villages. Most of them ran away. It will be harder for Vinh than Bac. But with luck we can try."

I wanted to get on a plane and go straight back to Vietnam. This wasn't possible for several reasons. The trip had put us in debt, and as freelancers we were now skating on thin ice financially. Even if we could return, would our presence change anything? I pinned my hopes on Vinh and Bac being accepted by the SOS Children's Village in Hanoi, and their father agreeing.

Weeks ticked by. Finally, we heard from Mrs. Duong that, in principle, an exception would be made for Vinh and Bac. On the next call, she told us she'd met with the children's father. He was agreeable but concerned the children would be so far away in Hanoi. He would prefer Haiphong, once the village was finished. So the plan was to keep in touch until it was ready for opening.

~

Sunny was back in California. He came up to visit us on Protection Island. We pored over photos and videotapes, reminiscing for hours about Vinh and Bac, and the beauty of Ha Long Bay. He cooked us Vietnamese food, and we took him out kayaking.

"We keep thinking about how amazing it would be to kayak in the bay," Dag told him. "Hey, Sunny, let's go back and do it! You could deal with the police."

"Dag, we would be in prison in a minute," Sunny laughed.

We learned he was a talented artist; he produced a series of sketches to head each of the chapters of the book I was writing about our trip through Vietnam. I loved having him with us in the house. He felt like a tangible link to Vinh and Bac.

After Sunny had left, one afternoon I was sitting at my desk, working on *Three Moons in Vietnam*. The phone rang.

"Hi, is this Maria Coffey? My name is Olaf Malver." I tried to place his accent, which turned out to be Danish.

"I work for the adventure travel company, Mountain Travel Sobek, in Berkeley, California. I've read your articles in *Sea Kayaker Magazine* and the *New York Times* about your round-the-world kayaking trip. And I've just finished *A Boat in Our Baggage*. It's fantastic!"

He hadn't rung up just to praise my writing. Olaf had been tasked to develop a program of international kayaking trips for the company. He had two questions for Dag and me.

"Would you consider working with me to develop and guide new trips? And could you suggest some amazing new kayaking destinations?"

I laughed. Could we ever!

Mountain Travel Sobek already ran trekking trips in Northern Vietnam. It had good connections with the Vietnamese government, and it had money to pay for permissions. A few months later, while I stayed at home to meet my book deadline, Olaf and Dag were on their way to Vietnam to scout the first commercial sea-kayaking trip in Ha Long Bay.

Dag called me from Hanoi. He'd been to see Mrs. Duong and got a tour of the SOS Children's Village. He described the comfortable houses, the garden behind each one, where the children tended vegetable plots and looked after chickens and ducks, and the sweet family groups. The well-kept grounds, with lots of trees and bushes and places to play. How healthy and happy the children looked.

"I got choked up," he said. "It would be perfect for Vinh and Bac."

Ms. Duong had been keeping track of them. The last she had heard, they were in Bai Chay, but when Dag arrived there they were gone. He had dinner at Mr. Song's restaurant and told him the whole story. He hadn't seen either of the children for a while, or their brother, but promised to keep an eye out for them.

In April 1996, I was back in Vietnam with Dag. A lot had changed in two years. Along the road from Noi Bai International Airport to Hanoi, huge billboards sprouted from paddy fields, advertising foreign cars, computers, and cameras. In the labyrinthine streets of Hanoi's Old Quarter, there were more motor scooters than bicycles, and boutique hotels were popping up on every corner. We were about to lead Mountain Travel Sobek's first official kayaking trip in Ha Long Bay, with a group of eight guests. But first we were going to see Vinh and Bac's father, along with Mrs. Duong and a colleague overseeing admission to the Haiphong SOS Children's Village, which was due to open in the summer.

I could barely contain my excitement as we got out of the car and walked back along the dyke. News of our arrival quickly spread, and children started running up toward us. I looked for Vinh's hopping gait, strained my ears to hear Bac call. But they weren't among the crowd. The village looked even more destitute than I remembered. We dropped down toward Mr. Le's house. This time, the door was shut, and he was sitting outside on a low stool. A woman stood next to him, shading her eyes with one hand, watching our approach. When we reached her, she barked something at the children trailing us, and they scattered. She wore a loose shirt over long pants. Her hair was wrapped in a scarf. She regarded us with a hard stare.

"I haven't seen this woman before," Mrs. Duong murmured to me.

There were no preliminaries. No offer of green tea. Mrs. Duong spoke gently to both of them. The woman answered, at length. Mr. Le stayed silent.

"There is a problem," said Mrs. Duong eventually. "This woman says she is married to Mr. Le, that she is the stepmother of the children. And that they now have a baby. If this is true, we need her permission also for Vinh and Bac to come to SOS Children's Village. She says the family can't survive without their wages. And that she won't give permission unless you send them money every week."

I felt a bubble of panic.

"Where are Vinh and Bac?" I asked.

"She says they are in Haiphong, with the baby, begging. They will be back later."

I stared at the closed door. I had a sudden strong sense that the children were behind it, listening, under strict orders not to make a sound.

Mrs. Duong looked at me sadly. "You know, of course, that we can't agree to her demands."

I could barely speak. "Please ask them one more time," I managed to whisper. "Please tell them that, in the long run, this will be the best for all the family."

"Maria, I will try."

The woman responded harshly. Mr. Le hung his head slightly.

"We have to leave now," said Mrs. Duong. "My colleague will come back to see if he can change her mind."

As we climbed back up to the dyke, I kept turning around, hoping to see the children emerge from the house and come running toward us. But there was only the couple, behind them the closed door.

≈

"I heard Vinh was at the Yen Tu Pagoda festival," said Mr. Song. "It's about 50 kilometres from here, in the mountains."

We'd taken our group to his restaurant for dinner. We were due to embark on a boat that would be our base for a week while we explored Ha Long Bay by kayak. The restaurant was still very basic; to get to the tiny bathroom, and its squat toilet, you had to walk right through the kitchen, and it wasn't unusual to see a rat scurrying around. But the food was delicious, and Mr. Song was charming. We'd already told everyone in the group about Vinh and Bac, and how Mr. Song was an integral part of the story. So, when he dropped this news about Vinh, we were all agog.

"It's a huge festival, from the start of the Lunar New Year for three months. Many Vietnamese pilgrims go there, and beggars, of course."

"What about Bac?" I asked.

Mr. Song shook his head. "I don't know. Mostly I see Vinh on his own. I haven't seen Bac since last year."

Mountain Travel Sobek had accessed the best boat possible, but it was still extremely rustic. The flush system of its only toilet was a bucket on a long rope dropped into the bay and then hauled up overflowing by one of the crew. For the first few days, we were hit by a storm that brought heavy rain that leaked into our cabins. The legendary islands were shrouded in mist, but we went paddling nonetheless. Dag wanted to explore new territory; one afternoon, as we passed a fishing village, an irate policeman waved an AK-47 at us, then shot off a round over our heads. The guests seemed to think this was all part of the adventure.

Finally, the sun appeared. Our sweet crew cooked us divine meals, gave us massages, and took us to hidden temples on tiny sand beaches and showed us how to make offerings to the spirits there. We paddled through long, dark caves that led to lagoons in the middle of islets, completely surrounded by sheer rock walls. It was all utterly magical. That we'd be returning here again in a few months seemed lucky beyond imagining.

At the end of the week, we returned to Hanoi and had a jolly final evening together. Early the next morning, after the last of the guests had left in taxis for the airport, we were on our way to Yen Tu Pagoda.

∾

Toward the end of the four-hour journey, we kept passing local buses on their way to the same place. I peered through the windows of our air-conditioned car, looking at the people crowded on board, imagining Vinh and maybe Bac among them, singing and begging. We were heading into a fairy-tale landscape of steep limestone mountains covered in thick forest, their sharp peaks wreathed in mist, separated by valleys filled with jewel-green paddy fields. We'd not had time to do much research on where we were going. All we knew was that, since the 13th century, Yen Tu Mountain – the highest in the area – had been a sacred Buddhist site, and that there was a steep trek to the main pagoda at its summit. Our driver, who spoke a little English, pulled up in a parking lot where pilgrims were spilling out of buses.

"How long?" he asked.

We had no idea. But it was almost 11:00, and we needed to return to Hanoi that night.

"Three hours?" we said.

He looked doubtful. "I am here."

Rough steps and rocky trails wound steeply through forests of pine and bamboo. We trudged up them, alongside elderly women and men bent over walking sticks; teenage girls in tight jeans and high heels; Buddhist monks in orange robes; and couples who looked like they were out on a date, the young women slender in their traditional *ao dais*, their consorts wearing pressed shirts and trousers with creases down the front. Despite the higher altitude – the mountain peak was over 1000 metres high – it was still hot and humid, and we were soon sweating.

"Where you from? What's your name?" cried a young man cheerfully, as he overtook us. "Many thousand steps more!"

We toiled on for over two hours. It turned out there were a couple of pagodas on the way up and one at the top. We gave each only a cursory glance; instead, we were searching the throngs of pilgrims to see if we could spot Vinh. I did wonder why we were doing this. It had been a knee-jerk reaction to Mr. Song's information. If we found Vinh, what then? We'd already raised his hopes, only for them to be dashed. Did we want to reassure him we were still trying on his behalf, or were we simply assuaging our own guilt, filling our own needs? I still don't know the answer, only that we felt compelled to somehow stay connected to the children.

We were puzzled by how few beggars we saw on the way to the summit. Where were they all? It was almost at the end of the three-month festival. Had most of them left already? Then we started our descent by a different route. Following a path through trees, we reached a very long, straight, stone staircase. On either side of it, for as far as we could see, were wrecked human beings. Lepers with half their faces missing, quadruple amputees lolling on the ground, wizened old women dressed in rags, young women clutching tiny babies, children with horribly deformed heads and twisted limbs. We stared down in horror. At the sight of two rare foreigners, the beggars nearest to us started howling, holding out arm stumps, deformed hands, and drugged babies. The noise alerted others further down, and they joined into the crazy, desperate chorus. We reached for the Vietnamese money we had on us, and, as we ran, we thrust notes at people, which made it all much worse. We were clutched and wailed at; the howling reached a new pitch. Some people crawled out to block our path, and we had to step over them. This was the epitome of desperate begging; these poor people were at the absolute bottom of society's pile. It was, quite literally, like a descent into hell.

At last, we reached the bottom and found our car. As we drove away, neither of us spoke for a long while.

~

We were finishing breakfast, sitting at Mum's kitchen table in Manchester. She'd moved there a few years after Dad's death, wanting to be closer to my brother John and his family.

At the time, John had offered to help her find a new home. She'd taken him at his word and given him clear instructions.

"It has to be a nice bungalow, with two bedrooms and a garden on a quiet road, in walking distance to a Catholic church, some shops, and your house."

No pressure. Amazingly, he'd quickly found a place that fitted all her criteria. She'd settled in and made friends fast. She worked a day a week at a charity shop. The church became a key part of her social life. She'd joined the Catholic Mothers and established a travel club, arranging day trips all over the country and local nights out. Most mornings, she walked over for Mass. She was happy there, and proudly independent.

Sunshine spilled through the window and onto the linen tablecloth. She'd cooked us bacon, eggs, sausages, and fried tomatoes. She'd asked Dag to make coffee from the freshly ground beans she'd bought specially for us. Had we had enough to eat? More toast? Another pot of coffee? She was beaming with pleasure to have us in her house, to be feeding us. It felt like she was feasting on us with her eyes. On me, especially. After our visits, Dag always laughed about the intensity of Mum's gaze, the way it hungrily followed my every move.

Three Moons in Vietnam had just been published in England. After the rounds of interviews and presentations, Dag and I were spending a few days with Mum. I'd told her about our encounter with Vinh and Bac, and kept her abreast of our efforts to help them. I'd admitted that for a brief period we had considered adopting them. Now she listened carefully as we related what had happened in Haiphong, a few weeks earlier, when we met Mr. Le and his new wife. My sense of the children being locked away.

"I know how hard this is for you," she said. "When I was 21, and pregnant with Mick, I tried to adopt a child."

She stared down at the tablecloth, smoothing it with her hand.

"You never told me that," I said, astonished.

She smiled. "Well, there's a great deal I haven't told you."

She had gone back to Ireland with Dad, visiting his relatives in Tipperary. It was always tense for her there. His family was staunchly Republican, and had been active in the fight for independence. Her father had been a member of the Irish Constabulary, in the pay of the British. She'd hear her in-laws whispering behind her back, calling her *seoinin*, a derogatory name for an Irish person who preferred England to their homeland. After Mass one morning, they'd visited one of Dad's sisters, Jula. Of all the siblings, she was the kindest to Mum.

"We were at their kitchen table like now," Mum said. "I'd heard a rumour about her youngest daughter having fallen pregnant, but that she'd never been sent away, and there was no sign of a baby."

She turned to Dag. "Usually girls in trouble got sent to awful places, laundries, run by nuns. The babies were taken from them, and then they were forced to wash sheets and clothes all day by hand. They were like slaves. The nuns were terribly cruel."

She paused and sipped her tea. She was a great storyteller, with an instinctive knack for pacing and building tension.

"So what do you think happened?" I prompted her.

"Well. The daughter was in the kitchen with us. She was only about 16, poor thing. I asked about a baby, and she looked scared and shook her head. Tom told me to shush."

Another sip.

"But I had a strong feeling. I went out of the kitchen and ran up the stairs. I looked in the bedrooms. Do you remember Jula's house, Maria? You stayed there with us once, you must have been about 22."

"Yes, of course," I said impatiently. "And then?"

"You might remember the narrow stairs to the attic. I went up them and opened the door. It was dark in there and musty."

She stopped and looked away, through the window. By now, Dag and I were leaning forward.

"There was a baby," she continued quietly. "A few months old. Terribly quiet. He'd been mostly alone. He'd had no stimulation."

Her chin was trembling. She took a handkerchief from her pocket, lifted her glasses, and wiped her eyes.

"I carried him down to the kitchen," she managed through her tears. "I told Tom we were taking him."

"Holy shit," said Dag.

"There was a terrible commotion. Tom said we couldn't keep the baby; it would be a shame on our family. The daughter was crying. Everyone was upset."

"Really, you wanted to keep him?" I asked.

"I did indeed. I would have brought him right back to England. But Tom was angry. He said we couldn't raise a bastard. I tried to stand up to him. It was hard; I was only a girl myself. In the end, I said I wouldn't leave until something was settled for the child."

"Mum, you were a hero," I said.

"There was a lot of discussion. Finally, Jula agreed to raise the child as one of her own. And she kept to that. He grew up thinking his mother was his sister."

"Wait a minute," I said. "I think I met him."

"You did. When you stayed with Jula, he was living there. He's never been quite right. His development was stunted by those months in the attic."

She paused.

"I often regretted not taking him. But in the end, you can only do so much. You tried your best with those poor children in Vietnam, Maria. Don't feel guilty."

Mrs. Duong and her colleagues persisted, visiting Mr. Le and his wife several times. They kept sending news. The oldest brother had left home and become a cyclo driver. Vinh's voice had broken, and he had started working as a shoeshine boy. Bac was now begging with her father. It was too late for Vinh to be admitted to the SOS Children's Village, but Mrs. Duong believed Bac was at risk, and they were prepared to take her. She had managed to talk to Bac once; she was keen to take this opportunity. Again, the stepmother refused. Mrs. Duoung promised she would keep trying.

In the spring of 1997, we were in Vietnam to guide a British film crew who were making a documentary about climbing in Ha Long Bay. It had been Dag's idea; he'd recognized that the multitude of islands could be a rock-climbing heaven, and he'd already been scouting some possible routes. They were only accessible by water, and the climbers and crew would reach them by kayak. While we were in Hanoi, and Dag was busy making final arrangements about permissions, I took a taxi to see Mrs. Duong at the SOS Children's Village. I was met by one of her assistants at the gate. We walked through the grounds, past kapok trees in full bloom, their pink and red flowers bright against the sky. School had just finished for the morning, and children in neat uniforms were running along paths, satchels slung over their backs, toward the cluster of houses.

Mrs. Duong poured green tea, asked after my health, Dag's, and that of our mothers. Then she sat back.

"My colleague went to see Bac's father and stepmother again, just recently. The father wasn't there. The stepmother said he had gone to Dongxing with Bac, to sing and beg. And she refused again to let Bac come to SOS."

I let this sink in.

"Where's Dongxing?" I asked.

"On the Chinese border."

The memory was sharp and painful. Bac sitting on my lap, Sunny saying, "Men come across the border from China. They pay a lot of money for a pretty young virgin."

Bac was only 10.

Mrs. Duong must have guessed my thoughts. "We don't know why they are there. But it is not a safe place for Bac."

Showing emotion is not considered proper in Vietnam, especially in more formal settings. But Mrs. Duong was sympathetic to my tears. She handed me tissues. She let me rant about how I had to go to Dongxing to find Bac. That Dag didn't need me in Ha Long Bay, and I could leave for the border the next day.

"Maria, it is a city," she said finally. "It would be hard, impossible maybe, to find them. And if you did, you would only make things worse for Bac. The family would start demanding money, and it would go on and on. I'm so sorry, but we can do nothing more."

~

Dag met Vinh once, outside Mr. Song's restaurant, when he was leading a trip on his own. The sweet little boy had turned into a teenager with a rather haughty attitude. His voice was deep. He was well dressed, in his own inimitable style. He wore a pair of jeans that he'd shorn off at knee level, and cut the hem into a ragged fringe. He was carrying his shoeshine equipment, a wooden box of brushes and polish that doubled as a stool. He remembered Dag and they chatted, but he didn't stay long. He was busy finding customers, taken up with his own life.

Bai Chay was already growing into Ha Long Bay City. We were leading trips there twice a year, but the boats we used had become progressively more luxurious. As soon as we arrived from Hanoi, we boarded and set sail for the islands. We didn't encounter Vinh again, but we heard about him.

Alongside pirated copies of Graham Greene's *The Quiet American* and Lonely Planet guides, street children in Hanoi, Bai Chay, Hue, Saigon, and other tourist spots were touting around photocopied versions of *Three Moons in Vietnam*. Once we found a whole pile stacked on a table outside a bookstore.

"Hey, my wife wrote this," Dag told the owner of the store.

"You joking," he retorted.

"I'm not, look," said Dag, opening up a copy to the photo section. "Here she is. Maria Coffey."

The bookseller looked at the photos, at me, and back at the photos.

"You famous!" he cried. "Will you sign all the books? Then I sell them for more."

It was so audacious I couldn't refuse. After I'd signed every one of the pirated copies, I asked, "Can I take one of these?"

"Yeah, seven dollars," he said. He was serious. Until I coughed up the money, I wasn't leaving with my pirated signed book. He got his seven dollars.

The paperback edition had a new postscript about our efforts to help Vinh and Bac. I started getting letters from people who were moved by the story and wanted to help. I always told them to check the details about SOS Children's Village in the postscript and to donate. But then other letters arrived, from people who had met Vinh in Bai Chay. They told me how he was doing, how they were helping him. One woman from Switzerland had given him money to expand his business, and now he was employing a couple of other shoeshine boys. "He's a smart young man," she wrote. "He's going to do fine."

We never heard a word about Bac.

~

It was summer on Vancouver Island, and we were getting ready to kayak around the Brooks Peninsula, a hunk of mountainous land that sticks out of the northwest coast of Vancouver Island like a giant thumb, attracting high winds, big seas, and some atrocious weather. But I couldn't concentrate on our preparations. I had missed a period, my breasts were swollen and sore, and I was convinced I was pregnant. It felt like the worst possible timing, in all regards. I was 45; the risks to the baby could be high. We had pulled off the freelance photographer/writer/adventurer lifestyle. I was working on my fifth book. We were developing and guiding kayaking trips for Mountain Travel Sobek in places around the world. Dag was doing seasonal stints as a large animal vet on the west coast of Ireland. We were getting invited to symposiums and conferences all over North America to present Dag's multimedia shows about our expeditions.

I loved our kaleidoscopic life. We weren't making much money, we certainly weren't saving any, and at times we were barely scraping by. But we only had ourselves to worry about. By the following spring, however, this could radically change. When I told Dag, he reacted with equanimity.

"Don't worry, Maria. It will be a different kind of adventure. We can call the kid Brooks."

"If it's a boy," I said. "If it's a girl, she'll be Bac."

I went to our local drugstore to buy a pregnancy test kit. I had been to its pharmacy counter countless times, but never before via the baby products aisle. I don't know how I got there. All I remember is standing, dazed, between shelves stacked with diapers. I stared wonderingly at the various packages: Why had I never realized how many different types of diapers there are? Then I noticed the people shopping around me – women with babies or toddlers in tow, a couple of them heavily pregnant. And all of them *significantly* younger than me.

On the way out of the store, I bumped into a friend. She took one look at my face and asked me what was wrong. We went for a coffee. We were the same age, but she had two children in their 20s.

"Both times I got pregnant, initially I was upset," she told me. "I was, like, why now, when I had all these other plans? But the thing is, it's never really the right time. You'll have months to get used to the idea. Then the baby will arrive, and all the hormones will kick in, and you'll be madly in love."

I had bought three sets of the test. I paddled home, sat in the bathroom, and took one after the other. They were all negative. My relief told me everything.

∾

I still have Bac's bag and spoons. In those first couple of years, when we had hopes of helping her and Vinh, I used to think about what it would be like to return the bag to her, once she'd settled into the SOS Children's Village. It would be among several presents I'd have brought from

Canada, all wrapped in pretty paper. The bag would be in the last present. She'd open it, push her hair out of her eyes, look up at me, and smile.

Bac will be in her 30s now. It's hard for me to think about where she is, how she lives, what she has experienced. I doubt she remembers the strange lady who took her on a trip to Ha Long Bay. But I remember her, often, and always with a heavy heart.

Fearing loss was one of the reasons I decided not to have children. Yet loss found me all the same.

Eight

That makes our heart sink more than
anything else, really, that the childless and
the mothers are equivalent, but it must be
so – that there is an exact equivalence and
an equality, equal in emptiness and equal in
fullness, equal in experiences had and equal
in experiences lost, neither path better and
neither path worse, neither more frightening
or less riddled with fear.

—SHEILA HETI

19

Over the years since our meltdown on the Irish ferry, I had grown steadily closer to Mum. She never mentioned that row, but a few years later we were shopping together when she pointed out some fridge magnets that read, "Stop me before I become my mother." I felt instantly guilty – had she known it was one of my fears around having children? But she laughed out loud, bought one for me, and insisted I put it on our fridge door.

That was in June 1998, when she came to Canada to celebrate her 80th birthday. By then, our house on Protection Island was in good shape, and she was thrilled by the new kitchen, the mature garden, and especially the sweet little writing cabin Dag had built for me. She stepped inside it, exclaiming at the stained-glass window, the shelves made from driftwood and held up with arbutus branches.

"Everything is so lovely," she said. Then she noticed the shelf holding one of each of my published books, including foreign translations. This had been Dag's suggestion, a self-esteem boost for when my writing confidence was low.

"I suppose all these books are your children," she said. There was no innuendo; I knew she was proud of my success as an author, but her words made me feel so bleak I had to turn away.

~

Dag and I had planned a huge surprise party. Our mothers had been born in the same year, a month apart, so we made it a joint celebration. On that Sunday morning, we arranged for someone to take them to church in Nanaimo and for a cup of tea afterwards, with instructions to keep them chatting as long as possible. While they were gone, an army of friends arrived. In the garden they put out tables and laid them with cloths and flowers, got the barbeque and drinks station set up, hung banners and strings of colourful lights in the trees. The illustrator of my first children's book had provided me with a sketch for the occasion, titled *Two Old Ladies Dancing*. In it, the figures had curly hair and glasses, and were lifting up their skirts in a joyful jig. I'd put the image on the front of invitation cards that went out to 90 guests. A neighbour who was a talented baker replicated it on a cake. We'd organized a string quartet for the afternoon, as Dag's mother, Justina, loved classical music, and a trio to play Irish music later.

I'd casually mentioned to Mum that we were going to have a few people over for drinks that day. So, when she returned from church and walked into the garden, she looked confused.

"Are you having one of your big parties?" she asked.

"Yes," I said. "It's for you and Justina."

She walked past the pond and across the grass, gazing at the decorations, at her and Justina's names on a big banner hung over the long head table.

"Oh my," she whispered. "Is it really just for us?"

Until that moment, it hadn't occurred to me that neither of them had ever been feted like this. One had married just before the Second World War, one right after. With little money, and no family support, the ceremonies were bare bones. Then their lives had been all about working to make a good life for their children and looking after their husbands. Saving and scrimping and – yes, I recognized it now – sacrificing for others. Never the centre of attention, never princesses for a day. One of our teacher friends had organized some island kids to help with the decorations. I had a quick word with them, and soon they ran over and asked Mum and Justina to bend down so they could place glitter-dusted crowns on their heads. Now they were queens.

Guests poured in. They arrived with gifts and congratulations, happy to be part of such a milestone celebration. I was racing around, organizing things, but from the corner of my eye I watched Mum shaking hands, laughing and chatting with people. She was glowing. A buffet table got loaded up with grilled wild salmon, salads, potatoes, desserts. Eventually, I carried the cake to where Mum and Justina sat at the head table. They stood together to cut it. Mum made a speech, completely off the cuff. She was poised and funny; she recited from memory a silly poem about getting old. Then a fiddler and guitarist serenaded her with a rendition of "Galway Bay," a song about the place she was born. Instead of getting emotional, like me, she sang along with the first verse:

If you ever go across the sea to Ireland
Then maybe at the closing of your day
You can sit and watch the moonrise over Claddah
Or watch the sun go down on Galway Bay

The dancing started soon after, and Mum, despite her recent knee replacements, was doing jigs on the lawn with Dag, laughing her head off. She carried on laughing and carousing until two in the morning. She wore out the musicians, who were half her age. I couldn't have been more proud of her.

~

Nine years later, she visited us again. Dag and I had moved from Protection Island and divided our time in British Columbia between a condo in the small city of Victoria and a remote, off-the-grid island where we had a share in a rustic property. Mum said she wanted to come and see our new life, "before it's too late." Though she was still remarkably fit for her age, during my most recent trips to England, I'd noticed the walks we took in the evenings were getting less brisk. She had shrunk – we used to stand head-to-head, but now I was taller than her. She'd started saying she didn't want to become "a burden" on anyone. That she'd never dream of wanting to move in with my brothers or me. She had cared for both of her parents at home, in each case for years, until they died. "It put a big strain on my marriage," she always said. "I wouldn't want to do that to any of my children."

She didn't mention alternatives. I preferred to assume she would live forever. And when I saw her come through the doors into the Vancouver airport's arrival hall, unassisted, pushing a trolley with her luggage, it was easy to believe this.

While she was in Canada, she told me about her plans for her 90th birthday party the following year. She'd decided to have it in County Mayo, Ireland, close to where her father had been born. My brother Mick and his wife, who lived in Tipperary, would help her to arrange it. She was going to pay for everything: rooms in the hotel where the 30 or so guests would stay, a big meal, a live band, and a dance.

"No one will have to drive home," she said. "They can all get as drunk as they like."

And so, exactly a decade after she had jigged in our garden, I watched her twirl on the dance floor at close to midnight.

"Jesus, she'll see her 100th birthday yet," said one of my cousins, who was standing next to me clutching a pint glass.

Mum thought so too. She'd been telling me that on her centennial she'd receive a telegram from the queen. "I don't want to miss that," she said.

~

I was guiding in Croatia when she turned 91. I gathered our kayaking group around my phone and got them to join in on a rendition of "Happy Birthday." Not long afterwards, I was in Manchester, getting out of a taxi, pushing open her gate, and pulling my case past rose beds to the bungalow. Before I could ring the bell, she had opened the door and was reaching out to embrace me. When we hugged, I felt the bones of her shoulders. Over the past months she'd been losing weight and had less energy. She claimed she felt fine; there was nothing to worry about.

"How was your holiday?" she asked me.

I'd long ago given up trying to convince her – or most people for that matter – that Dag and I actually worked. Carrying on with our mission to "keep life interesting" in lieu of having kids, we'd been piling on projects and travel like there was no tomorrow. In 2000, we had set up our own adventure travel company. A few years later, we established its conservation branch, Elephant Earth, piggybacking time onto trips we were guiding to do research work in Southeast Asia. Dag produced a photo exhibit and installation about the plight of captive elephants that was shown in India and at several festivals across North America and Europe. And we'd travelled to attend all the openings.

In the midst of all this, I was furiously writing and had published more books. I'd written parts of them aboard a small, open sailboat in the Salish Sea, leaning against logs on wild beaches during a kayak circumnavigation of Vancouver Island, and sitting under a thatch shelter in Laos, watching mahouts bathe their elephants in a river. I'd proofread manuscripts in hotel rooms in Bangalore, Hanoi, Dubrovnik, and Chiang Mai. My last book, *Explorers of the Infinite*, was extremely research heavy and challenging to write. By the time I finished it, I was exhausted. Dag then told me he needed help with the administrative side of the travel business, which he'd been dealing with almost single-handedly. So I'd swapped my author hat for that of an entrepreneur. I poured my creative energies into the company and it blossomed. With our office tucked into our laptops, we were circling the world, doing work that engaged us and gave us the adventure hits we craved.

All this had far surpassed my childhood dreams. I often had to pinch myself to believe it really was my life. But there was a toll. Sometimes I felt we were going at such a speed we could barely take it all in. We were always on the move. I was beginning to wonder what "home" meant for us, apart from being together. The stress factors were building up: the endless arrangements and emailing; the seven-day workweeks; the long-haul flights; being on call 24/7 when we were leading trips. And there was another element. I felt increasingly torn about my mother. The push-pull of wanting to get on with my own life but wanting to see her; knowing she needed me and would do so even more in the future. On this visit, suddenly all that came to a head.

~

She'd always been anxious to get out and about with me as much as possible, for shopping trips, lunches, and walks. But this time we didn't leave the house much. I sat with her in the living room while she dozed.

I helped her hang out the laundry in the back garden, and then did some weeding as she followed me, leaning on a cane, pointing to plants I'd missed.

One day, she told me she had a rash on her torso. We went to see her doctor, who dismissed it as a reaction to a new washing powder. It got worse overnight, and painful; we returned to the doctor, who diagnosed shingles. It was caught just in time for Mum to take the anti-viral drugs, but she felt very poorly for the next few days.

I remember thinking if I was single, I would just stay with her from now on. That's what would be expected of me as the unmarried, childless daughter, and that's what I would do. I imagined settling into the little spare bedroom with its pictures of the Virgin Mary, the bedside table with a crocheted doily and old-fashioned lamp, the net curtains on the window. It wasn't the worst option; I would have a simple, clear purpose: to make the end of my mother's life as comfortable as possible. But I wasn't single. I had a man who loved and needed me, and a life we'd built together. Mum's words, "I sacrificed everything for you," echoed down the years. Could I finally sacrifice my needs for hers? Tell Dag I wasn't coming home?

Of course, I returned to him. But only for a few weeks until Mum suddenly became very ill and was admitted to hospital.

There had been no pain to signal the spread of ovarian cancer. And now it was at an advanced stage. Treatment wasn't an option, but if it had been, she told us, she would not accept it. She was in hospital for almost a month. I became her chief advocate, badgering nurses and doctors for information, doing whatever was needed to make her more comfortable. I helped her to the bathroom each day to wash. She would sit on a stool as I crouched in front of her, bathed her feet in a bowl, dried, and powdered them.

"Ah, that is so comforting," she'd say.

As a family, we talked about next steps. Returning home was the best option for her emotionally, but with the amount of care she would need, as her illness progressed, it wasn't feasible. With my sister-in-law Gail, I toured around nursing homes. I came away from all of them feeling distressed. How do you make a decision like that?

There were two possibilities. One place had good recommendations but was in a smallish building, going through renovations, so residents who weren't bedridden spent much of their days squashed into the temporary day room. And Mum would initially have to share a room with someone else. The other place, run by Catholic nuns, was in a rambling, Victorian-era building. Lofty ceilings, high windows, wide hallways, and a chapel where Mum could attend Mass daily. This, I thought, was ideal. I couldn't have been more wrong.

"Go home to Dag," she instructed me, a couple of days after she moved in. "You've been away from him for five weeks. You need to look after your marriage. I'll be fine now."

I talked to her doctor. I explained about living in Canada, working around the world.

"Because of your mother's advanced age, and her previous good health, the cancer could progress slowly," she told me. "She could live on for many months, even a year or two. It's impossible to say at this stage. My advice would be to do your travelling now, before she gets any worse. But don't be away for too long."

Soon John was calling me in Canada. Mum hated the nursing home. The nuns were curt and inept. The helpers were poorly trained. She didn't like the food. She wasn't interested in going to Mass in the cold, drafty chapel. Eventually, she snapped at him, "Whose idea was it to leave me in this horrible place?"

A private room came up in the other nursing home, so John and Gail moved her there. Instantly, she was much happier. I decided to go to Kenya with Dag, to help scout a new trip and do some elephant research. I booked a flexible ticket I could change at anytime. After ten days, I got a call in the middle of the night. Mum had suddenly become very confused, and kept asking for me. The doctor was concerned.

"We just don't know what's going on, Maria," said my sister-in-law. "I don't want to drag you back if it turns out not to be necessary."

Next day, I was on my way to Nairobi for a red-eye flight to London. Before I boarded, I called Gail. The crisis had already passed. As soon as Mum learned I was coming, she had started to improve dramatically.

When I turned up at the nursing home, I was jet-lagged, and my defences were down.

"She's in the day room," said the care assistant who let me into the building. "It's still the temporary one, so it's a bit crowded right now. Pop in and surprise her."

I stood in the doorway. She was sitting in a high-back chair, engrossed in a copy of her favourite newspaper, the *Daily Mail*. A few other people occupying the closely spaced chairs were reading or knitting. But most were beyond that. Some stared into space; one woman was waving her hands back and forth in front of her face; several people were talking to themselves. Next to where I stood, there was a bathroom for the disabled. I fled inside it, locked the door, and sat down on the toilet lid. Clinging to the support railing, I pressed my face against the white-tiled wall, crying uncontrollably. Seeing my mother surrounded by people with dementia had completely undone me.

Minutes passed before I could compose myself, splash cold water on my eyes, and walk into that room. Mum looked up in delight, put down the paper, and reached out her arms to me. She turned to the woman next to her. "Here's my daughter!" she cried.

I had no idea then that I would get to know and care for those people who at first had repelled me. When the nurses were examining Mum, or washing and dressing her, I would go down to the day room. Renovations had been completed, and now residents sat in a large, sunny space with windows looking out onto a garden. I would pull up a chair, hold hands, listen to the stories of those who were still capable of telling me about their lives. Others, who were lost to dementia, still seemed happy to have me chat to them, and when their relatives came, I asked them questions. I learned that the man in the room next door to Mum (one of her staring-into-space day room companions) had been a champion footballer. I saw photos of him in his heyday, wearing his team's jersey. When I held up the pictures to his face, there was a flicker of recognition in his eyes. The woman who waved her hands in front of her face had been a dancer and piano player, and when I spent time with her I realized how beautiful those hands were, the fingers long and graceful, the nails perfectly manicured by the esthetician that came every week.

One of the slumped-over people turned out to have a rare neurological disorder that had completely paralyzed her. When she was in the day room, I read her short stories.

"Do you want a job here?" the caregivers joked.

My life had so suddenly shifted it almost felt possible. I had moved in with John and Gail. Along with their youngest daughter, Hannah, who lived and worked in Manchester, we had formed what we called "Team Coffey," aided by my sister-in-law Eileen when she came from Ireland. As Dag had taken over all my work, I was the team member with no other commitments. I turned up at the nursing home every day after breakfast, and usually stayed there until the evening when Mum was ready to go to sleep. She had stopped saying anything about me needing to be with Dag, to look after our marriage. She constantly told me how grateful she was to have me with her, the comfort I was bringing her.

Dag and I were in daily contact. We had no idea of how long we'd be separated. I missed him terribly, but otherwise I settled into the routine of caring for Mum. It was a peaceful time. Everything else had fallen away. And it was the closest I'd ever felt to my family.

In the day room, Mum always sat next to a woman called Joan, who, like her, was fading in body but not in mind. They would chat and gossip until they both became tired and shut their eyes for a while.

"Your mum is a treasure," Joan told me, again and again. "She always makes me feel better about everything."

The staff loved Mum too. "She's so cheerful and funny," said a nurse. "She appreciates everything we do for her. She keeps telling us about the terrible nursing home she was in before here."

Ah, the guilt. Was that what kept me with her from morning until night? Guilt for that month of misery with the nuns? Guilt for being the wayward daughter who had opted for an adventurous, wandering lifestyle, instead of staying close to her and having a family? Guilt was a part of it, but it was also a need in me. I wanted to do anything I could to help make her comfortable and more content in these hard circumstances. To nurture her. To mother her.

You always hear about the tables eventually turning, the child becoming the parent, and I could feel it happening. But right to the end she remained my mother. The one who could make me feel better in special and simple ways. When I arrived on very cold mornings, she'd say, "Here, let me warm your hands." She'd hold them underneath the bedcovers until she felt the heat return to my fingers. She did the same for Hannah. We both loved it; we agreed it was like being cuddled and comforted. It was something only my mum and her nana could do for us.

Mostly her brain was sharp, her memory amazing. But strange things began happening. She told John he should hide all her candies, because the staff were taking them when she was asleep. Once she accused him of stealing chocolates.

"I bought them for you, Mum," he said. "And then you told me to help myself."

"I did no such thing," she snapped back. "How could you think of robbing an old, bedridden woman?"

One morning, I was sitting next to her, tapping out an email on my computer.

"Maria, look!" she cried. She was staring wide-eyed at the opposite wall. "Jesus is dancing across that shelf. What a good dancer he is! Do you see him?"

"No, Mum," I said. "I can't."

She was pointing and laughing. "There he is! He's dancing so well!"

Moments later, she turned to me, her face serious. "Of course, nothing was there," she said. "I think the cancer is going to my brain."

There were no tests to find out where the cancer was spreading. Her care was all palliative. She had a corner room, with windows on two sides. Through them I had watched the leaves turn yellow in late September, then get blown off by the October winds. We brought knick-knacks from her house, including all the framed family photos from her living room. And clothes – the wardrobe next to her bed was filled with her winter coat, tweed skirts, twin sets, scarves. We took her out for meals sometimes, pushing her in a wheelchair. In early November, I took her shopping, and she bought a lovely cashmere sweater that was on sale.

"I've little use for that sweater now," she said to me sadly the next day. "And I'm never going home, am I?"

I couldn't speak. I just held her hand and stared down at the gold rings and watch, loose now on her once plump fingers and wrist.

In mid-November, she decided it was time to die. Every evening, as I was leaving her, she'd say, "I won't be here in the morning." Then she'd start praying out loud, asking Jesus to take her during the night. Next morning, I'd check in with the nurses before I went up to her room. "She had a comfortable night," they'd say. "Fast asleep whenever we looked in."

And there she'd be, propped up against her pillows, ready to tell me what she'd had for breakfast.

"I'm not going to be here at Christmas," said Mum, sometime in December. "So don't buy me any presents." From then on, she repeated this daily.

"Of course you'll still be here," I'd say.

"Well, if I am, what use will I have for presents?" she'd retort. "Promise me that none of you will buy any."

So we didn't.

Since I'd first moved to Canada, and then started travelling so much, I'd missed most Christmases with my family. The festivities depressed me, and I came across as a grinch, so the distances had been a useful excuse. It was always a huge disappointment for Mum. Now, finally, we would spend the whole day together. But she was asleep when I arrived on Christmas morning, and she never really woke up. Her breathing seemed to get increasingly shallow. I was convinced she was dying, but the nurses kept telling me, no, she's fine. I called John and Gail every hour. They were delaying dinner until I got back, but I felt I couldn't leave. What if I stepped out, and she died, alone, on Christmas of all days?

"Maria, go home to your family," said one of the nurses firmly, at close to eight o'clock. "If there is any change, we'll call you immediately."

As usual, Gail handed me a large glass of wine when I walked in. I knocked it back and got a refill. After a long, boozy dinner, I fell into bed. I woke with a start before dawn. Reaching for my phone, I called the nursing home.

"I checked in on her ten minutes ago," said the nurse who picked up. "She's sleeping like a baby. Which is what you should be doing."

John and Gail went to see her later in the morning, while Hannah and I had breakfast. We were just finishing when my phone buzzed. John's number flashed on the screen. I snatched it up.

"Yes? Everything okay?"

"Houston, we have a problem," he said.

When they arrived, Mum had been wide awake, cheerful, and full of questions about Christmas dinner. How big the turkey was, and how long Gail cooked it for. What vegetables she served with it. What kind of wine we had. If we had plum pudding afterwards. And what presents we gave each other.

"Then," said John, "she asked when you and Hannah were coming in." He was standing in the hallway outside her room, speaking quietly. "I told her you'd be arriving in an hour or so. And she said, 'Okay, I'll wait until then to open my presents.'"

"Presents?" I squeaked, staring wide-eyed at Hannah.

"Yep. She seems to have forgotten she didn't want any. Can you rustle something up?"

Hannah got on her computer and found out that a big supermarket nearby was open. We sped around it, buying Christmas packs of soaps, talcum powder, and bath salts, nail polish and hand cream, boxes of chocolates. Back at the house, we wrapped up everything prettily. We found a festive hairband with a Christmas tree and reindeers stuck on top, and Hannah wore it as she led us all into the room, the presents in her arms, calling out, "Happy Christmas, Nana!"

Mum was too weak to open the parcels by herself, so Hannah sat on the bed, helping her with the ribbons and paper.

Right after New Year, the head of the nursing home returned from a two-week skiing holiday. While she was away, a couple of the residents had died.

"Both times, the phone went in the middle of the night," she said. "When I heard it, I thought, *This must be Bee*. I honestly thought she would be gone by the time I got back. I can't believe she's managing to hang on."

By then, Mum had stopped asking Jesus to take her to heaven in her sleep. Mick was visiting regularly from Ireland, his daughter Laura from a previous marriage took the train up from London several times, as did Hannah's brother, Charlie, and their sister Louise came over from Hong Kong.

"It's so lovely having everyone around me," was Mum's new mantra. "I don't want to leave you all."

In January, she kept going to the brink and pulling back. A priest was called to her bedside on three separate occasions to give her the Last Rites. Each time, she woke up some hours later and asked for a cup of tea.

I was exhausted. The staff at the nursing home were urging me to have a break, go on a holiday, before I burned out completely. But when I wasn't with her, I worried. And I felt I was atoning. For the sadness I'd caused her by living so far away. For the ways in which I could have been a better daughter. The daughter she had always wanted. I remembered how, when I was young, she said that people who chose not to have children were selfish. I had been puzzled by this. But now it began to make some sense.

One morning, during what would turn out to be the last week of her life, I arrived to find her propped up against the pillows of the bed, with the *Daily Mail* on her lap. A photo of Prince William and his fiancé dominated the front page. Mum was a huge fan of the royal family.

"Would you read me the article about William and Kate?" she asked. I guessed she didn't have the strength to lift the paper.

"Kate's a lovely girl," she said, when I'd finished the piece and showed her the photos. "I hope Harry finds someone like her. He's a troubled boy. Losing his mother so young, and the way she died, it hurt him badly. It would be so nice to see him settled down with a family."

Then she gave me a long look. The thick lenses of her glasses made her eyes appear huge.

"Can I ask you something?"

"Of course," I said. "Anything."

"Have you ever regretted not having children?"

I was taken aback. It was an age since we'd discussed the possibility of Dag and I producing offspring. Suddenly, I understood why she thought people who decided not to have children were selfish. I had broken a cycle. A grandchild from me would have completed her, passing on not only genes but the experience of motherhood from one generation to another. It would have brought her more happiness than anything else I could have done.

Her question hung between us. What could I say? That I was painfully sorry for denying her such joy? But it was something I just couldn't do for her?

I took a deep breath.

"No, Mum," I said. "Never. I'm really happy with my life."

Her face broke into a smile.

"I'm so relieved, Maria. I've always worried about it." She put her head back against the pillows. "I need a little rest now."

I held her hand and watched her sleep.

20

Dag and I have always left ourselves open to chance and serendipity. By axing our secure careers, and not having children, we created the space and freedom to be able to seize opportunities when they arose, to develop ideas that popped into our heads. Often we didn't know where a new direction would lead us and were surprised by how things turned out. And so it was with elephants, leading us to Agnes.

Back in 2007, Dag was planning to fulfill a long-held dream: to trek across the sub-Sahara with a camel caravan to the fabled salt mines north of Timbuktu. This was to be the real deal, with real salt miners, walking for two weeks and 800 kilometres through searing heat to where blocks of salt were dug up and strapped to the camels' backs. And then turning around for the return trip.

Initially, I was keen to go with him. I had once told my mother I would walk across the Sahara when I was 70, but doing it at 55 sounded more sensible. Then Dag warned me that it involved being on the move for 18 hours a day, only stopping to rest when the sun was highest in the sky. That water was highly rationed. And that anyone who couldn't keep up got left behind. I decided that walking across the Sahara wasn't the best thing for me, at any age.

Dag wanted to be a useful member of the team, not a tag-along tourist. He had already worked with large animals in Wales and Ireland; now he decided to study camel medicine. The best place to do that, it turned out, was the veterinarian department of a university in Rajasthan, Northern India. He went there in May, while I was leading trips in the Galapagos Islands.

Toward the end of his stay, a local vet contacted Dag to ask if he would accompany him to the stables of Amer Fort, home to a large number of captive elephants used in the tourist industry. One of the elephants had just had a baby. Elephants don't breed well in captivity, and this was the first time in almost a hundred years that there had been such a birth in Rajasthan. Along with excitement over this auspicious event was worry about how to monitor the health of the newborn. As a Western large-animal vet, Dag was considered an expert. No one had thought to ask about his experience with elephants, which was just as well, as it was zero. But he wasn't going to turn down the chance to get his hands on an elephant – and an 11-hour-old one at that – for the first time.

He described it all to me in a long email. The stable was a cavernous space, like a warehouse, containing over a hundred concrete pens, one for each heavily chained elephant. Dag was led to the pen where the new mother stood. She was calm and relaxed, as her 70-kilo daughter stumbled around beside her. The baby had wrinkly, loose skin and fuzzy hair on her head. Her eyes weren't properly focusing yet. And she was having trouble controlling her trunk. With the local vet translating, Dag spent ten minutes talking to the mahouts and examining the baby in the way he would a newly born calf. Taking her rectal temperature, examining her stools to check that they contained meconium, asking if she had suckled yet. Everything seemed fine. Everyone was relieved.

While this was going on, other mahouts were preparing food for all the elephants, mixing up rice and grains in pails. The elephants were impatiently straining against their chains, reaching out their trunks toward the pails, and not paying any heed to Dag. But, as he left the mother's pen, suddenly one elephant grabbed his wrist with her trunk.

"It felt like a hugely powerful snake wrapped around my arm," he wrote. "There was no way I could pull my hand free or resist the elephant. In a split second she had pulled me so close that my face was almost touching hers, and I was gazing into her eye. The eyes of other large animals – horses, cattle, sheep – are big and liquid. This eye was small and beady, dark amber in colour, with a round pupil. It moved like human eyes do, looking upwards and sideways. And it was full of intelligence. It felt like an aperture to the universe in which this animal lived, a huge dimension I couldn't comprehend but only sense: a whole world of emotion, thoughts, feelings, moods. I don't know long we stood there, eye to eye. Time seemed to stop, but eventually – maybe only seconds later – the mahout tapped her on the trunk with his cudgel, and she let me go."

In those moments, much changed for Dag – and for me. Camel medicine and the trek to and from Timbuktu were abandoned. Instead, he wanted to learn everything about elephants, to help these creatures in some way. I was enthusiastic about the plan. Six months later, we were on our way to India to start researching the welfare of captive elephants in temples, tourist camps, and the logging industry. From there, it spiralled into us setting up the conservation branch of our travel company, and doing work with elephant welfare and conservation groups in Laos, Thailand, and Myanmar, as well as India.

In 2010, the resurgence of the ivory poaching crisis led us to East Africa. We quickly made contacts among the tightly knit network of Kenyan elephant researchers. We decided to work with Max Graham, whose small NGO at the time would grow into Space for Giants, and began funding one of his projects. We also learned about ecolodges run by local communities and conservationists, and we started to plan for some new Hidden Places trips.

~

In September 2011, we arrived back in Kenya for a safari with a group of 12 women hailing from Canada and the US. Most of them had travelled with us before. Ranging in age from their 20s to 70s, they included a mother and daughter, and two sisters. They were single, divorced, widowed, or travelling without partners. On game drives in Masai Mara National Reserve and Naboisho Conservancy, we got close to elephants, lions, leopards, giraffes, zebras, and hippo. We saw a cheetah chase an antelope at high speed. We watched a herd of migrating wildebeest stampede across a river, frantically avoiding crocodiles. Then we flew in a small plane to Laikipia, passing close to the slopes of Mount Kenya, gazing down at the edge of the Rift Valley. We landed on a dirt airstrip carved into a high plain covered in long grasses and dotted with spindly acacia trees. Waiting there, ready with some Jeeps to take us to her ecolodge, was our host Anne Powys.

Anne was a striking figure. She had perfect posture, high cheekbones, and piercing blue eyes. A wide-brimmed, weather-beaten hat stuck with an array of large feathers topped her mane of curly blond hair. She was dressed in her regular attire of a loose cotton shirt over cargo pants and desert boots. She wore heavy ethnic jewelry made from silver and aluminum on her wrists, fingers, and around her neck, and multiple silver hoops in each earlobe. I could tell our group was already in awe of her.

Dag and I had met Anne a couple of years previously through Max Graham. Her father, Gilfred, was a third-generation white Kenyan. A legend in the area, he was a hunter turned conservationist, who in his late 70s still roared around in a Cessna plane and went on long walkabouts with his camels, searching for rare plants. He raised cattle on the family's sprawling ranch, which he kept unfenced so elephants, lions, and other wildlife could roam through it. Anne had taken after him in many ways. She was a free spirit; she'd grown up running wild in this landscape and understood it inside out. She helped Gilfred with the cattle operation, she wrote papers and books about botany in the area, she worked with local community groups on forest and elephant protection, and she'd built a small off-the-grid lodge in one corner of the ranch.

We settled in for a few days. We slept in rammed-earth, thatch-roofed cottages tucked between huge boulders; we went on walkabouts and game drives with Anne; we ate meals at a long table under an old acacia tree whose widely spreading branches were festooned with weaver birds' nests; and at night we sat around the firepit gazing up at the star-packed sky. After this, we would fly to the tiny island of Lamu and stay in a historic house right on the Indian Ocean. It was an astonishing trip in all regards. Yet the highlight, everyone agreed later, was what happened in Nalare village.

On the night of our arrival at Anne's lodge, while having drinks by the fire, we told the group about our first visit to Nalare, 11 months before. A couple of hours' drive away, the settlement sprawled across an elephant migration path. When the giants moved through, they raided crops and, if taken unawares, sometimes attacked people. They were regarded as an enemy that brought only bad things to the community. Anne had been trying to recalibrate that, showing how elephants could, in a roundabout way, help the local economy. She had advised a group of women on how to set up a cooperative and introduced them to the concept of making paper from elephant dung, then beading it with traditional patterns and selling it at tourist lodges. The business was established, but the women needed more assistance for it to grow, and Anne had asked if we'd like to meet them.

When we drove into the village, a man dressed in a check shirt and beige pants had been waiting for us at the side of the dirt road. Behind him was a scattering of small buildings, some with breeze block walls and corrugated iron roofs, others built traditionally from mud, sticks, and thatch. He had greeted us warmly, and Anne made the introductions. Joseph Lekipaika was the head teacher of the village school, and he was also assisting the Women's Papermaking Cooperative. As he led us across the red, sun-baked earth, he explained that he was allowing the women to store their materials and finished products in the schoolhouse.

"They have no place of their own to work, and their husbands aren't supportive of this project," he said. "I am different to my male peers. I believe in the rights of women. I think initiatives like this are a stepping stone for Samburu women to gain more control over their lives."

Only later did I learn that, traditionally, Samburu women have very little power; that they aren't allowed to own property and are excluded from community meetings and decisions; that, in championing their cause, Joseph was a remarkably enlightened man.

The eight members of the cooperative were sitting in the dappled shade of a tree, next to a long table. They had high foreheads and fine cheekbones. Their hair was cut very short or shaved, their earlobes lengthened from years of heavy earrings. They wore layers of brightly patterned cloths called *shukas* and huge, beaded necklaces made from many loops of wire. More beaded jewelry adorned their wrists, ankles, waists, and foreheads. As we approached, the woman who looked the oldest stood up. She was painfully thin, but her handshake was strong. Grasping my arm, she began speaking rapidly to us in Samburu, with

Joseph translating. She showed us the heaps of fresh elephant dung she and the other women had collected that day, and the equipment they used to make this into paper: big pots for boiling the dung into a pulp over a fire, sieves to remove stones and bits of vegetation, frames for spreading out the pulp to dry in the sun. She directed our attention to the tabletop and the sheets of grey parchment dotted with fibre, covered with traditional Samburu patterns made with tiny, colourful beads. As we looked through them, the women crowded around us. Then my new friend grabbed my arm again and began an urgent speech.

"She is saying what I told you before, that they have to do all their work outdoors, in the sun and the rain," Joseph translated. "She says if they had their own place, they could make more paper and have a little shop. Tourists could come to buy cards and the jewelry they make. But their husbands won't help them to build a house. She is asking if you can offer that help."

At this point, we didn't have many funds in Elephant Earth, so any donation would come directly from us. We asked how much such a building would cost. Anne and Joseph came up with an estimate for a construction made of breeze blocks, but it was too high. Dag suggested a structure built in part from traditional materials – termite soil for the walls, acacia branches for beams. The women said they could collect these. Anne did a rough calculation of the cost of extra timber, screws, tools, wire, rainwater tanks, guttering, tractor hire, and so on. As for the more skilled building work, asked Dag, could some of their husbands help? At this, the women fell silent.

"The men won't be happy about their wives getting a bit of independence," said Anne. "But let's see what we can do."

We came to an agreement. A couple of months later, we had sent money to Anne to buy the necessary supplies. The women in the village collected soil and wood. But the project stalled. The jealous husbands had refused to contribute labour, so extra costs would have to be incurred. We needed to discuss all this with the papermaking cooperative. We wanted to spend an afternoon in Nalare, and our group was keen to come along.

~

This time, as well as Joseph, the whole papermaking cooperative was waiting for us by the road. The women were done up in their finery, and they hurried toward us with ululations and handshakes. Again, we gathered under the tree by the table, and Joseph translated their forthright questions. Had Anne told us about their problem? What did we think? Could we assist? The matter was quickly settled. We reconfigured a budget, and Anne agreed to make all the arrangements for the outside crew. Then the sales pitch began: Would our group like to buy cards? And how about jewelry? From cloth bags, gorgeous beaded items were produced and laid alongside the elephant dung paper in front of 12 eager and curious shoppers. Anne leaned in too, and while transactions were going on, Joseph took Dag and me to one side.

"I have a request," he said. "There is a young woman in our community who needs help. Her name is Priscilla Lekorere, but she goes by Agnes. She was my star pupil. She passed all her higher exams with top marks and was offered a place at the University of Nairobi. This is a great opportunity for a young person from a Samburu village. But her father and the community Elders will not give her the financial support she needs. They are punishing her for having refused for a long time to undergo FGM – female genital mutilation."

He paused, as if to gauge our reaction. Dag and I were silent, taking this in. There had been a lot in the local news about FGM, which had just been declared illegal in Kenya. Circumcision was regarded as a necessary rite of passage into adulthood for both men and women. It was performed as a ritual and followed with big celebrations. Male circumcision involved cutting off the foreskin. For females, it was far more complicated – a brutal process of cutting away the clitoris and sometimes other external genital parts, without anesthetic. It often led to long-term medical problems: complications during childbirth, fistulas, chronic infections, not to mention painful sex, depression, and post-traumatic stress. Despite the recent ruling, it was still rife, particularly in remote rural areas where uncircumcised women were regarded as "unclean" and a disgrace to their families.

"Agnes has been very brave, fighting this," Joseph continued. "Only her mother and I have supported her decision."

"How can we help?" Dag asked.

"If someone is prepared to pay her fees and expenses for university, her father cannot stop her going. I have spoken to Agnes's mother, Mary, and she gave me her permission to make this request of you."

He nodded toward one of the papermaking women, who was standing slightly apart from the others, watching our exchange. She was small and slight. When our eyes met, she smiled shyly and looked away.

"But we haven't mentioned this to Agnes," Joseph continued. "I tried before with a local land conservancy, run by an Englishwoman, which gives support to women's education. But for them the FGM question was an issue – they didn't want to upset the Samburu community."

Anne had already told us about the delicate relationships that she and other ranchers had with their Indigenous neighbours. The Samburu, like the Masai further south, wanted to freely graze their livestock across what they claimed as their traditional lands. But during colonial times some of those lands had been granted to white settlers, and some of their descendants, like Anne and her father, had become avowed conservationists, turning their properties into corridors for wild animals, including elephants, the keystone species. With too much grazing, the vegetation needed by elephants would be destroyed. The whole ecosystem would be thrown off balance. Anne had long been in negotiation mode over land issues. There had been clashes in the past, and some of them had turned violent; she was anxious to stay in the good graces of her neighbours. But if we wanted to assist this Samburu girl, we would need Anne's help. I walked over to where she was busily translating the transactions around the table, tapped her on the shoulder, and quietly relayed what Joseph had told us. She didn't miss a beat.

"Let's talk to her," she said.

I asked Joseph if Agnes could meet with us.

"Please don't raise her hopes yet," I said.

He nodded. "I will tell her you wish to ask some questions about village life. And that I have chosen her to speak because her English is so good."

I briefly explained the situation to our group. Leaving the paper-making women packing up their supplies and jewelry, we moved to another clump of acacia trees and sat in a semi-circle beneath them. Joseph returned with Agnes. She was as tall as him and heavy-set, with a full face. She wore a loose, red T-shirt and a calf-length skirt. A blue scarf was wrapped around her head and numerous long braids fell beneath it to below her shoulders. I stood up to shake her hand.

"Thank you for coming to talk to us," I said.

"It is my pleasure," she replied. "I am happy to tell you about my village and culture."

I led the discussion, asking Agnes about elephants coming into the village, about her views on the papermaking project, about her school years. She answered clearly, pitching her voice so everyone could hear. She was poised and confident.

"We heard from your teacher that you got stellar marks in school," I said finally. "And that you have been offered a place at the University of Nairobi."

"I cannot take the place," she said. "My father and other village Elders won't support me."

"Why not?" I asked her.

She paused for a moment, then held her head high.

"Because I will not be cut."

∼

Though I have never asked Joseph, I can guess why he didn't tell me about Agnes during our first visit to Nalare. He wanted to make sure we were the sort of people who would keep to our promises. If the house for the papermaking cooperative had failed to materialize, the women would have been terribly disappointed. But it was only a building; it was worth the risk. With Agnes, however, it could be disastrous.

Only later, as we grew closer, did I gradually learn the extent of what Agnes had been enduring. When she was 10 years old, there was a presentation at her school about HIV. The course instructor told the students that the virus could be spread through the knives and blades used during

FGM. Agnes was already scared of the pain of circumcision; now she had a new fear to add to that.

"I gathered my courage to say no," she wrote to me in an email. "But it was very hard. In our culture, it is a taboo not to undergo FGM. Women in the village kept asking me when was I coming for my initiation ceremony. I would brush them off and politely say never. My peers thought I was not brave enough to undergo the cut, and they said I would never be a true Samburu woman. And my dad was angry. Other men would ask him how he could be a community Elder yet have a daughter who doesn't follow the culture. He kept hoping that, by the time I graduated high school, I would give in and undergo the cut."

After high school, instead of taking her university place, she helped her mother run a small shop in the village. She took computer courses in a nearby town. Mostly, she languished.

"Before I met you, every evening I would cry myself to sleep," she confided in another email. "I was very depressed and put on a lot of weight. I felt trapped. One night, I asked God why he allowed me to perform so well in high school when clearly he knew I couldn't go to university. And, just like that, God sent you."

∼

Agnes sat and talked to the group for a while. She told us about her seven siblings, how she was the oldest of the two girls in the family, and that she was going to do all in her power to protect her sister from going through FGM. While I listened, my mind raced. Memories of what had happened when we tried to help Vinh and Bac resurfaced. I wanted to find out from Anne and Joseph what helping Agnes would involve financially. If it was even possible, given her father's stance. How could Joseph be sure he would let her leave the village? What if he tried to use our offer as a bargaining chip and demand more money? What if this separated her from her culture? Eventually, I thanked Agnes and said we had to get back to Anne's lodge. She shook everyone's hands, wished us a good journey to the coast, and walked away. When she was out of earshot, we went into a huddle. Joseph assured me Agnes's mother was prepared to step away from community norms and make a stand against her husband; that she would not let him prevent their daughter from taking such an opportunity; that she had a rare strength in this regard. He and Anne made a rough estimate of the cost of university fees, accommodation, and expenses for four years.

Agnes had inspired everyone in our group; they were all eager to help. In my notebook, I wrote out our pledge under the title "Agnes's Scholarship Fund." Joseph sent a couple of children to call her back, and to tell her to bring the papers with her grade results. She returned looking puzzled. Joseph read out from the papers – top marks consistently. Everyone clapped. Then we told her about our decision, and her puzzlement turned to astonishment. There is a photo of Agnes and me, heads close together, as she reads the pledge in my notebook. Another one, taken right after that, arms wrapped around each other, before she hugged everyone in the group.

"When you and Dag and your friends left the village, I went straight to my small room, locked myself up, and started crying," Agnes wrote to me later. "I could not believe what just happened. I didn't eat, I went to bed early, but I couldn't sleep. I prayed a lot that night and cried some more. Then I resolved never to cry myself to sleep again. The next morning, my mother and siblings had a small party for me. They were very happy and proud. All that day I was just in my little world of imagination. I asked myself questions like, how will university life be? Will I cope being alone in the big city of Nairobi?"

⁓

Of course, it could all have gone sideways – and early on I feared it would. It was then late September. The university semester had already started; Agnes would have to wait until January to enroll. Her father was furious about our support; that his daughter was about to get what she most wanted, despite being in an "impure" woman in the eyes of the community. His fury caused her to leave the village and move in with relatives on the outskirts of Nairobi. But she wrote to tell us she was safe, that her father just needed time to accept what had happened.

January rolled around. Just after Agnes became an undergraduate at Nairobi university's Faculty of Business and Management Studies, Dag and I returned to Kenya for a long trek with Anne. With six camels and a support team of four men, we set off to walk for three days and 110 kilometres across the high plains of Laikipia to the Karisia Hills. Cloaked in dense forest, the hills acted like a water tower for the surrounding area and provided a natural sanctuary for fauna small and large – the largest of which were elephants. But poaching was on the rise, and Anne wanted us to meet a group of community anti-poaching scouts. They were the first line of defence against people who were increasingly killing elephants for their ivory. They worked voluntarily, and they needed basic equipment – radios, tents, boots, and clothing. Dag and I quickly agreed to support them through Elephant Earth. Then we walked back.

After the trek, we visited Nalare to meet the papermaking cooperative and see the progress on the house. The site had been chosen, the foundations were laid. Rain had transformed the land – green grasses covered the red soil, and there was foliage on the trees. Agnes's mother Mary was with us, and she had a small goat on a lead. I didn't think too much about it. Goats and cattle are a huge part of Samburu life. They represent wealth, so I reckoned it was a bit like having a wallet full of money – around 50 US dollars in this case – that maybe she wanted to keep an eye on to make sure it didn't go missing. I've always loved goats, and I admired this one, with its pretty markings and long, soft ears. As usual, Mary smiled shyly. But as we were preparing to leave the village, she approached me and, with Anne translating, made a speech.

"You have given my daughter a great gift," she said. "I can never thank you enough." With that, she handed me the end of the rope around the goat's neck. I looked at her in confusion. I turned to Anne.

"This goat is for me?"

"It's a great honour," said Anne. "Mary had been hoping we could stay in the village tonight. She wanted to arrange a goat roast, and you would have been presented with the liver to eat."

"This goat's liver?"

Mary was curiously watching our exchange. I knew I was being a ridiculous foreigner. I rearranged my face. Giving Mary a grateful hug, I explained we had to return to the lodge that night. We kneeled down on either side of the goat, each of us with a hand on its neck, and posed for a photo. The goat was loaded in the back of Anne's Jeep. I kept it company for the bumpy, two-hour drive, stroking its soft ears. By the time we reached the lodge, I was very fond of it. Anne's cook was clearly delighted to see it too, but for different reasons. For the next few days, I avoided the meat dishes he served us.

We sent money for Agnes's fees and accommodation via Anne, who made sure it went to the right places. When she was in Nairobi, she checked in on Agnes and kept us updated on her progress. From time to time, Agnes emailed me, her messages full of gratitude for the opportunity we, and the "Hidden Places Ladies," had given her. Partway through her second semester, she wrote that she had decided her calling was law, not business. The switch meant extra years at university. Dag and I agreed that, whatever the rest of the group decided long-term, we would support her.

From then on, Kenya kept drawing us back. We started running fundraising treks to the Karisia Hills. We walked 150 kilometres in a week, accompanied by a train of camels and a big team of Samburu warriors, camping along the way. Participants raised money from family and friends, which went to the anti-poaching scouts we met at the end of each trek. And we always stopped for a visit in Nalare.

Each time we were in Nairobi, before or after a trek, we tried to meet up with Agnes. Within a year she had completely transformed. The extra weight that depression had piled onto her was gone. She was elegant and citified. She wore high heels and dresses that emphasized her slim figure and long legs. She always greeted us with her dazzling smile, but she was still shy and rather formal, and I was probably the same. Emotionally, I had kept my expectations low. I had learned a lot from our failure to help Vinh and Bac; I knew so much was out of our control. Of course, this was a completely different situation. From the beginning, I knew Agnes was a strong woman, and that even if she didn't manage to complete her university studies, she would somehow use the opportunity we'd given her. I thought about how lovely it would be to have her as part of our lives in the long term, but I wasn't banking on that. Her emails kept coming, though, sometimes with news of exams passed, always with gratitude.

In late September 2014, I went to Kenya alone to lead one of our fundraising treks. After a week of walking, we set off on the eight-hour drive to Nairobi. By late afternoon, dusty and tired, we were back in our regular lodge in a leafy suburb of the city. I was flying to Canada in the early hours of the next morning and had to be at the airport around midnight, but I'd arranged for Agnes to come over and have dinner with me. The lodge had a small outdoor restaurant, with tables set on a veranda overlooking a central garden and pond. It was a cold evening, and Agnes arrived bundled up in a heavy coat, which she kept on throughout our meal. I told her about our visit to Nalare during the trek, how we met her mother and danced with the women of the papermaking cooperative. She talked about how her studies were going, how her little sister was thriving at school, and how she had reached a truce with her father. She was now involved in the anti-FGM movement and was returning to the village to give talks to the pupils at her former school. She told me about the plan to set up alternative rites of passage for young women in Nalare. Instead of being "cut," they would be taught about Samburu culture and traditions, about health and sexuality and life skills. Then, during a celebration, they would receive a certificate announcing their passage into womanhood.

As we talked, frogs started croaking in the pond. I had the sense that something was bothering Agnes. I had noticed straightaway that her face had filled out, and I was concerned she was depressed again. But our relationship was still quite formal; I didn't feel I could probe.

"Is anything the matter?" I asked hesitantly.

Moths flapped around the lamp that hung over our table. Agnes's smooth cheeks gleamed in the soft light.

"Everything is fine," she said. "Don't worry about me. When is your flight? The traffic is very bad, you should leave with lots of time to spare."

~

I was only home for six weeks before setting off with Dag on a three-month trip to six countries for a mixture of scouting, leading trips, attending a film festival, and doing elephant conservation work. I had a lot on my mind, but at the back of it all was a growing concern. I hadn't heard from Agnes since our meeting. I'd tried emailing, texting, and phoning her but got no reply. Anne was spending some time in England, so I couldn't ask her to go and find Agnes in Nairobi. I wrote to Joseph, but he said he had no news.

My emotional barrier was still up. I wasn't disappointed in her, or cross that she wasn't writing. But as weeks turned into months of silence, I had a growing sense of disquiet, that something bad had befallen her.

I finally heard from her at the very end of our travels, in China. We were about to fly from Beijing to Canada; our bags were packed, and I was sitting on the bed in our hotel room, downloading emails. Dag was at the reception desk arranging for a taxi. I saw Agnes's name in my inbox. The subject line of her email read, "Resuming Studies." I clicked on the message:

> I am sorry for the long silence. Last time we met at Wildebeest Ecolodge, I wanted to discuss something with you but I couldn't because you were going to catch your flight. Actually I was pregnant then and I had the baby on December 14th. I am so sorry for this but I promise to discuss everything when we meet again. I feel so bad about myself, I never thought that I will repay Dag and you in this unkind way. Please Maria kindly forgive me and I beg you to continue your support on my education. I can't do without your help.

I stared at her words. A baby? I hadn't even considered this as the reason for her silence, but *of course*...I remembered her full face when we last met, the bulky coat. I counted back – she would have been six months pregnant. How stupid of me not to have realized. She was probably waiting for me to ask. But we had been together for a few hours – why couldn't she tell me? Was there some terrible reason? I felt a wash of fear. I tapped out a quick reply.

Without question, we would continue to support her, I wrote. "But please let me know about the baby. Did you have a boy or a girl? Where did you give birth, and how was the labour? Who is helping to look after the baby? Are you in a relationship with the father? I so hope the pregnancy wasn't the result of a bad experience. Please write to me with full news very soon."

Dag walked into the room. "The taxi will be here any minute, so we should check out." He saw my face. "What's happened?"

"I'll explain on the way to the airport," I said.

∽

Sitting in a transit lounge at the Chengdu airport, I picked up her reply.

I am in tears as I write you this mail. I can't believe that I still have your support. I thought you would be disappointed in me, that I would lose my scholarship. Thank you once more for being true friends to me. I have never thought anyone would love me this much. This will also be a relief to my mother since she has been scared about my career. The baby is a boy, called Adrian Saitabau. He is healthy and playful. I will attach some pictures. I gave birth at Cottage Hospital in Nanyuki. I was in labour for twenty-two hours. That pain was crazy but it was worth enduring it. I am back in the village with him, but we will be returning to Nairobi and my grandmother will be looking after him while I study. I will be expressing breast milk for him till he is at least six months. I am in a relationship with the father of my baby. He has been supportive to us. But I would like to make a kind request that, if possible, you add me a little more accommodation money. I will need it more than ever since I will have to get a room for the baby and me. The hostels I was staying in before don't allow students with babies. I will appreciate your assistance on this.

The extra money wasn't a problem. A couple of the women in our group withdrew their support when they found out about the baby, but others stepped in with even more help. But I didn't know until much later how high the stakes had been for her; why she had held back from telling me. If our group had withdrawn our support, she would have had to give up her studies. That itself was a terror, but worse still, it meant her father would have had power over her again. He would have insisted that, as an impure Samburu woman, she was not fit to raise a child, and the baby would be taken away from her. Losing her child, her education, her entire future: the thought was unbearable. So she warded it off for as long as possible by keeping her silence. She arranged for a break from her studies after the birth without consulting Anne or us. It was only just before she was due to go back to university, at the very last minute, when her mother was insisting, that she wrote me the first short email I picked up in Beijing.

The baby brought us closer. I let down my emotional barriers and allowed her to land fully in my heart. We began to write more, to share confidences. I met little Adrian in Nairobi. Agnes asked me if I thought she should marry his father. She wasn't sure, she felt like keeping her independence. I told her it was her decision entirely, that she should only take that step if and when she felt ready. I had promised earlier that, when she graduated, Dag and I would attend the ceremony, but by then she had decided she wanted to become a barrister. The support from our safari group had ended, so we agreed to cover the fees ourselves. As the graduation ceremony didn't coincide with any trips, instead of us paying for flights to Nairobi, we added that money to her education fund.

Agnes is a barrister now. She works on children's rights and on anti-FGM issues. She's raising her family alone, and she keeps me updated on her life, her successes and milestones, regularly sending me messages and photos through WhatsApp. I have a special file on my computer for all the photos. The ones of Adrian date from now, proud in his school uniform, long-legged and with a dazzling smile, just like his mother, back to the ones that were attached to the email I picked up at the Chengdu airport. Adrian Saitabau, immediately after his birth, his head extended from the forceps delivery, his umbilical cord curling from his belly, his hands over his face with just one rather angry eye showing. Then Adrian at 2 months old, lying on his side in a cot, sleeping peacefully. Gazing at those for the first time under the bright lights of the transit lounge, I had felt a sudden jolt of joy. Back then, it was an unexpected and surprising feeling. Now I'm used to it. When my phone pings as messages and photos of Adrian and his baby sister, Serenoi, arrive, I remember what my mother-in-law, Justina, once said: When you have a child, happiness and love grow. And with each child that comes, the love expands to encompass them.

21

I was 59 when I met Agnes. On learning my age, she was openly shocked. I was older than her grandmother, older than the oldest woman in the papermaking cooperative, who seemed so ancient. But, of course, those women's lives had been inordinately harder than mine: decades of punishing outdoor work and cooking inside smoky huts, rudimentary health care, the trauma of FGM, and a litany of pregnancies, starting from their early teens. It was little wonder I looked years younger than them.

But even in my own, highly privileged culture, a reveal of my age had for long raised eyebrows. At my mother's funeral, a man I hadn't seen for two decades started in astonishment when we met. "What are you on?" he demanded.

My genes had been kind to me. Dag complained he was doing the aging for both of us. This, plus our hectic lifestyle, and without growing children to mark the passage of time, had allowed me to exist in a kind of Neverland: I had simply forgotten I was getting old.

When I turned 60, I declared myself Age Neutral and announced I was racking up "youth miles." We had a weekend-long celebration in Canada. Several of the guests thought I was joking about which birthday it was. "You do mean 50, don't you?" exclaimed one woman, and she wasn't just being polite.

Then things began to quickly change. Deep wrinkles appeared at the sides of my mouth, finer ones around my chin. Flubber crept onto my stomach, crepiness onto my thighs and upper arms. My neck suddenly belonged to a turtle. Comments about how young I looked rapidly dwindled. A specialist I saw about a shoulder issue kept referring to "ladies of your vintage," as he injected me with cortisone. And, in one way or another, people had started asking about when I was going to retire.

~

We were having dinner with a young couple who were establishing a company to run kayak tours from a remote island in British Columbia. They were interested in how we had set up our business, how it had evolved.

"So," said Dave, as we started on the cheese course. "What's your exit strategy for Hidden Places?"

We both gawked at him. "Exit strategy?" I spluttered.

The truth was we didn't have one. We'd never had a business plan, or any long-term plans in any area of life. Our modus operandi had always been to first decide what we didn't want to do. Uncertainty was our stimulus; we embraced it, following our instincts. We had developed trips in areas we wanted to explore, that inspired us, rather than for purely commercial reasons. Creating and running Hidden Places had been a big adventure, a haphazard, exciting journey. I didn't want it to stop.

"I suppose our strategy is – we DIE!" I snapped at Dave, who looked mortified and changed the subject.

"It was a fair question," said Dag when we were in bed that night. "It's obvious we can't keep this pace up indefinitely."

I stared into the darkness. "I love our big life. I'm terrified of it becoming small. That will come soon enough."

"What do you mean?"

"When we're old."

"Maria," he said gently. "You're almost 64. Next year, you'll officially be a senior. You'll get old age pension. Life will have to change eventually. You've got to be open to that."

~

Later that year, two good friends, Tara and Andrew, visited us with their small daughter. Excitedly, they told us about the co-housing project they were helping to establish in the interior of British Columbia.

They explained the concept: an intentional, multigenerational community living in privately owned houses clustered around shared areas and facilities – gardens, workshops, a communal house for events and meals. Committees would run everything by consensus. They wanted to do this so their daughter would grow up surrounded by other children, with a sense of community. On a lakeside acreage, with mountain views and close to a ski hill, they were building 24 houses, beautifully designed and appointed, and very reasonably priced. Some of the houses were already spoken for, mostly by young couples with small children. For our friends, the multigenerational part was key. They wanted some older people in the mix. They asked us to consider selling our Victoria condo and moving there. They had known us for a long time; we were like family.

"We need elders," said Andrew. "People with experience of the world they could share."

"Grandparent figures?" I said. I was teasing, but he nodded.

"I think of you guys as ever young," Tara chipped in tactfully. "I know you're going to be racing around the world for years. But this would be a good base for you, and one day you might like the companionship and support our community will offer. And, anyway, it would be awesome to have you living there."

After they had left, we talked about it. Dag was drawn to the idea of sharing resources – he and Andrew had chatted about the possibility of building cedar-strip kayaks in a communal workshop. And before their visit I had been thinking about the lack of physical connection with our friends in British Columbia. I had none of the social routines most of them had had for years: book clubs, yoga classes, "girls' nights," regular hikes, and bike rides. Shared activities that cement friendships. And now lots of them were becoming grandmothers, and that was cementing them further. Sometimes I wondered if we should try to spend more time at home and establish a more stable community. The co-housing idea sounded like a ready-made solution. We knew Tara and Andrew would create a lovely environment and surround themselves with like-minded people. There would be children around; we could be de facto grandparents. We were touched they wanted to include us. But the place they planned was too far from an airport, or the coast, for our needs. And it also felt too soon to be more settled.

In early 2016, through a friend, we heard about a house for sale in a community co-housing project that was close to the ocean and an airport. Dag developed one of his sudden enthusiasms for the idea.

"Maybe we should try it out now," he suggested. "And if it doesn't work, we could move on, while we still have the energy for that. If we wait another ten years to try it, we could get stuck."

The sellers were asking prospective buyers to visit the community for a couple of days before making an offer. There was a guest room in the communal house where they could stay. They would be toured around, invited to a meeting, an event, and a communal dinner, and be able to interact with the 60 or so residents. A number of parties were interested, and the only available time slots coincided with me being in Kenya for a fundraising trek, then going on to India for a kayaking trip.

"Do you think I should check it out on my own?" asked Dag.

I hesitated.

"Do you really want to?" I was relieved to have a solid excuse not to go.

"I guess I might as well."

"Well, okay then."

He booked a slot.

~

I was out of cell phone range for most of the trek. I sent Dag a couple of text messages via my inReach device and got a short one back saying his visit had been "very interesting." But I was too entranced by the high savannah, the herds of elephants, giraffes, zebras, and antelopes, the sweetness and care of our Samburu teams, the camels that plodded along behind us carrying all our gear from one campsite to the next – not to mention the soreness of my feet after each 20-kilometre day – to think about a co-housing project in Canada.

Back in Nairobi, while I waited for the first of my overnight flights to India, I picked up emails and scrolled through Dag's messages and photos. The place had exceeded his expectations. The house was really nice.

He liked the people he met. He thought we should go for it. We had to decide soon – the owners were taking offers within a week.

I thought about it on the plane. Did I want to do this? Maybe in a decade, but now? Over the next few days, as I met our group and started kayaking in the Kerala backwaters, I dithered. I trusted Dag, his taste, his judgment. But making a decision like this from such a long distance seemed crazy. Dag didn't pressure me, but I knew he was waiting for my answer. The dithering was distracting me from my work. And it was exhausting. Finally – and I really don't know why – I agreed.

"It will be different," Dag wrote. "But if we don't love it, we can simply move on."

~

Several of the Kerala group had travelled with me before and knew me quite well. One evening, I told them about the community co-housing project. How Dag had said the other residents were mostly "our age." There were only a couple of families with small children, including our next door neighbours, but others had grandchildren who visited frequently. I said I'd been imagining kids running in and out of our house, hosting parties for neighbours, Dag creating beautiful wooden furniture in the communal workshop alongside some new like-minded chums. Yoga lessons in the common house, just two minutes' walk away.

"What do you think?" I asked, when I stopped for breath.

No one responded at first.

"From what I've heard about such places, people are expected to participate," said one woman. I could tell she was carefully choosing her words. "You and Dag are always travelling. Honestly, I'd think hard about this before deciding."

I didn't tell her our offer had been accepted, and Dag had made the deposit.

~

From the parking area, on the perimeter of the ten-acre property, we followed paths to a horseshoe-shaped arrangement of identical duplexes, one of the three housing "pods" in the development. The front windows faced a lawn with a couple of trees, a double swing seat, and a wooden picnic table. As we approached the house that would soon be ours, the door was flung open.

"Welcome!" cried a slender, blond-haired woman. Behind her stood a lean man with short grey hair and a goatee.

"It's so good to meet you, Maria," he said. "I feel like I know you from your books."

Dag had already told me something about Jan and Fred. They were stalwarts of this community, but some tragic family circumstances were forcing them to move to Vancouver. They ushered us inside and gave us a quick tour of the house, then led us out of the back door to tour the whole property. The meadow, the communal gardens and workshop, the kayak shed, the recycling shed.

"We left the best for last," said Jan.

The communal house was huge and sturdily built, with big wooden beams and high windows. In the porch, a diary board showed upcoming events: knitting club, book club, yoga, exercise class, coffee mornings, a house concert, and a whole slew of meetings for committees looking after gardening, parking, trees, maintenance – the list went on. In the spacious dining/living room area, next to an industrial kitchen, we sat across from Fred and Jan on a couple of sofas.

"There are usually two communal meals here a week," said Jan. "You don't have to join in, but it's encouraged. Everything is arranged by the meals committees."

I ran my hand over the fabric covering the sofa Dag and I were sitting on. It was an old-fashioned design, similar to one that had covered my mother's "three piece suite" in her living room.

"It took forever for us to get proper furniture in here," said Fred. "The committee in charge had endless meetings about the style, the price, and so on. It was 18 months before they reached an agreement."

"Eighteen months?" I parroted.

"Well, decisions made on a consensus basis can take longer than usual."

We had lunch back at their house. Jan insisted I took the "view" seat at the table, facing out to their small garden and the meadow beyond it.

"In the spring and summer, the meadow's full of wildflowers," she said. "In the evenings, you can hear frogs singing from the creek. Dag told us how much you love frogs."

They were so kind. They didn't want to leave this place, yet they were doing everything they could to make us feel welcome and appreciated as its new owners. But I had an overwhelming sense of unease. I concentrated on the delicious lunch – squash soup, various salads, local cheeses and bread – and attempted to make appreciative noises. Then some people emerged into my view. Silver-haired, bent-backed, moving slowly, pushing wheelbarrows across the meadow, they were like spectres rising from the grass. I put down my knife and fork and sat very still, watching them.

"They're from the gardening committee." Jan's voice sounded distant. "They meet every week at this time to do some work in the communal garden."

I kept staring. I was seeing myself in the future. Old. Out there in the meadow.

With a sharp intake of breath, I looked away from the window and met Jan's concerned gaze.

"Are you okay, Maria?"

Her voice sounded normal again. I realized my lower lip was trembling, that tears were pricking my eyes.

~

We moved in June. At first, we received a warm welcome. Soon, however, our new neighbours made it clear they didn't want us to use this place as a base. Our model of parachuting in and having gatherings to catch up socially before leaving again didn't work for them. The dinner parties we hosted were awkward affairs. We were quizzed about when we would be staying for longer periods, which committees we planned on joining, if we'd signed up for communal meals. And while people had got to know Dag a bit during his pre-purchase visit, it appeared I remained an enigma.

"Even when you're here, we don't see you out and about," commented a woman called Madeline. "We thought you would at least come to the coffee mornings to meet people."

I described my demanding work schedule. How when I took a break it was usually to walk downtown for some shopping. I would go out through the back of the house and follow the path through the meadow to reach the road. I loved that meadow; it always lifted my spirits.

"That helps to explain something. There's a rumour going around you're agoraphobic."

I laughed.

"That's hardly likely, with all the travelling I do for our business."

"Where are you going next?"

I told her about the Himalayan trek in September, a fundraiser for snow leopard conservation. Straight after it, I'd join Dag in Greece to lead a kayaking trip. And in the winter I'd be heading to Antarctica.

There was silence around the table.

"That's a lot of time away," said the man sitting next to her.

I stayed quiet for the rest of the meal.

~

Dag was trying harder than me. He had joined the Maintenance Committee. One day, he got a call. In the garden area, the irrigation piping in a culvert had got blocked.

"That sounds easy," he said, as he headed out. "I should be back soon."

It was two hours before he returned.

"When I arrived, there were four guys staring at the pipe," he told me. "I took one look and knew how to solve the problem. I could have fixed it in 15 minutes. But everyone had to offer their suggestion, then everyone else had to discuss it. Consensus decision making over a blocked pipe! I got so frustrated I left."

My first big problem arose because of a rotary washing line. It had four metal arms with nylon lines strung between them, like a web, mounted atop a long metal leg. The arms could be folded down to lie alongside the leg, which fitted into a base buried in our lawn. Jan and Fred had explained it was shared by three houses – theirs and the houses on either side of them. They said it was typical of the community to combine resources like this rather than overconsume. But that the only other person who regularly used the line was Raynor, a single woman living in the next duplex, separated from their house – now ours – by a narrow stretch of bushes and trees.

As the wildflower meadow bloomed, I had become increasingly annoyed by my view of it being impeded by the rotary washing line, even with the arms down. One morning, I pulled it out of its base and leaned it against the wall of our house, which was four steps away. This seemed logical to me. It only took seconds to replace the line in its base. I was a bit uneasy. I knew I should have first discussed this with Raynor, but she was away on a hiking trip. And I was a bit intimidated by her. A decade younger than me, she was a founding member of the co-housing project, and her passion for it was intense. A counsellor who offered sessions for "transformational change," she had a direct, steady gaze and a preternatural aura of calm and inner control.

The remote island property we had a share in was up for sale, so we were spending a lot of time on it during what we knew would probably be our last summer season there. One morning, I was on my computer in the cabin when I noticed an email from Raynor arrive. The subject was "Moving my clothesline." She wrote that she was uncomfortable about me taking the clothesline out of its base. She had checked with the Wild Space Committee, and it had agreed she could put the line in the meadow. She had no idea when we would be returning, so she planned to move it the following day, but to let her know if we had any other ideas. I was taken aback. A clothesline in the meadow? And what was this about "my" clothesline? I had a huge pile of work emails to deal with, so I wrote a quick note, apologizing for the misunderstanding. I said we'd return within a week, and I would drop by then to see if we could find a different solution.

When I walked into the house, through the dining area window I immediately saw the washing line, hung with Raynor's laundry. But it was no longer in our garden. It was in the meadow. Around it was a big bare circle – the red poppies, white Queen Anne's lace, purple vervain, and golden grasses all trimmed to extinction.

I should have calmed down before I marched to Raynor's back door and knocked. Waiting for an answer, I realized I couldn't see the washing line from where I stood. The view of it was blocked by her bushes. The door opened; I spun around.

"Raynor, I wish we could have discussed this," I blurted out. "It's awful to destroy part of the meadow for a washing line. Can't we – "

"Can't we what?" she shouted. Her face turned red; her usual aura of calm and inner control vanished, replaced by fury. "I spent fucking hours getting the area ready and digging a new hole for the base. It was fucking hard work. And it's MY washing line. I bought it."

I took a step back and gathered my thoughts.

"But I thought it was communal property."

"No, it's MINE. I paid 50 dollars for it."

"So why was it in our garden?"

"Before you arrived, everyone agreed it was the best place."

"But if it's your line, why not put it in your garden?"

"Because then I would have to look at it when I'm sitting on my back patio."

I was so astonished by this I laughed out loud. Which only made things worse.

"I know the history of this community and how things work, and you clearly don't and haven't bothered to find out," she raged on. "I told you in my email that the Wild Space Committee had agreed to the new placement of the line. And, anyway, it's my line, and I don't need your permission for what I do with it."

Sensing she was close to tears, I suggested we talk about this another time.

"That went well," said Dag wryly when I walked into the living room. He'd been hovering in our back doorway and had heard everything.

I wrote Raynor an email. I apologized for the mix-up and suggested we meet over coffee or a drink to sort it out. A long message came in return. She agreed we should meet. But it had to be in a neutral space, like the Common House. There had to be someone else in attendance, one of the Conflict Resolution Committee, or an independent mediator of our choice. And only Dag or I should be there, because with both of us she would feel outnumbered.

"You should go," I told Dag.

"You're right," he said.

He came back shaking his head.

"I think you're going to have to live with the washing line in the meadow. And, apparently, she hadn't said the F-word to anyone for years. She said you triggered something in her."

"Triggered what?"

"I'm not sure. I don't think it's worth finding out."

Of course, I had been largely to blame. The culture of the place was based around participation. I clearly wasn't making an effort, by this time neither was Dag, and people were annoyed with us. Not long after the incident with Raynor, we drove into the parking lot and got out of our car as a woman from another pod walked past with her dog.

"Hello," I said.

"Hello, *Maria*," she replied testily. "You don't know my name, do you? I happen to live here too, in case you hadn't noticed."

Dag and I both felt trapped. It was like we had ended up in the wrong skins and didn't know what to do about it.

∿

In late January 2017, to celebrate Dag's 59th birthday, we arranged a getaway with friends on one of the remote Nuchatlaht Islands, off the west coast of Vancouver Island. To get there, we would have to drive for four hours, partly on rough logging roads, then go by water taxi for an hour. Friends from Victoria drove up to spend the night with us before we all set off the next day. It was their first time visiting us in the new house. They burst through the door, brandishing bottles and yelling at us in astonishment.

"What the hell are you guys doing here? We wandered past all these identical houses and knocked on the wrong doors twice."

"It's like something out of *Peyton Place*!"

"No, *Trailer Park Boys*!"

"Have you lost your minds?"

They teased us mercilessly that night and on the drive the next day. However, when we boarded an aluminum motorboat in the tiny settlement of Zeballos, and roared down a fjord, everyone fell under a spell of beauty, gazing up at steep, forested, snow-dusted peaks reflected in the still water. The boat dropped us at the dock below a cabin, and we hauled our bags, groceries, and bottles up the ramp. We arranged a time for the driver to return in three days. There was no cell phone coverage, and no Wi-Fi, so we wouldn't be able to contact him.

We settled into our rooms, got the food stored away, put the beers, champagne, and white wine to chill, and went out for a walk through the woods and along the shore. Dag was in fine form, laughing and joking with his buddies. But during dinner he grew quiet. He'd only eaten a few mouthfuls before he excused himself, took a flashlight that was hanging by the door, and went outside.

The toilet was a double outhouse, connected to the building by a boardwalk. For the next two days, he spent a lot of time either there or in bed dealing with a nasty stomach flu. He was feverish and couldn't eat. I checked in with him regularly, but he wanted to be left alone. Between his outhouse forays, he curled up like a sick animal. He missed most of his party, but everyone else made up for him. We hiked and kayaked, did yoga in the living room, cooked huge meals, and drank far too much. And I talked endlessly about how unhappy I was with our living situation. One friend, who is a life coach, plied me with all the right questions – and lots of wine. Soon I was admitting what a colossal mistake it had been. By the time the weekend was over, I knew what to do.

Dag was starting to recover, but he was quiet on the drive back, and as soon as we got home, he went to bed and stayed there until the next morning. Finally, he woke up, looking bright, and announced he was really hungry. I made a big brunch. After days of silence, he was back to his chatty self. I can't remember what he was talking about. I was staring at my eggs.

"Maria, is something wrong?" he asked.

I looked up. "I've got something to tell you."

His face filled with concern. "What it is?"

I had a whole speech prepared. I was going to say that while I still wondered about the need to create a more stable community, I knew for sure I didn't want be in a place like this, away from people who felt like our tribe. That community co-housing might suit many people, but it was the wrong choice for me.

"I can't live here anymore," I began. And that was as far as I got.

"Oh! What a relief, I thought you were going to say something terrible!" cried Dag. "I totally agree. Let's get the hell out."

$\approx$

We set a record for the shortest stay ever. We moved to a loft apartment in the downtown core of Victoria, which we could rent out while we were travelling. Later that year, in Catalonia, we bought a small village house. It was on a steep, narrow lane with no car access, and, like our city apartment, it had lots of stairs. In the eyes of many, these were poor choices for a couple aged 60 and 65. For us, they were exactly right.

Nine

We do not actually know it, but we sense it:
our life has a sister vessel which plies an
entirely different route.

—TOMAS TRANSTRÖMER, *THE BLUE HOUSE*

22

Our house in Catalonia proved to be a good jumping off point for work travels in India, Africa, and Southeast Asia. And it was close to our family and friends in other parts of Europe. In the spring of 2018, I flew from Barcelona to London, dropped off my bag at a friend's place in the Barbican, and walked across the city to Covent Garden for a haircut. The temperature was unseasonably high. Warmth radiated from the stone walls of ancient buildings, sunlight winked against futuristic high-rises. I arrived early for my appointment and sat outside a tiny coffee shop, sipping an iced latte. I thought about Dag drinking coffee in the sun on the rooftop terrace of our little house. I felt ridiculously happy, for what we had created and done together during our marriage, for the adventures that lay ahead.

"Do you live in London?" asked the stylist as he examined my hair.

I explained that long ago I'd moved to Canada, and now had a second home in Catalonia.

"I wish I could travel about like that," he said. "But I've got two little kids, so I'm grounded for now. I suppose I'll have to wait until they grow up and I can retire."

The conversation turned back to my hair. The grey that had invaded its underlayers some years ago was now showing up all over my head. Should I finally consider colouring it?

"Leave it for a while," he advised. He picked up some lighter strands. "But you do have highlights," he observed. "Who did them?"

"The sun and the sea," I replied, and he laughed out loud.

The cut took longer than I expected, making me late for meeting my nephew Charlie. He lived across London, and he'd been texting me for updates on my ETA. I hurried to the tube station. Hearing the rumble of a train, I ran down the escalator to the platform.

I love London tube tunnels. The smells of metal, dust, and earth, the whoosh of hot air as the train approaches, then the rattle and screech as it passes with a flash of windows, finally shuddering to a halt. When I admit this to my London friends, they always shake their heads.

"That's perverse," one had commented. "Do you like the rats as well?"

The doors of my train hissed open. As I stepped aboard, a young man sitting next to the opposite glass partition looked at me. He was strongly built and dressed in carpenter's overalls and boots with reinforced toes. Concern washed across his face; he stood up, indicating I should take his seat. It was unnecessary – the compartment was more than half empty – but out of politeness I accepted his offer. As I sat down, my phone buzzed with an incoming text from Charlie. Quickly, before I lost the signal, I tapped out a reply, telling him I was on my way. It was only when I looked up from the phone that I saw the sign across from me:

PRIORITY SEATING.
WOMAN WITH INFANT.
PREGNANT WOMAN.
DISABLED PERSON.
ELDERLY PERSON.

I stared at "ELDERLY PERSON," and the drawing of a bent-backed figure leaning over a stick under the words. Then I glanced at the kind man in overalls. Our eyes met again. He must have registered my horrified expression because he looked away.

Okay, I told myself, I'm 66, what else did I expect? Very quietly, barely moving my lips so the young man wouldn't think I was mad as well as old, I spoke the words in rhythm with the rocking of the train: sixty-six, sixty-six, sixty-six. Sibilant – a susurration. I considered how the numbers looked. 66: the rounds like pot-bellies, the forward bends like stooped backs.

Outside the station, Charlie's familiar form loped toward me. It was over 30 years since his christening, when, as his godmother, I'd stood in a Catholic church denouncing the devil on his behalf. Now he was tall, and strong from workouts and football. We walked along a canal lined with funky houseboats, through a park and to his flat. I was so happy to see him, I forgot about the incident on the train. Later, with his girlfriend, we headed out for dinner. On the way, Charlie told me about having to find quiet restaurants when his father, my brother John, comes to town, because he can't hear well amid a hubbub. John is three years my senior. We arrived at a Vietnamese restaurant, which Charlie had picked, he said, because he knew I love that cuisine. It was very quiet in there. As we were ordering, a group of 12 women arrived and sat at a nearby table, laughing and talking loudly. Charlie looked concerned.

"Is this place okay, Maria?" he asked. "Would you prefer somewhere else?"

Over the years, I'd been to lots of noisy pubs and restaurants with Charlie. This was the first time he'd asked if I minded the din. I remembered the tube train. I saw myself through the eyes of these two young men: an ELDERLY PERSON, her faculties fading.

$\sim$

Dag was bemused to discover I had swung from denying old age to fretting about it. He was affected in all the usual ways by the advance of years, like the shock of looking in the mirror and seeing his father. But he was calmer and more accepting about it.

"You were right," I told him one night. "We can't keep up this pace forever. But what will happen when we're really old and frail?"

"We'll find out when we get there," he said. "That's how it's always worked for us, right?"

I wasn't so sure it would work this time.

I remembered a friend from my university days, Ann, who was an artist, a free spirit, a political activist. A few years after we'd graduated, I'd gone to visit her in Wales. She'd told me about her work in the women's movement and the Anti-Fascist League. While we chatted and drank wine, I noticed the balls of wool and yarn at the end of the table, the needles and knitted squares.

"I've been learning how to knit and crochet," she had explained. "It's important to have skills like this so you'll have something to do when you're old. And it will be good for manual dexterity then. I'm learning piano too."

I was perplexed. Why start preparing for old age in your 20s? I lost touch with Ann after I moved to Canada, but I heard she'd had twin girls. Now I wondered if, in her 60s, she was using those knitting and crocheting skills. Of course she is, I thought, she'll be making clothes for her grandchildren. Maybe manual dexterity had only been a small part of her future planning – becoming a mother being a much bigger piece.

~

Back when Dag had finally agreed with me about not having kids, that seemed done and dusted for us both. So he was puzzled when now I began to wonder aloud if parenthood makes the reality of the last stage of life less daunting. If a grandchild is not just a comfort in old age but also a big distraction.

"Well, I guess it's like seeing a rocket head into the future," he said. "Another life unfolding, with endless possibilities, with a bit of you attached. So you never really die – or at least you can tell yourself that."

That didn't help much. All those warnings during my reproductive years about not having children started looming up again: *You'll regret it. You'll be lonely when you're old.* At the time, I'd easily sloughed them off. Now I kept thinking about where parenthood might have led us: to be revelling in grandparenthood, like many of our friends, or heartbroken because our child had followed my example and moved to the other side of the world, or –

"Or I'd have long since fled the settled existence you wanted for a kid," said Dag bluntly. "Honestly, Maria, regret is such a waste of time."

It wasn't regret. I'd been honest with my mother when she had asked me that question. But there were other emotions – and always had been – that I couldn't find words to describe. Couldn't ever really understand.

My mother had known about my sadness over Bac. And even though I hadn't admitted them to her, perhaps she also knew about other things. The brief, indefinable longing I sometimes felt when I held a newborn baby and breathed in the musky, milky scent of its scalp. The quick stab to my heart when friends proudly showed me photos of their new grand-children. My moroseness every Christmas, when the decorations, the lights, the presents, the jollity all brought on the sense of being a misfit; the one who hadn't made her own family.

I chewed this over with a journalist friend. She told me she got preg-nant with her first child accidently, at the start of a new relationship. "A burst condom," she said. "I had thought that was a myth." She married the father, and they quickly decided to have another baby, then be done with it. Now their sons were in their late 20s.

"Before I got pregnant, I was always ambivalent about becoming a mother," she said. "I sometimes wonder what my life would be like if I hadn't had kids."

"So what is that?" I asked. "It's not regret. There has to be another word. Or we have to make one up."

"There's a term in psychology," she said. "Counterfactual curiosity. Wondering about ways you could have lived life differently."

That's what those feelings were all about. The pangs, the Christmas depressions, the new bouts of fear about the future – they were an aware-ness of a sister vessel to my life, the one I didn't board, the route it would be plying now. A parallel me, a Maria who had given birth and raised a child or two. I knew I was a nurturer, that I would have enjoyed mother-hood and made my own mother happy. But the life I chose was the life I wanted. If I could go back, my choices would be the same.

∿

In February 2020, Dag and I celebrated my 68th birthday in the Catalan city of Valencia. We walked for hours through its historic, leafy streets. We had a long, late lunch sitting in a square under the shade of large orange trees. I wore the "FCKYRASS" dress that I'd almost worn for our wedding. It still fit, albeit more snugly around the middle. I knew that, as averages go, I was lucky for a woman approaching 70: strong, healthy, and with a happy relationship that nourished me in numerous ways. I was starting to feel relaxed about getting older. I had decided it was like being caught in another riptide, but this time I was better prepared. I knew what to do. I couldn't fight it; I just had to relax and trust that everything would turn out well.

Then came COVID. And Dag's accident.

23

October 2020

The morning after his bike crash, Dag was moved from Emergency to the trauma unit. By the time I got there, two surgeons were with him.

"There is a great deal of swelling in the leg, so we can't operate until it goes down," the head surgeon told me. "It may take ten days or more."

He was handsome, with a compact, athletic build. I guessed him to be in his mid-40s. Under his white coat he wore casual clothes. Around his neck was a fine gold chain with a tiny dolphin, on his wrist, a diver's watch. His junior was tall, thin, pale, and a bit stooped. He swiped the screen of an iPad to show me X-ray images. Dag's left tibia – in pieces.

"Jesus," I said. He nodded.

"It will be complicated to fix. We will do our best."

~

Serious cyclists flock to the mountain roads of Catalonia to train for races; these surgeons had patched up a fair few of them after crashes, though never one who had dragged himself a long way across steep terrain to safety. I was grateful for their expertise, and hugely relieved I could be with Dag. All COVID patients from our area were being transferred to a larger hospital in a nearby city, and one visitor per in-patient was permitted.

His room looked onto a courtyard, with trees and a view of hills. It became our world for the next two weeks. I arrived each day around eight with freshly squeezed orange juice, coffee, boiled eggs, and bread. I brought him cheeses, salads, smoked salmon, and fresh fruit for his lunches and dinners. I ate the hospital food he couldn't face – the soups and paellas and lamb stews and custardy desserts. He was in a lot of pain. The morphine had initially been replaced by a drug that gave him violent headaches, so he'd come off that. Every little movement of his leg was excruciating. Some of the nurses and aides tended to forget this. They would hurry in with a gurney to take him for an X-ray or a test and grab his legs by the ankle. Then they would jump back, like I did the first time, when he howled in pain. I became like a hawk, fending them off with my claws, opening my wings protectively around him. Together, we worked out a system for moving him off the bed, getting him onto a wheelchair, and into the bathroom, with minimum pain.

Sometimes he went into an almost transcendent state. Appreciative of every little comfort, every touch of kindness. Of the sheer miracle of being alive. I would arrive to find him staring out the window at birds in the tree branches, amazed by their beauty, their interactions. Often he became very emotional, thinking about other people's suffering. Torture victims. War victims. He needed to talk and talk about the accident, how he got himself to safety, the massive effort it took, the agony of moving. By then, we'd learned he'd also broken his hand in the fall. Because of the intense pain in his leg, he hadn't noticed it at first.

With Dag, I maintained a front of being calm and in control. He had enough on his plate without knowing that most of the time I was close to being overwhelmed. I was navigating an unfamiliar medical system in my rudimentary Spanish and almost nonexistent Catalan. I was constantly worried about his pain and his mental state; the outcome of the operation; how long it would take him to recover; what his mobility would be long-term, if and when we could get back to Canada; and where we would live before then. The surgeons had said he would need to keep his leg extended for weeks, and he would be dependent on a wheelchair and crutches for months. Our house in the village had three flights of narrow, winding stairs without handrails, so we'd need somewhere else to live. On top of all this, I'd discovered he had let his insurance lapse, and the costs for medical treatment were mounting.

~

Nine days after the accident, at around 4:30 in the afternoon, he was taken to the operating room. We had been told the procedure to piece the bone back together and secure it with titanium plates would take about two hours, and that it would be done under local anesthesia, so he'd be out of the recovery area quite quickly. I sat by his empty bed, trying to work on my computer. I couldn't concentrate. I paced around. I walked up and down the hallways. I watched the light fade over the trees in the courtyard. At 7:00, I went to the trauma nurses' station. Any news about my husband? One of them made a call. He was still in surgery.

His evening meal arrived on a tray: soup, an omelette, cheese. I picked at the food, then went back to the nurses' station. It was just after 8:00. They saw me coming through the window; they shook their heads. No news yet. I paced some more. My phone buzzed. A FaceTime call from our friend Charlie, a consultant neurologist in London.

"They may have been late starting the operation," he said, after I'd given him an update. "Or it might have turned out to be a bit more complicated than expected. But no news is good news."

I'd been leaving messages for Sara, a dear friend who is an ICU nurse in Oregon. When she had a break, she called me back.

"What's up?"

I gabbled out my concerns.

"When did they take him down to surgery?"

"Four-thirty. And it's almost nine now."

I should have remembered that Sara doesn't have many filters. She tells it like it is.

"Hmm. That is a long time. With such a bad break, you never know how things will go. Maybe they've had to amputate. Though they'd need his permission for that."

I can't remember what I said. I just remember running to the nurses' station in tears. They made another call. He was still in surgery.

Shortly after 10:00, the junior surgeon walked into the room. He was more stooped than usual. He looked exhausted.

"The nurses say you have been calling and are upset, so I thought I should come to see you," he said. "The operation was very hard. It was like solving a jigsaw puzzle, so many pieces. It took us four hours, but we did it. In the end, we had to give him a general anesthetic, so he will be in the recovery area a while longer."

It was close to midnight before he was brought back to his room. I decided to spend the night with him. Despite the morphine, he was in a lot of pain and discomfort. He told me that, for the first two hours of the operation, he could hear sawing, the whine of the drills, and the surgeons talking.

"They sounded really tense. Then I began to feel a deep, burning sensation in my leg, and I knew the local anesthetic was wearing off."

I held his hand. Gave him sips of water.

"I'm so glad you're here," he said.

A nurse brought me a blanket, and I stretched out across a couple of chairs.

We both dozed until dawn.

~

We'd had lots of scrapes and near misses in the past. Dag had contracted cerebral malaria in the Solomon Islands, and we both had serious pneumonia in a remote part of Thailand. In Kenya, we got caught up in a riot. Kayaking around Vancouver Island, we dealt with huge standing waves, strong currents, whirlpools, and storms. Each time, we'd emerged unscathed and carried on. It had been easy to be lulled into a sense of infallibility. And, of course, we were younger then. Now it felt like life was saying, *So you think you can just keep gadding about the world and not consider how you'll cope when you're elderly? Well, try this on for size.*

Right after the accident, when Dag was in the emergency department and I was back in our house, unable to sleep, the niggling concerns about stability I'd sometimes wrestled with over the past few years ganged up on me. We'd never been present enough in one place to build a deep-rooted community. We didn't have children. Now we were in our 60s. What the hell do old childfree nomads do when shit hits the fan?

I had gone downstairs and poured myself a glass of wine. I'd sent messages about Dag to neighbours in the village, but I hadn't yet been in touch with anyone else. I opened up WhatsApp on my phone and tapped out a message to my niece Hannah. It was two in the morning in Catalonia; Vancouver was nine hours behind. She would still be working. She replied immediately.

~

I'd always considered myself a hopeless aunt to my four nieces and two nephews. The oldest, Laura, was 4 when I moved to Canada. The youngest, Hannah, was born just as I was starting my worldwide travels with Dag. We only saw them on brief visits back to the UK. As the years passed, it became clear they viewed us as their eccentric aunt and uncle. Cool, maybe, but peripheral to their lives. Totally unlike the aunt I grew up with.

My mother's older sister, Madge, had never married – there was some vague story about a relationship with a pharmacist back in Ireland who broke her heart, but I could never get more details. She lived close to us and was always included in family events. An illness in her 30s had left her very deaf, and the hearing aids she used couldn't cope with noise from multiple directions, so at meals and gatherings she would sit quietly, excluded from the conversation unless someone tried to holler in her ear. Perhaps this made her particularly observant and patient. When I was 9 years old, it was Madge who noticed I had started favouring my left hand over my right; Madge who put that together with the fact that I had become withdrawn, and wondered if there was a problem at school; Madge who gently got me to open up about a teacher who was bullying me. My mother went into Mama Bear mode and found a solution, but Madge was key to catching it in time.

Her life was structured and predictable. She loved routine; each week was strictly divided into days for laundry, ironing, shopping, housework, confession, Mass. I always knew when and where to find her. Throughout my teens and 20s, I often went to see her on my own and talked to her about my problems with Mum. She listened sympathetically. She never judged or criticized. She was the one who explained to me that Mum was going through menopause, and why it was making her behave erratically at times. The one I talked to after the disastrous Christmas visit with my Jewish boyfriend; when my mother was freaking out because I was leaving for a year in Peru; after I'd told Mum I was giving up my teaching job to be a nanny in Canada. Madge was a solid point in my life, a rock where I could haul up to take stock of my situation and decide how to carry on.

For my nieces and nephews, I was the aunt who went off and did exciting things. But I wasn't the aunt who was there for them from babyhood through growing up.

Then Hannah decided to come to Canada. During her university years, while we were still living on Protection Island, she spent a summer working in Vancouver. I remember the first time I bought her a float plane ticket to Nanaimo, and I watched her disembark and walk along the dock toward me. Like the rest of my family, she had always been reserved emotionally, maintaining a British button-up-your-feelings mode. Since losing Joe and finding Dag, I'd become much more open. My motto: If you love someone, tell them. She seemed a bit embarrassed when I gushed about how happy I was to see her. We introduced her to kayaking, to fishing, to sushi, to swimming in bioluminescent waters. It made an impression; after she graduated, she returned for another visit. She started talking about moving to Canada. I introduced her to a friend who offered her a position in his company. She arrived in Vancouver to start work in the fall of 2012, just as we were heading overseas for a long period. Some friends of ours took her under their wing, and she stayed with them until she found her own place.

Whenever we were home, we visited her in Vancouver, or flew her over to spend weekends with us. We took her out for meals, spoiled her, invited her to our big parties. I revelled in her company, but, like with Agnes, I kept up a guard. I didn't want to seem dependent on her, or make her feel she was obliged to keep in regular touch. I didn't want to act like my mother. Nonetheless, she and I grew closer. We shared confidences, sought each other's advice.

After a few years, out of the blue she wrote a sweet post on Facebook, describing what Dag and I meant to her, that we were her "rocks" in Canada. The next time we met, I told her how much this meant to us – especially to Dag, who had never really been able to gauge what she thought of him. I hadn't realized this went both ways. She recounted how, on one of her weekend visits, she had overhead Dag on the phone, telling the person on the other end that his niece was staying with us.

"I was so touched when he said *my niece*. It's always been comforting to know I'm not alone here. But when Dag said that, it made me realize you aren't looking out for me because of obligation but because you both genuinely care about me. That you would both be there, if I needed anything."

Which, of course, was absolutely true. Eventually, as she found her feet in Vancouver, developed a big circle of friends, and met her partner, she needed us less. Which is how things should progress.

And now we needed her.

$\sim$

Hannah became our command centre in Canada. She liaised with a friend of ours who insisted that, as soon as Dag was allowed to fly, she would use some of her many air miles to book us business class flatbed seats to Vancouver. As Dag wouldn't be able to get up the steps of the small plane from Vancouver to Victoria, Hannah checked the COVID rules and found out she was allowed to pick us up and drive us via the ferry to our apartment. She got in touch with folks in Victoria about getting the place ready and stocked with food and wine.

"Your Canadian support crew is coming together at this end," she wrote in one of her many WhatsApp messages. "Don't hesitate to give me tasks. I'm grateful to be able to help."

Meanwhile, our neighbours in the village were rallying. One of them sourced a wheelchair for us. We were offered the use of three different easy-access apartments to stay in when Dag was discharged. Five days after the operation, we moved into a place that had a sunny atrium and garden. The owners made it clear: anything we needed, we just had to ask. Three weeks later, a friend drove us to the Barcelona airport, helped me wheel Dag and our luggage to the check-in desk, then drove our van back to the village and stored it safely for us until we could return.

Hannah was waiting in the arrivals area of the Vancouver airport. It had been over a year since we'd last seen her. "Don't you dare go away for so long again," she said as we drove to the ferry. "You're the only family I have here."

~

When we got to our apartment, I finally realized how much I'd been running on empty for the past five weeks. For me, our two-week quarantine drifted by in a haze of pottering, catching up on paperwork, resting, and sleeping deeply. A whole gang of our Victoria "peeps" tirelessly shopped for us, dropped off homemade bread, soup, and cookies, care packages of wine, cheese, and chocolate. A farmer friend who raises free-range animals gave us a lamb shoulder. Two other friends arranged for the delivery of meal kits. Hannah sent messages or phoned most days. And Agnes was in touch from Kenya. When Dag had his accident, she was doing anti-FGM work in villages and was out of cell phone range. It was almost two weeks before I told her the news. After that, she wrote regularly, full of concern, wishing she could help.

I felt overwhelmed again, but this time with gratitude. I stopped worrying about creating a community. I realized it was already there. It was in all the places we'd touched down. That we were part of a huge web stretching around the world, connecting us to our far-flung tribe.

I also realized the importance of recognizing and valuing the people who hold you in their thoughts. Who you can call on in the middle of the night, full of fears, after something terrible has happened. Who will still remember you, tell stories about you, long after you have gone from the earth. Whose children will be like rockets heading into the future, taking a little bit of you with them.

Epilogue

Christmas Day, 2020

Dag was on crutches in the kitchen, cooking our dinner. I was on WhatsApp in a long text conversation with Agnes. I had just broken the news that we had to postpone the fundraising trek in Laikipia we had planned for the following February. Agnes and her son Adrian were to be our special guests. And it was to be a very special trip, walking across their homelands, arriving in the village where I met Agnes, being greeted by her mother and the other women of the papermaking cooperative, singing and celebrating with them. But the ongoing problem of COVID-19 – not to mention Dag's accident – had scuppered that dream.

Agnes had been sending me photos of Adrian's birthday party – earlier in the month, he had turned 6. He looked grown up, wearing khaki long pants and a T-shirt with a surfing logo, his hair fashionably shaved at the temples.

"We have been having conversations about you," she wrote. "He is always asking who you are. I told him you are my fairy godmother."

"Oh, that is lovely!" I replied. "I've been meaning to tell you I am writing a book about my decision not to have children. I will be describing how children – like you – came into my life later on. And now I can say I'm a fairy godmother."

There was a pause. Dots appeared and disappeared as she started to write something, then erased it. More dots and, finally, the message.

"You are the best thing that ever happened to me. There is something I have been meaning to ask you, but I had been holding back until we met."

"What is it?"

"I hope one day you will grant me permission to call you Mother."

This time the pause was on my end. I was stunned. Blinking back tears, I tapped out a quick reply. Of course, she had my permission. It was an honour. A gift.

"The heavens knew I would meet you," she wrote back. "You are full of love and care. I love you and always will do, Mama."

Becoming a mother, at 68, on WhatsApp, on Christmas Day – it was something I could never have imagined. It was perfect.

Acknowledgements

In the fall of 2019, when this memoir was a mere proposal with a different focus, I took part in the Mountain and Wilderness Writing program at the Banff Centre for Arts and Creativity. Our group of three editors and nine authors bonded fast. And we've stayed that way: since the program ended, the majority of us have continued working together on the emerging books via Zoom. It's hard to adequately express my thanks to our superb editors Marni Jackson (who has gone the extra mile for me on countless occasions), Tony Whittome, and Harley Rustad, and to my fellow alumni Louise Blight, Gloria Dickie, Martina Halik, Brian Hall, Michael Kennedy, Kate Rawles, Rhiannon Russell, and Katherine Weaver. In Banff, and beyond, your feedback, suggestions, and encouragement have been invaluable, and buoyed me throughout the writing of *Instead*. It's been a happy, creative journey with firm friendships made along the way.

For reading and commenting on my completed manuscript, thanks to Marni, Michael, and Louise from our Banff Zoom group, and to Claire Graham, Joanna Streetly, Alison Watt, and Sara Whitner. Extra thanks to you all, and to Christin Geall, Margaret Horsfield, Deb McVittie, and Carol Matthews for pitching in with title ideas.

I wrote most of *Instead* while sharing close quarters with Dag, including a small sailboat. Once in a while, when I needed more space, generous friends provided it. Thanks to Alison Watt, Liz Hammond-Kaarremaa, and Di Roberts for your lovely island homes, to Hélène Cyr for your inspiring studio, and to Donna Konsorado and the late, greatly missed Eleanor Jean Macleod le Cheminant for your very special "Missoula."

For your advice, support, and contacts, thanks to Bernadette Mc-Donald, Bruce Kirkby, Wade Davis, Kevin Patterson, Angie Abdou, and Jon Turk.

Joanna Croston and Paul Scully, thank you for inviting me to bring *Instead* to the Banff and Kendal Mountain festivals. To have my work, past and present, included in these gatherings of the "tribe" means more than I can say.

To all my family and friends around the world – please know how much I appreciate every one of you, and how lucky I feel to have you in my life. Thank you for always welcoming me when I parachute in, and for not making me feel bad when, all too soon, I take off again.

My grateful thanks go to: The Banff Centre for Arts and Creativity, and all involved with its Mountain and Wilderness Writing program. The BC Arts Council for Creative Writers grant that allowed me to start work on *Instead*. Extra special thanks to Don Gorman and his team at Rocky Mountain Books, for believing in my story and bringing it to life.

Some short passages in *Instead* first appeared in different forms in the anthologies *Nobody's Mother* (Touchwood, 2006), edited by Lynne van Luven, and *Waymaking* (Vertebrate, 2018), edited by Helen Mort, Claire Carter, Heather Dawe, and Camilla Barnard, and also in my books *Fragile Edge* (Chatto and Windus, 1989, and Mountaineers Books, 2000), *A Boat in Our Baggage* (Little, Brown, 1994), *Where the Mountain Casts Its Shadow* (St. Martin's Press, 2003), and *Explorers of the Infinite* (Tarcher Penguin, 2008). I have also used a chapter, with some edits, from *Three Moons in Vietnam* (Little, Brown, 1996). My thanks to all involved in those publications.

While writing this book, I was inspired and informed by other authors who have tackled the subject of choosing not to have children. They include Sheila Heti, Emma Gannon, Meghan Daum, Pam Houston, Elizabeth Gilbert, Nina Jervis, Jen Kirkman, Laura Carroll, Laura S. Scott, Ruby Warrington, Kate Kaufman, Amy Blackstone, Ann Patchett, Bernadine Evaristo, Marcia Drut Davis, Jeanne Safer, and Ellen Peck.

My biggest thanks go to Dag: for making our life together an ongoing adventure; for never ceasing to amaze, amuse, and inspire me; for loving me so steadfastly and bringing me more happiness than I could ever have hoped for; and for patiently playing your violin on the roof to give me quiet times to write *Instead.*

ABOUT THE AUTHOR

Maria Coffey is an internationally published and award-winning author of 12 previous books. *Fragile Edge: Loss on Everest* won two prizes in Italy, including the 2002 ITAS Prize for Mountain Literature. *Where the Mountain Casts Its Shadow* won the Banff Mountain Film Festival Literature Prize in 2003 and a National Book Award in 2004. For these titles, along with *Explorers of the Infinite,* Maria was awarded the 2009 American Alpine Club H. Adams Carter Literary Award. She has also written extensively about her travels with her husband, Dag Goering, who is a veterinarian and photographer. As tour operators and guides, Maria and Dag have led many trips around the world, including fundraising treks for conservation causes. They are based in British Columbia, Canada, and Catalonia. Maria can be reached via @bookscoffey and www.hiddenplaces.net.